Canadian Issues
and Alternatives

Canadian Issues and Alternatives

Robert J. Clark, Editor-in-Chief,
Assistant Professor, Faculty of Education,
University of Western Ontario,
London, Ontario.

Robert Remnant,
History Department
Lasalle Secondary School
Sudbury, Ontario

John Patton,
Ottawa Board of Education,
Ottawa, Ontario.

Cary Goulson,
Associate Professor, Faculty of Education,
University of Victoria,
Victoria, British Columbia

Macmillan of Canada / Toronto

ISBN 0-7705-1192-9

For permission to reprint copyright material, grateful
acknowledgment is made to the authors and publishers indicated at the end of each selection. Additional acknowledgments can be found on page 243,
which is hereby made a part of this copyright page.

Cover photos: Canadian Pacific, Keith Branscombe,
Toronto Star Syndicate, United Nations

Printed in Canada for
The Macmillan Company of Canada Limited
70 Bond Street, Toronto, Ontario M5B 1X3
Affiliated with Maclean-Hunter Limited

To the Student

This book examines four of the basic issues that have beset Canadians:

1. How should a Canadian Prime Minister gain, maintain, and exercise power?
2. How should we cope with the question that has faced generations of Canadians: Québec in Canada, or Québec and Canada?
3. What strategies should we employ to maintain a distinctive Canadian identity on the North American continent?
4. How should our urban environment be shaped to serve human ends?

The book will present you with a great range of evidence relating to these four questions, and you will be asked, ultimately, to make judgments about the issues involved.

Each unit of this book is devoted to one of the four issues noted above. These units are carefully designed to encourage you to organize your study around a framework of ideas. In "Canada's Prime Minister", for example, you will be examining notions of power, authority, influence, and decision-making, and such ideas will provide the scaffolding you may use to build a systematic examination of the unit. Here are some additional features of the units:

1. Different disciplines are introduced to present different kinds of evidence, and methods of investigation. In "Canada and the World", for example, you will be presented with the views of historians, political scientists, journalists, and politicians on aspects of our foreign relations.
2. The dimension of time is an integral part of each unit. Most of the issues raised in the book have confronted Canadians over a long period of time, and hence flash-back information is given where it is deemed necessary. Most of the data, however, refers to events since the turn of the century and, in particular, since 1945.
3. The format of the book is varied. In one sub-section of Unit 2, "Terror, Murder, and Panic in 'The Peaceable Kingdom'", narrative and documents are woven into a continuous story. Other sections are organized to make possible a more open form of inquiry. A problem is raised, and evidence is marshalled to help you test and revise your initial interpretations. In other sections, you are given considerable freedom in choosing where to begin your examination, and how to order your investigation. In such cases, you must carefully weigh the data you choose, considering its balance, accuracy, and relevance.
4. Introductions are included if you need background information, help in making transitions to a new aspect of the study, or assistance in tackling the new evidence presented. They have been kept to a minimum in order to promote open inquiry.
5. Evidence has been varied. Each form of data should be evaluated according to its particular nature. Newspaper comment, cartoons, and excerpts from fiction and non-fiction need to be weighed for the contribution they can

make to your study. Photographs, for example, have been carefully selected to add a visual perspective to the evidence in the book. In some cases, they have been grouped to form a single component of a study.

6. Guidelines for Inquiry are introduced in order to give guidance in examining a particular piece of evidence, or groupings of evidence. They will help you to recall the main points of an argument, to analyse particular aspects of the evidence, to combine threads from different forms of information, and to make evaluative judgments.

In a certain sense, the elements of the book that have just been described are the "mechanics" of good investigation. The book will, however, demand your active participation. In order to encourage this, components have been introduced that may be described as "inquiry sequences". For example, the unit entitled "The Americans and Us", or the first part of "Canada's Prime Minister", can be so described.

In such sequences, you will be given fragmentary evidence from which to devise a possible explanation for the problem at hand. Then you will be presented with additional evidence in order that you may test your interpretation. This evidence must be weighed carefully, and you should ask yourself questions such as the following: Who said this? What are his/her qualifications for commenting on this issue? When did he/she say it? Why did he/she make these comments? What clues are there within the excerpt as to the motives of the commentator? Is the data relevant? Is it accurate? Can this evidence be supported by reliable data found elsewhere in your investigation?

After you have weighed the evidence carefully, you may be asked to make some conclusion about the problem being investigated, based on the logical implications of the evidence before you. In some cases, you will want additional data that is not provided by the book, and there may be suggestions within the book to assist you in your further exploration. If not, you should consult your school resource centre for additional material. Whatever your conclusions, they should not be considered as final, but rather as being subject to scrutiny and possible revision in the light of new evidence.

The entire inquiry process, which is heavily emphasized in the book, is explained very carefully in Part One of Unit 1. Refer to this material in order to clear up any difficulties you may have with this way of thinking.

It has been assumed throughout the book, however, that nobody lives and thinks in a vacuum. We all have values — those standards by which we judge the events and people around us. Such values give shape and intensity to our judgments. Inevitably, you will be making value judgments throughout your study of the issues raised in this book. In addition, you will be invited to participate in activities that explicitly emphasize valuing processes. It is assumed that your views will stand the scrutiny of rational consideration, and open oral discussion with fellow students.

You will notice, finally, that each unit in the book has been prepared by a different author. Thus, each study reflects the particular approaches and interests of one person, while the book has sufficient unity to be a valid core for a year's work.

ROBERT J. CLARK

Contents

unit 1: Canada's Prime Minister

by Robert Remnant

Duncan Macpherson, Reprinted with permission—the *Toronto Star*

INTRODUCTION

We are going to be governed whether we like it or not; it is up to us to see to it that we are governed no worse than is absolutely necessary. We must therefore concern ourselves with politics. . . .

PIERRE ELLIOTT TRUDEAU

"It is up to us." Today, more than ever before in Canada, *us* means *you*; government is no longer the concern only of the old. Now that the right to vote at eighteen is established in most parts of Canada, no high school student is more than five years from exercising his or her full rights as a citizen, many are only two or three years away, and some have reached that point already. What kind of government will you help to create? What kind of leaders will you vote for, and how will you judge them? What can and should you expect from your national leaders? Do our leaders have too much or too little power? To what extent do we manipulate them and do they manipulate us? This unit is designed to help you think about questions like these, and to assist you in developing your own ideas and standards of judgment about Canadian political leadership.

[In our state] each individual is interested not only in his own affairs, but in the affairs of the state as well. . . . We do not say that a man who takes no interest in politics is a man who minds his own business; we say that he has no business here at all.

PERICLES

Part One: How Do You Judge?

A. THE POLITICAL CARTOONIST AND THE ART OF CRITICISM

One of the crucial tasks for a citizen in a democratic society is evaluating the effectiveness of a political leader's performance. What skills and information do the citizens need, and where does this information come from? How should they organize and analyse this information to help them make their judgments?

Political cartoons afford one valuable medium for assessing leaders and governments. They focus attention on important issues, and afford useful critical models. The cartoons included in this section cover a period of several years in the mid-1960s. They are not intended to provide you with a complete assessment of the period or of the political figures involved; the purpose of this section is to help you use political cartoons as one form of evidence for making critical judgments.

What evidence do political cartoons provide?

While the best political cartoons are an art form and not easily analysed, most of them have the following characteristics:

(a) a single basic theme or situation
(b) political figures shown in an historical, literary, or other unusual situation
(c) a message that is conveyed by suggestion
(d) exaggeration

The following cartoon will help you see these elements. It was drawn during the 1965 federal election campaign; the three figures involved are, from left to right,

Duncan Macpherson; reprinted by permission of *Toronto Star*

Lester Pearson (leader of the Liberal Party and Prime Minister), John Diefenbaker (leader of the Conservative Party), and Tommy Douglas (leader of the New Democratic Party).

Guidelines for Inquiry

1. (a) What is the cartoonist's basic message?
   (b) What is the historical situation in which the political leaders have been placed?
   (c) What is the value of placing them in that setting rather than simply showing them at a contemporary election meeting?
2. What advantage does this cartoon have over a written account which has the same message?
3. Identify any implied criticisms of Canadian politicians and/or voters.

B. A WAY OF THINKING

In addition to understanding how a political cartoon conveys its message, you should develop some skill in critical thinking, in order to make full use of the cartoon. A useful method of critical thinking can be built on the following pattern:

(a) Analytical Questions

The most important kinds of questions that can be asked about a problem in politics are those for which there are a variety of possible answers, all of which are more or less acceptable, depending on how well the answer is supported by evidence. Many of the questions you will be asked in this section are of this kind: they do not involve simply discovering some factual information, but rather using factual information to support a political opinion.

(b) Stating an Hypothesis

Once an analytical question has been asked, you need some organized and effective way to begin to answer it. One way is to propose a possible answer, which you may think acceptable, but which you are prepared to change if you cannot find adequate evidence to support it. This possible (or tentative) answer to the question is known as an *hypothesis*. To illustrate what is meant by this term, let us imagine the following situation. You have a choice between two candidates in an election. You ask yourself, "Which of the two candidates would represent me best?" On the basis of your initial information you propose the following hypothesis to yourself: "I think Candidate A would be best." You then begin to collect more complete evidence about the candidates, such as their backgrounds, experience, and policy statements; in the process you may find that Candidate B suits you better. In that case you would change your original hypothesis and develop a conclusion (or decision) based on the hypothesis that Candidate B could best represent you. The main points to note in this process are that, first, you have established a starting point for your thinking, and second, you have not opted for a particular answer before you have adequate information on which to base a decision.

(c) Collecting Evidence

The last part of this process, the gathering of evidence, has already been referred to, but it requires clarification. All the information available to you on a particular topic has to be considered. Information only becomes evidence when it can be related to your hypothesis: for example, if you found that one of your two candidates had a relative who had once been convicted of careless driving, that would be considered information about the candidate, but it could hardly be considered evidence, because it would have no bearing on whether or not the candidate would make a good representative. The most important point about collecting evidence is to keep your mind open; do not reject evidence just because it does not fit some preconceived idea. And if the evidence points to a different conclusion than the one you might have liked, be prepared to change your mind. The way of thinking outlined here will be referred to and used extensively in the cartoon analysis which follows.

C. THROUGH THE CARTOONIST'S EYES

1. Introduction

You will now be asked to look at a series of cartoons related to two of the most controversial political leaders in our recent history, John Diefenbaker and Lester Pearson. A series of questions will be asked after you have had a chance to examine the cartoons, and you will be asked, at the end of the assignment, to develop an hypothesis related to them.

Cartoon number 1

THE MAN WHO FORGOT TO GET OFF THE BUS AT WESTMOUNT

Westmount is a wealthy, largely English-speaking section in the predominantly French-speaking city of Montreal.

Duncan Macpherson; reprinted by permission of *Toronto Star*

2. Background Material

Some knowledge of the events of the time is necessary for understanding a political cartoon. The comments which accompany some of the cartoons, and the following background material, will provide a minimal outline of the situation in which the cartoons were created.

(a) John Diefenbaker—the leader of the Conservative Party and Prime Minister from 1957 to 1963; leader of the Opposition from 1963 to 1967.

(b) Lester Pearson—leader of the Liberal Party and leader of the Opposition from 1958 to 1963; Prime Minister from 1963 to 1968.

(c) Minority Government—from 1962 to 1963, John Diefenbaker led a Conservative minority government, and

Cartoon number 2

Duncan Macpherson; reprinted by permission of *Toronto Star*

from 1963 to 1968, Lester Pearson led two Liberal minority governments. A minority government exists when a single governing party has less than half of the seats in Parliament.

(d) Election Results, 1958 to 1965
    Total seats in Parliament: 265
    (i) *Standings after the 1958 Election*
Conservative	208
Liberal	49
C.C.F.	8

    (ii) *1962 Election*
Conservative	116
Liberal	100
Social Credit	30
N.D.P.	19

    (iii) *1963 Election*
Liberal	129
Conservative	95
Social Credit	24
N.D.P.	17

    (iv) *1965 Election*
Liberal	131
Conservative	97
Social Credit	5
N.D.P.	21
S.C.R.	9

Cartoon number 3

"CHARGE!"

Duncan Macpherson; reprinted by permission of *Toronto Star*

Printed during the 1965 election campaign.

Cartoon number 4

Duncan Macpherson; reprinted by permission of *Toronto Star*

Davie Fulton and George Hees were two leading Conservative M.P.s who were thought to be interested in replacing Diefenbaker as leader.

Cartoon number 5

'NOW FOR MY NEXT ACT—'

The Rivard Affair, and the Dorion Inquiry which followed it, involved a scandal in which some prominent Liberal M.P.s were allegedly associated with criminal elements.

Cartoon number 6

—BUT THERE'S NOTHING WRONG WITH US'

Schizophrenia is a psychological disorder in which the individual displays contradictory personalities at different times.

"Opting-out" meant that a province could decide not to become involved in a co-operative federal-provincial program, meant to apply to all Canadians. In such a case, the federal government paid its share of the program directly to the "opting-out" province, to be disposed of as the province saw fit.

Cartoon number 7

REFLECTED GLORY

Cartoon number 8

"NOTHING TO BE ALARMED ABOUT OFFICER, JUST A LITTLE FAMILY GET-TOGETHER"

Erik Nielsen was the Conservative M.P. most noted for bringing Liberal scandals to public attention.

Cartoon number 9

Duncan Macpherson; reprinted by permission of *Toronto Star*

"THE STAKE OUT"

Cartoon number 10

CROSSING THE STYX

The River Styx, in Greek mythology, separated the land of the dead from the world of the living. It was considered impossible to cross without the assistance of Charon, the boatman, because of the many monsters which inhabited it.

Duncan Macpherson; reprinted by permission of *Toronto Star*

Guidelines for Inquiry

1. For cartoons 1-4, identify the main theme or idea.
2. What qualities of the political leadership of John Diefenbaker does the cartoonist illustrate in cartoons 1-7? Support your opinions with specific evidence from the cartoons.
3. Political cartoons do not always deal with negative features. Sometimes they illustrate a strong or admirable

feature of a politician's personality or abilities. In 1958, John Diefenbaker led the Conservative Party to the greatest electoral victory in Canadian history. What explanations for this success can be found in cartoons 1-4?

4. In 1962, Diefenbaker's government lost the majority gained in the previous election. What explanations for this failure can be found in cartoons 1-4?

5. What qualities of the political leadership of Lester Pearson does the cartoonist illustrate in cartoons 5-7? Support your opinions with the evidence from these cartoons.

6. In both 1963 and 1965, the Liberals seemed almost assured of winning a majority of seats in Parliament, but both times they could only gain enough seats for a minority government. What explanations for Pearson's failure to lead the Liberals to these expected victories can be found in cartoons 5-7?

7. Develop an hypothesis in answer to the following question, and use specific evidence from all the cartoons to support your hypothesis: Which of the two leaders seems to have been more effective?

D. COMPLETING THE ASSESSMENT

The cartoon unit you have just examined was designed mainly to assist you in developing your ability to make critical political judgments. But it also introduced you to a particularly stormy period in Canadian politics and to two of our most controversial political leaders. What further information do you need to make a more complete assessment of the leadership provided by Diefenbaker and Pearson? How you can check on the validity of the judgments made by the cartoonist? The following information will help you to deal with these questions.

1. Election Results, 1963 and 1965, by Province

1963

	Seats	Elected				Popular Vote							
		PC	L	NDP	SC	PC	%	L	%	NDP	%	SC	%
Nfld	7		7			45,491	30.1	97,576	64.5	6,364	4.2		
NS	12	7	5			195,711	46.9	195,007	46.7	26,617	6.4	401	0.1
NB	10	4	6			98,462	40.4	115,036	47.3	8,899	3.7	21,050	8.6
PEI	4	2	2			35,965	52.0	32,073	46.4	1,140	1.6		
Que	75	8	47		20	413,562	19.5	966,172	45.6	151,061	7.1	578,347	27.3
Ont	85	27	52	6		979,359	35.3	1,286,791	46.3	442,340	15.9	56,276	2.0
Man	14	10	2	2		169,013	42.3	134,905	33.8	66,652	16.7	28,157	7.0
Sask	17	17				224,700	53.7	100,747	24.1	76,126	18.2	16,110	3.9
Alta	17	14	1		2	249,067	45.3	121,473	22.1	35,775	6.5	141,956	25.8
BC	22	4	7	9	2	172,501	23.4	237,896	32.3	222,883	30.3	97,846	13.3
Yukon & NWT	2	2				7,783	53.8	6,114	42.3			560	3.9
Total	265	95	129	17	24	2,591,614	32.8	3,293,790	41.7	1,037,857	13.1	940,703	11.9*

*Other parties, and independents, got 30,112 votes, and 0.4% of the popular vote.

1965

	Seats	Elected					Popular Vote									
		PC	L	NDP	SC	RC	PC	%	L	%	NDP	%	SC	%	RC	%
Nfld	7		7				47,638	32.4	94,291	64.1	1,742	1.2	2,352	1.6		
NS	12	10	2				203,123	48.6	175,415	42.0	38,043	9.1				
NB	10	4	6				102,714	42.5	114,781	47.5	22,759	9.4	352	0.1	1,081	0.4
PEI	4	4					38,566	53.9	31,532	44.1	1,463	2.0				
Que	75	8	56			9	432,901	21.3	928,530	45.6	244,339	12.0			357,153	17.5
Ont	85	25	51	9			933,753	34.0	1,196,308	43.6	594,112	21.7	9,791	0.4	1,204	0.0
Man	14	10	1	3			154,253	40.7	117,442	30.9	91,193	24.0	16,315	4.3		
Sask	17	17					193,254	48.0	96,740	24.0	104,626	26.0	7,526	1.9		
Alta	17	15			2		247,734	46.6	119,014	22.4	43,818	8.3	119,586	22.5		
BC	22	3	7	9	3		139,226	19.2	217,726	30.0	239,132	32.9	126,532	17.4		
Yukon & NWT	2	1	1				6,751	45.2	7,740	52.0	431	2.9				
Total	265	97	131	21	5	9	2,499,913	32.4	3,099,519	40.2	1,381,658	17.9	282,454	3.7	359,438	4.7*

*Other parties, and independents, got 90,334 votes, and 1.2% of the popular vote.

[J. M. Beck, *Pendulum of Power*, Prentice-Hall of Canada Limited, 1968]

Guideline for Inquiry

To what extent does a comparative analysis of the 1963 and 1965 federal elections support or contradict your hypothesis about the leadership qualities of Diefenbaker and Pearson?

2. It Isn't Too Much To Come Out Of an Election

This is an account of the 1965 election taken from *The Pendulum of Power* by J. M. Beck. It is a mixture of factual account and critical assessment and deals with approximately the same period as the cartoon unit.

On September 7, 1965, Prime Minister Lester Pearson announced Canada's third election in four years. Those who heard him wondered if he was trying to convince himself of a decision he had declared to be his and his alone. At any rate, Canadians would pronounce upon two and a half years of Pearson rule. Undoubtedly his government had shown both imagination and courage in tackling some of the country's problems, but in the process it had also demonstrated its astonishing lack of political finesse. Its

early troubles hinged around the Prime Minister's promise of "sixty days of decision". He might have wanted to forget that promise, but the newspapers did not; "a daily tabulation of the administration's accomplishments became a favourite sport"[1] with them. . . .

Fate also conspired to confront the Pearson government with difficult problems. In its earliest days Premier Lesage presented the demands of Quebec's Quiet Revolution in a so-called ultimatum. Desperately the government sought to "find an unmarked channel of co-operative federalism between the Scylla of national needs and the Charybdis of provincial rights."[2] History may later credit Pearson's diplomacy with doing much to save the Canadian federation in these troubled days. . . .

The bitter controversy over the flag further [inflamed] relations between the Liberals and the Conservatives. Parliament heard 270 speeches in 33 sitting days spread over 6 months, before the Prime Minister decided that public opinion permitted him to invoke closure in December 1964. The debate served to increase the antipathy between Pearson and Diefenbaker. . . .

. . . In November 1964 there was the

sordid case of an active worker for the Liberal party in Quebec, Lucien Rivard, whom the United States was seeking to extradite for narcotics smuggling. Had an executive assistant to a cabinet minister offered a bribe to secure his release on bail? Had a parliamentary assistant applied pressure to the same end? Had Guy Favreau, the Minister of Justice, dealt properly with the evidence in his possession? Eventually, Chief Justice Dorion, acting as a one-man royal commission, found that the executive assistant had offered the bribe, that the parliamentary assistant had applied improper pressure, and that Guy Favreau had shown bad judgment in not seeking an opinion from his legal advisors on the evidence. The executive assistant was charged, the parliamentary assistant resigned from the Commons, and Favreau left the Justice Department but remained in the cabinet. . . .

Despite all its troubles, the government's position remained surprisingly stable. In March 1965 the Gallup Poll indicated its support had fallen only from 47 to 45 per cent, while that of the Conservatives had fallen from 32 to 29. Bad as the Liberals appeared, the feeling existed that the Conservatives would not be a suitable alternative until they changed leaders. . . .

In succeeding months the omens continued to be good for the government . . . [and] strategists Walter Gordon, Tom Kent, and Keith Davey wanted a dissolution, and [in] a cabinet meeting on September 1 only one minister was strongly opposed to it.

This election, wrote Peter Desbarats, was the first to bear the authentic Pearson imprint. In his three previous campaigns as leader, Liberal strategists had tried to give him "at least a glimmer of glamour and . . . put [him] through all the hoopla of American-style electioneering," but the surveys had shown that his popularity actually decreased during the campaigns.[3] This time

the Liberal high command decided that he would conduct what virtually amounted to a non-campaign. Above all, they did not want it to "deteriorate into a titanic duel between two aging political gladiators" in which their man would be no match for John Diefenbaker. Instead they proposed to present Pearson as a man above politics, "as a personification of the national consensus on all of the broad basic issues. . . . "

Pearson none the less spent an unprecedented amount of the election period in Ottawa "prime ministering", and the result was to cut drastically the number of his public appearances. . . .

When the Prime Minister did participate in the campaign, he emphasized, above all, the theme of majority government. . . .

Pearson's real failure . . . was not in his arguments but in his manner of presenting them. Why his strategists believed he could enact the exacting role they had assigned to him in 1965, after his disappointing performances of 1962 and 1963, is somewhat mystifying. Indeed, their own action indicated they did not believe he could do it. Realizing his inadequacy before the television camera, they resorted to a gimmick that John F. Kennedy has used successfully; they filmed informal living-room encounters between Pearson and "typical" citizens who wanted to have specific issues explained to them. But it seemed too artificial. Scoffingly Charles Lynch wrote that "given a few more elections, the party brass may fathom some of these hitherto unfathomable mysteries."[4]

The strategists had likewise failed to find a solution to Pearson's ineffectual performance before large audiences. This time his speeches were short, and virtually the same night after night. To one observer he seemed "even more adept than usual . . . in ringing all the flat notes in the oratorical scale."[5]

. . . [Diefenbaker's] defects were of another kind, and one of the first tasks of the Conservative national campaign committee was to repair a party riddled by the defections he had caused. . . .

Although John Diefenbaker held out the olive branch to the rebels, he promised them nothing. To him it was simply a case of the disloyal returning to a fold they ought never to have left. . . .

The defectors were returning not to Diefenbaker, but to the Conservative Party. Except in the Prairie provinces, "Conservative spokesmen tended to follow one of three courses: to ignore their leader altogether; to argue that he was a changed man; or to point out that he would soon be stepping down."[6] The Conservative party, which had been masquerading for some time as the Diefenbaker party, emerged in its old true-blue colours in newspaper advertisements. "The Chief" none the less got into the campaign early and stole the show almost from the start. Indeed, it is a sad commentary on democratic elections—or on his opponents' lack of political talents—that one offering so little could be so successful. . . .

"A bore for the voters, but for the politicians . . . a nightmare," was Peter Newman's description of the campaign.[7] George Bain of *The Globe and Mail* found that the voters were not greatly concerned with programmes but were mainly interested in the personalities of the leaders and the candidates.[8] Even the normally Liberal Leslie Roberts felt that Pearson had accepted the advice of his strategists to stage a general election over nothing. "Hence the national yawn. Hence the state of boredom which has laid its heavy hand on the Canadian people."[9] What, wondered *The Globe and Mail,* were the issues? The politicians "do not debate. They are little men posturing a hundred sideshows up and down the country, while the country yawns. It had better weep." Yes, said the same paper, it was "a long, shabby sham of an election campaign," and "there has been little in the tide of words that eddied around [the voters] that offered their country any clarity, any purpose, any dignity."[10] The evidence bears out this dismal picture to some extent; issues such as defence and foreign policy were not discussed at all, and the voter turn-out, which had been 79 per cent in the three previous elections, fell to 75 per cent.

Both Pearson and Diefenbaker campaigned with serious liabilities. Pearson's apparent reluctance to deal firmly with lapses in conduct had created doubts that he could be sufficiently hard-hearted. Consequently he had to "maintain the fiction that all is well in his government."[11] John Diefenbaker had the even more difficult task of persuading the voters that he was credible as a prime minister in view of his previous record in that office. It had been said during the British election of 1964 that all a Labour candidate had to do was say, "Think of another five years of Sir Alec Home," and he would be greeted by stunned silence to be succeeded shortly by rage and, finally, by despair. "Substitute John Diefenbaker for Sir Alec Douglas Home in this harsh context," wrote Peter Newman, "and you have one expression of the nation's mood on the eve of its 27th general election."[12] Indeed, this factor led some observers to feel that Pearson would get at least a small majority. For the first time John Diefenbaker was not running ahead of his party. The Gallup Poll indicated that only 29 per cent of the electorate approved of his conduct as leader of the opposition, the same percentage that supported the Conservatives in the immediate pre-election poll. . . .

Seldom has there been so strange a contrast as exists between Mr. Pearson and Mr. Diefenbaker. The Liberal is richly endowed with good sensible ideas about the direction of Canada's future. He is also, perhaps, the worst strategist and tactician who has ever held high place in this country. Mr. Diefenbaker is utterly absorbed with these latter matters but has few glimmers about policy. . . . If our two leaders could be placed in a blender and thoroughly shaken up, we might get an ideal prime minister—unless, of course, what emerged was the worst in both of them.[13]

1 *Canadian Annual Review* (Toronto: University of Toronto Press, 1963), p. 50.
2 *Canadian Annual Review,* 1963, p. 65.
3 *Montreal Star,* October 26, 1965.
4 *Ottawa Citizen,* November 2, 1965.
5 *Montreal Star,* October 26, 1965.
6 *Canadian Annual Review* (Toronto: University of Toronto Press, 1965), p. 98.
7 *Toronto Daily Star,* October 23, 1965.
8 *Globe and Mail,* Toronto, November 5, 1965.
9 *Montreal Star,* October 16, 1965.
10 *Globe and Mail,* Toronto, October 13 and November 8, 1965.
11 *Toronto Daily Star,* October 23, 1965.
12 *Ibid.,* November 2, 1965.
13 Quoted from the *Montreal Star* in *Canadian Annual Review,* 1965, p. 119.

[J. M. Beck, *Pendulum of Power,* Prentice-Hall of Canada Limited, 1968]

Guidelines for Inquiry

1. What evidence is there in the cartoons to support or refute the judgments made in this account about Diefenbaker and Pearson?
2. To what extent has this article led to a revision of your original hypothesis about the leadership of Diefenbaker and Pearson?
3. In order to make a more complete assessment of the leadership of John Diefenbaker and Lester Pearson, you might consult the following books:
   (a) Fox, Paul. *Politics: Canada*. 3rd edition. Toronto: McGraw-Hill Ryerson, 1970.
   (b) Johnston, James. *The Party's Over*. Toronto: Longmans, 1971.
   (c) LaMarsh, Judy. *A Bird in A Gilded Cage*. Toronto: McClelland and Stewart, 1968.
   (d) Newman, Peter. *The Distemper of Our Times*. Toronto: McClelland and Stewart, 1968.
   (e) Newman, Peter. *Renegade in Power*. Toronto: McClelland and Stewart, 1963.
   (f) Regenstreif, Peter. *The Diefenbaker Interlude*. Toronto: Longmans, 1965.

Part Two: Assessing Canada's Prime Minister

You will now have developed ideas about evaluating data on Canadian political leadership, and you will have some standards on which to judge the performance of our present and future leaders. You are ready, then, to explore this topic on your own; the rest of this unit is organized to let you do this, giving guidance where it may be needed. You will be looking at three aspects of political leadership:

(a) How our leaders are chosen
(b) How our leaders woo voters, and how the voters respond
(c) How our Prime Ministers exercise power, once they have attained it

A. WINNING PARTY LEADERSHIP

1. Backgrounds of Conservative Leadership Candidates

Year	Candidates in order of rank on first ballot	Age	Religion	Occupation	Province
1927	R. B. Bennett	57	United Church	Barrister	Alberta
	Hugh Guthrie	61	Presbyterian	Barrister	Ontario
	C. H. Cahan	66	Presbyterian	Barrister	Quebec
	R. J. Manion	46	Roman Catholic	Physician	Ontario
	R. Rogers	63	Anglican	Merchant	Manitoba
	Sir Henry Drayton	58	Anglican	Barrister	Ontario
1938	R. J. Manion	56	Roman Catholic	Physician	Ontario
	M. A. MacPherson	47	Presbyterian	Barrister	Saskatchewan
	Joseph Harris	49	Presbyterian	Businessman	Ontario
	Denton Massey	38	United Church	Businessman	Ontario
	J. E. Lawson	46	United Church	Barrister	Ontario
1942	John Bracken	59	United Church	Professor	Manitoba
	M. A. MacPherson	51	Presbyterian	Barrister	Saskatchewan
	John G. Diefenbaker	47	Baptist	Barrister	Saskatchewan
	H. C. Green	47	United Church	Barrister	British Columbia
	H. H. Stevens	64	United Church	Businessman	British Columbia
1948	George Drew	54	Anglican	Barrister	Ontario
	John G. Diefenbaker	53	Baptist	Barrister	Saskatchewan
	Donald M. Fleming	43	United Church	Barrister	Ontario
1956	John G. Diefenbaker	61	Baptist	Barrister	Saskatchewan
	Donald M. Fleming	51	United Church	Barrister	Ontario
	E. Davie Fulton	40	Roman Catholic	Barrister	British Columbia

1967	Robert L. Stanfield	53	Anglican	Barrister	Nova Scotia
	Duff Roblin	50	Anglican	Businessman	Manitoba
	E. Davie Fulton	51	Roman Catholic	Barrister	British Columbia
	George Hees	57	Anglican	Businessman	Ontario
	John G. Diefenbaker	70	Baptist	Barrister	Saskatchewan
	Wallace McCutcheon	61	United Church	Businessman	Ontario
	Alvin Hamilton	55	Protestant	Teacher	Saskatchewan
	Donald M. Fleming	62	United Church	Barrister	Ontario
	Michael Starr	56	Ukrainian Orthodox	Clerk	Ontario

[John C. Courtney, *The Selection of National Party Leaders in Canada,* Macmillan of Canada, 1973]

2. Backgrounds of Liberal Leadership Candidates

Year	Candidates in order of rank on first ballot	Age	Religion	Occupation	Province
1919	W. L. Mackenzie King	44	Presbyterian	Indust. rel. advisor	Ontario
	William S. Fielding	70	Baptist	Journalist	Nova Scotia
	George Graham	60	Methodist	Journalist	Ontario
	D. D. McKenzie	60	Presbyterian	Barrister	Nova Scotia
1948	Louis St. Laurent	66	Roman Catholic	Barrister	Quebec
	James G. Gardiner	64	United Church	Teacher	Saskatchewan
	C. G. Power	60	Roman Catholic	Barrister	Quebec
1958	Lester B. Pearson	60	United Church	Civil Servant	Ontario
	Paul Martin	54	Roman Catholic	Barrister	Ontario
1968	Pierre E. Trudeau	48	Roman Catholic	Barrister	Quebec
	Paul Hellyer	44	United Church	Businessman	Ontario
	Robert Winters	57	United Church	Businessman	Ontario
	John Turner	38	Roman Catholic	Barrister	Quebec
	Paul Martin	64	Roman Catholic	Barrister	Ontario
	J. J. Greene	47	Anglican	Barrister	Ontario
	A. J. MacEachen	46	Roman Catholic	Professor	Nova Scotia
	Eric Kierans	54	Roman Catholic	Economist	Quebec

[John C. Courtney, *The Selection of National Party Leaders in Canada,* Macmillan of Canada, 1973]

Guidelines for Inquiry

1. What appear to be dominant characteristics of candidates for the national leadership of the Conservative and Liberal parties respectively?
2. To what extent are there similarities between the two parties? How do they differ?
3. What elements of our society seem to be excluded from attaining the national leadership of political parties? How do you explain this situation? To what extent do you think it should be remedied?

3. National Leadership Conventions

[Each of the major Canadian political parties holds a national convention to select a leader when the need arises.] Any winning candidate must have the stamina to campaign strenuously, and the kind of personality that impresses itself on delegates and ordinary voters; he must have some kind of past role in his party to justify his running; he must have mastered the ordinary political skills of debate and written argument.

But those kinds of qualities are available in a large number of men in any [strong] political party. What makes the difference for the man who wins?

High-level support inside the party is usually an important ingredient of success. Studies of voting at the 1967 P.C. convention showed the party elite strongly in favour of Stanfield, while rank and file delegates seemed to prefer Roblin; the result was a Stanfield victory. Pierre Trudeau, too, won his victory with the support of most of the prominent cabinet ministers who were not themselves running.

The existence of a strong regional base of support is also important, so that a candidate can work for voters elsewhere while assured of strong support from a particular area. Stanfield, for example, could count on the Maritimes, just as Trudeau carried with him strong backing as the major Quebec candidate. . . .

Then there is the media impact of any candidate. This can be crucial, as it was in the case of Trudeau; in the pre-convention period, as Laval political scientists discovered, Trudeau received 26% of all newspaper coverage of the leadership candidates— far more than any other contender. The result was a sudden and escalating public interest in the man, and a response from party delegates as Trudeau's popular appeal spread. Somewhat similar media support for Stanfield came during the convention period in Toronto, when Toronto dailies featured the Nova Scotia premier with increasing prominence. The bandwagon effect of this helped Stanfield win.

All this reflects the major criterion which delegates tend to stress: who can bring their party the greatest popular support in an election? Particularly in the Liberal and P.C. parties, this question is often framed brutally as a campaign develops. And the press response to candidates is often a good indication of likely popular reaction to a potential leader.

There are, however, other significant factors in leadership choice. Especially in the N.D.P., policy positions will be a central concern; how closely a candidate can match the mood of radicalism in a convention will affect his possibility of winning. This factor operates in the other parties, too, but in a less obvious way; candidates are simply not taken seriously if they stray too far from the usual party consensus.

The background of any candidate will also be important. Parties out of power in

Ottawa tend to look for leaders who head provincial governments; thus Stanfield and Roblin were the strongest P.C. candidates, just as it was Douglas who won the N.D.P. leadership ten years ago. Parties in power federally tend to look for a federal cabinet minister to succeed a retiring P.M. That meant the single Liberal candidate from a provincial cabinet, Eric Kierans, could get little support despite a vigorous campaign.

In the end, though, convention decisions reflect a complex combination of all these factors; and they represent a fairly frank appraisal of how forceful, able, and honest a personality is each candidate who seeks party leadership. That, in fact, may be the best argument for conventions. They set each candidate in a context of tension, crisis, and constant grueling scrutiny. The man who can survive and surmount that brutal atmosphere is perhaps the man best equipped to face the constant pressures, critical choices, and cruel assaults of modern political life.

[Stephen Langdon, "The Political Convention Process", *Quarterly of Canadian Studies,* Spring 1971]

4. Is There a Better Way?

National conventions are purely and simply an import from the United States and they are not really proper in a parliamentary system such as we have in Canada.

The parliamentary system of leadership is, or ought to be, based on several assumptions: That members of Parliament will, through their ability to work with their fellow members, their capacity to react quickly to changing circumstances, general parliamentary ability and intellectual qualifications, prove themselves capable or incapable of assuming a position of leadership in the party.

Members of the comparatively small parliamentary group are better qualified than the general public, assembled in a convention, to determine which members of the group are likely to provide the best leadership.

The parliamentary system has been short-circuited by the national convention which operates best in conjunction with a presidential system, but not with a parliamentary form of government.

Inasmuch as the convention now selects the party leader, it is not likely that the leader will be a member of the parliamentary group. Thus, it is likely that the leader will often be totally lacking in ability to operate in the House of Commons.

The make-up of a convention is perhaps the single most imporant reason for its failure to live up to its theoretical promise.

It is composed of delegates who know little about the candidates except what they have read in the newspapers or what they have seen on television.

Also, the delegates to a convention rarely represent anything other than the hand-picked choices of the local or regional party organization.

Many just do not wish to participate in a meeting lasting several days, where objective decisions are well nigh impossible, where only a few insiders have any idea what is going on and where "hoopla" and drum majorettes provide a constant if not mindless diversion.

Cut off from sound judgment by a tumultuous crowd masquerading as public opinion, just how could any delegate function properly?

The delegates, even if they have a free choice, are likely to select a candidate who has gained national prominence by his competence in fields outside of the House.

For example, in recent history, Lester

Pearson was picked essentially because of his reputation in the field of foreign affairs.

TRUDEAU'S VIEWS KNOWN

Trudeau had been in the House of Commons for only four years before he became party leader. Prior to that he had been a journalist and lawyer known for his federalist views in Quebec.

Robert Stanfield, of course, had been Nova Scotia's premier.

It is too bad that so many have given up any critical analysis of our political conventions. Television has undoubtedly helped to make conventions a great spectacle.

Few among the watchers can remain impassive through the dramatic episodes or resist the appeal to the senses of so much color and movement.

Generally, in conventions there is an elaborate respect for form and delegates pretend to deliberate many issues which usually are settled by a handful of "wire pullers" in the obscurity of private caucuses or hotel rooms.

ANOTHER FACTOR

There is another factor to be considered. When the parliamentary group selects the leader and knows his qualifications for the post, it is much more likely that he will retain the confidence of that group.

When the convention picks someone whom it does not know intimately, it is likely to be much more fickle. When campaigns go awry, there soon arises a demand for the resignation of the party leader.

Finally, it is questionable if the national conventions do what they are also intended to do—promote harmony. In fact, most national conventions endanger unity and thereby weaken the party.

Even the 1967 convention left a great deal of bitterness felt by unreconciled Diefen-

baker supporters, a fact that Mr. Stanfield has spent years trying to erase.

In the final analysis, the convention system seems to have an unerring instinct for picking leaders unprepared for the rigors of leading the parliamentary group.

[Bruce Whitestone, "System of Selecting Leaders Needs Overhauling", *Toronto Daily Star,* August 16, 1972]

Guidelines for Inquiry

1. What factors important to the selection of a national political party leader are identified in Langdon's article?

2. To what extent to you agree with the contention that a person "who can survive [the political convention process] is perhaps best equipped to face the pressures . . . of modern political life"?

3. Where do you stand in regard to Whitestone's argument that national political conventions are an American import and are ill-equipped to select national political leaders in Canada? You might want to consult John C. Courtney, *The Selection of National Party Leaders in Canada* (Toronto: Macmillan of Canada, 1973), or Thomas A. Hockin, *Apex of Power* (Toronto: Prentice-Hall, 1971), in researching your answer for this question.

4. Consider the following qualities of an ideal Canadian leader: education, age, religion, occupation, provincial background, personal wealth, political experience, Parliamentary experience, image, and physical stamina.
   (a) What qualifications would you consider to be ideal under each category? Why?
   (b) Rank order the categories. Justify your ranking.

B. THE SHOWDOWN: A NATIONAL ELECTION

What follows is a case study of the federal election held on October 30, 1972. Issues that might be considered are: To what extent do election results reflect party platforms, local issues and candidates, and traditional party allegiances? To what extent are they a verdict on the performance of a national leader? What qualities do Canadians appear to expect in their national leaders? Are candidates being falsely "packaged" in order to attract votes?

1. Before the Election

(a) If Candidates Are Right, We've Got Bad Trouble

My nerves are shot and I can't sleep nights.

No wonder.

It's this damn federal election.

After October 30, one of three men will run the country for the next four or five years—Pierre Trudeau, Bob Stanfield or David Lewis.

That seems obvious enough.

However, Trudeau says Stanfield and Lewis are incompetent.

Stanfield insists Trudeau and Lewis are incompetent.

And Lewis gives his word that Stanfield and Trudeau are incompetent.

Obviously, no matter which way we vote, we're going to wind up with a dummy for a prime minister.

Break it down even further.

What happens if we vote Liberal?

If we do, according to Lewis and Stanfield, we're just asking for unemployment, inflation and corporate bums to bleed us dry.

That's not much of a ticket to run on.

However, if we vote NDP, we'll get higher taxes, a cold war with Washington and the destruction of the middle class as we know it.

Both Stanfield and Trudeau agree on that.

That leaves the Tories.

But if we vote for them, Trudeau and Lewis guarantee we can look forward to depression, the separation of Quebec, and colder winters.

The prospects are bleak, indeed.

What do we do?

Unfortunately, somebody has to win the election. There isn't much we can do about that.

But which candidate do we select—the one accused of being "dangerous" or the one who's "insensitive"?

Perhaps the "arrogant" leader is your choice.

Just to be on the safe side, I have instructed my wife to convert our assets into Swiss francs; the children are getting instruction in karate; and all livestock on the premises has been spayed.

I have also made inquiries about steamship sailings to South America, departing these shores from October 31 on.

And why not?

If everything the candidates are saying about each other is true, we're in for some bad times.

[Gary Lautens, "If Candidates Are Right, We've Got Bad Trouble", *Toronto Daily Star*, October 25, 1972]

(b) Party Strategists Strive to Polish Up Images of Leaders

OTTAWA—Beneath the speeches and promises on the surface of the election campaign, Ottawa's party strategists are honing the leadership images that they admit ultimately matter most.

Voters will see Prime Minister Pierre Trudeau as the hard-working, decisive leader of an optimistic and basically happy country.

Conservative Leader Robert Stanfield will be honest, decent, a good manager and man you can trust.

NDP Leader David Lewis will be an aggressive critic, the man who, as Opposition leader, could keep Trudeau in line.

The parties have all taken extensive surveys to find what voters like most and least about their leaders—the same kind of surveys car manufacturers make before they bring out a new model. The findings shape almost every aspect of the campaigns for your vote.

Liberal sources say their polls show Trudeau's basic appeal is his image as a strong leader, a man who makes up his mind and sticks to it. The impression was made when he used the harsh War Measures Act to crush terrorism in Quebec two years ago, and won overwhelming public support for it.

But Trudeau's strength, his eccentricities and his raw edges are the very things that turn other people against him. And most people are either for or against—few are indifferent.

With that in mind, the Liberals have designed a campaign to present Trudeau as a hard-working Prime Minister capable of handling tough decisions. They hope this image will hold the voters who are attracted by the bold personality, and neutralize the irritation and disgust which some felt at his antics.

The main campaign picture will show Trudeau working at his desk in a shirt and tie. There will be none of the frivolous stunts that fueled Trudeaumania in 1968, and the Prime Minister agreed several months ago to restrain any caustic or rude expressions. . . .

The Liberals hope the opposition leaders' criticisms will make them look dour and pessimistic in contrast.

Reinforcing the image of a businesslike Prime Minister, Trudeau will probably spend about half his time in Ottawa. The cabinet will continue to meet weekly and trips will be short jaunts in and out of the capital on a chartered DC-9. Other cabinet ministers will be used extensively for rallies while Trudeau minds the shop at home.

"There won't be any cute tactics," says Robert Andras, minister of consumer and corporate affairs and the Liberals' campaign chairman in English Canada. "Slickness is suspect in an electoral campaign."

Nevertheless, the Liberals will spend more than ever before on television advertising built around the Prime Minister.

In contrast to the arrogant and authoritarian rule they think Trudeau has given, Conservative strategists want to depict Stanfield as a man who can listen to people and work with them.

"The theme is confidence," one Conservative explained. "People can't have confidence in the government because of its mismanagement of the economy, and the secrecy."

Stanfield's campaign will be geared to "a guy you can trust. We can all get together and work with this guy."

The Conservative slogan is "a job for Canadians". Apart from the obvious reference to unemployment, it is intended to depict Stanfield as the man who can bring the country together to set its goals and directions.

Conservative party polls show two issues that Stanfield is in a good position to exploit —rising prices and a backlash against welfare.

Stanfield will propose price and wage controls to combat inflation, and welfare reforms—better co-ordination and work incentives—to tap the hard-hat vote without appearing reactionary or callous.

The Conservatives are also mounting a big advertising campaign, modelled in some ways after the ads for Premier William Davis that saturated Ontario in the provincial election last fall.

Although he has spent more time touring the country than any other leader in the past year, Stanfield will open the campaign with a quick, cross-country hike. In the second phase of his tour he'll spend time in each region of the country, and probably end up with another cross-country trip at the end.

While Stanfield is campaigning to form a government, Lewis is out to become the official Opposition leader—the man who can handle Trudeau.

The party's slogan—"We need more New Democrats in Ottawa"—brings out its strengths in opposition.

In the first part of the campaign, Lewis will hit hard at specific issues like his "corporate welfare bums". The strategists expect him to keep to specific problems, and offer solutions, to avoid the negative impression of constantly poor-mouthing everything.

Although it is spending almost twice as much on advertising as it did in 1968, the NDP can't afford to compete with the Liberals and Conservatives in that game. Therefore, Lewis will rely on trenchant descriptions of problems in each region to generate news coverage.

The emphasis throughout will be Lewis standing up for the little man who feels exploited by big corporations and cold bureaucracies.

The NDP's target group is the young marrieds—people who haven't developed rigid political views and the ones who hurt most from high-priced housing, taxes and rising food costs.

Although all the parties say they are well prepared for the election, they are all leaving their plans for the last few weeks fluid so they can adjust to the moods created by the campaign itself.

[Eric Malling, "Party Strategists Strive to Polish Up Images of Leaders", *Toronto Daily Star,* September 2, 1972]

Guidelines for Inquiry

1. Why did Lautens claim he was a nervous wreck? Humour aside, what advice would you have given him about deciding how to cast his ballot?
2. What images of their respective leaders were Liberals, Conservatives, and New Democrats attempting to project in the 1972 federal election? What factors were considered in deciding on these particular images? Does this represent an attempt to dangerously manipulate the electorate or does it merely involve giving the electorate what it wishes? Comment.

(c) Trudeau Appeal Surpasses Party

. . . Field work for this survey was carried out by Canadian Facts Co. Ltd. during the last four days of September. A national sample of 1,262 eligible voters was asked by phone to "forget for a moment which political party you happen to prefer or like" and to choose one of the four party leaders they felt "would make the best prime minister".

Preference for prime minister	(%)	Vote intention	(%)
Trudeau	39	Lib	31
Stanfield	22	PC	21
Lewis	13	NDP	13
Caouette	3	SC and others	4
Other	2		

Undecided and refused*	21	Undecided and refused*	25

*6 per cent say they will not vote or will spoil ballot.

Preference by regions:

	Atlantic (%)	Que. (%)	Ont. (%)	Prairies (%)	B.C. (%)
Trudeau	35	46	41	26	37
Stanfield	28	14	22	29	24
Lewis	15	6	14	17	18
Caouette	4	8	1	2	1
Others		2	3	5	1
Undecided and refused	19	24	20	21	19

. . . After expressing a preference, people gave reasons for their choice in their own words. . . .

Reasons for preferring Trudeau (39 per cent):

	First mention (%)	All mentions (%)
Doing a good job, gets things done	26	32
Intelligent, educated, knows what he's talking about	10	15
He is the best for Canada	11	14
He's popular, has personality, like him	7	8
Straight-forward, not afraid to say what he thinks	5	8
He's a good politician, he is a leader	4	6
Aggressive, energetic, dynamic	4	6
He's honest, means what he says, not making a lot of promises	3	5
Done a good job in foreign relations	3	4
New ideas, will/has changed policies	3	4
Miscellaneous	17	32
No reasons given	2	

Reasons for preferring Stanfield (22 per cent):

	First mention (%)	All mentions (%)
Time for a change	10	13
Honest, sincere	8	10
Sturdy, reliable	8	10
Don't like Trudeau	7	10
Intelligent, educated, knows what he's talking about.	6	9
Like his policies, has a good program	7	8
Sensible, serious	5	8
Works hard, will get things done	4	7
He's a good leader	3	7
Would provide better government, keep tighter rein	5	6
He's best for Canada	4	6
For all the people, the working people	3	6
He's a gentleman, a good man	3	6
Miscellaneous	24	32
No reasons given	3	

Reasons for preferring Lewis (13 per cent):

	First mention (%)	All mentions (%)
Need a change	13	15
Like the man, the best man	9	12
Original thinker, new ideas would change things	4	12
He's interested in people, understands people	9	11
He's more for the working class	6	11
Better program, policies	7	9
Brings important issues into the open	7	9
Like the NDP, the best party	7	7
Aggressive, dynamic, has guts	6	6
Sincere, genuine, honest, would keep promises	5	6
Would do a good job	4	5
Would not favour big business as much	2	5
Don't like Trudeau, hasn't done a good job	2	5
Miscellaneous	17	21
No reasons given	2	

Prime-ministerial preference:

Vote intention	Lib (%)	PC (%)	NDP (%)	SC (%)	Undecided (%)
Trudeau	89	11	13	7	20
Stanfield	2	66	8	8	16
Lewis	3	5	66	—	7
Caouette	—	—	1	71	7
Other	1	5	2	2	1
Not sure	6	13	11	13	50

[Peter Regenstreif, "Trudeau Appeal Surpasses Party", *Toronto Daily Star*, October 19, 1972]

Guidelines for Inquiry

1. What polling methods did Regenstreif employ?
2. Compare the public's images of leaders with those defined by party strategists. What significance do you attach to your results?
3. Which leader has the broadest regional appeal?
4. Which leader would appear to be most appealing on the basis of his personal characteristics?
5. What qualities do Canadians appear to value in all of their national political leaders?

(d) PC, Liberal Voters' Intentions Linked Directly to Appeal of Party Leaders

These [results] emerged from a national survey of 1,262 people eligible to vote carried out during the last four days of September. The survey showed that the Liberals are supported by 31 per cent, the Conservatives by 21 per cent, the NDP by 13 per cent, and Social Credit and others by 4 per cent. Another 25 per cent were either undecided or refused to say who they would vote for and another 6 per cent said they would either not vote or spoil their ballots.

After people answered questions about which party they would vote for, they were asked to explain in their own words the reasons for their choice. Some people gave more than one reason. . . .

Reasons for voting Liberal (31 per cent):

	First mention (%)	All mentions (%)
I like Trudeau. Trudeau is a good leader, he's younger, clever, good personality	26	32
They will do more, doing a good job	18	21
General liking for party	15	18
Like the local candidate	8	9
Like their platform policies	6	9
Always been Liberal	6	6
Give them another chance	5	7
Don't know enough about the others	3	3
Don't like Stanfield	2	2
They are popular, the leading party	1	2
Miscellaneous: they are for everyone, for the people; do more for Quebec; don't care for Conservatives; other mentions	5	8
No reasons given	6	

Reasons for voting Conservative (21 per cent):

	First mention (%)	All mentions (%)
I like Stanfield, good leader, he's trustworthy, mature	17	21
Time for a change	15	17
Like local candidate	11	12
I don't like Trudeau	9	12
General liking for party	8	11
Liberals haven't kept promises, haven't done well	6	9
Like their platform, policies	5	9
They will do better job than the Liberals	5	7
Always been Conservative	6	7
Will do more for the West	1	3
Like Claude Wagner	2	2
Don't like NDP—too socialistic	1	2
Would bring more stable government	1	2
Would do more for working man	1	2
Miscellaneous: against bilingualism, do more about taxes; do more for the Maritimes; other mentions	6	12
No reasons given	7	

Reasons for voting NDP (13 per cent):

	First mention (%)	All mentions (%)
Time for a change	19	26
They're for the working man, common people	15	19
Like their platform policies	12	16
General liking for party	8	11
Like the local candidate	8	8
They will do a better job	5	8
Don't care for Liberals, present government	6	6

I like Lewis	4	5
Don't like Trudeau	3	4
NDP would do more about taxes	2	4
Would handle American investment better	2	3
Better opposition party	2	3
Handle separatists, Quebec better	1	3
Do more about inflation	2	2
Will keep "corporate welfare bums" in line	1	2
Do more for old people	1	2
Miscellaneous: will create more jobs; would like a socialist government; do more for youth; other mentions	4	9
No reasons given	6	

Reasons for voting Social Credit (4 per cent):

	First mention (%)	All mentions (%)
Time for a change	34	44
I like Caouette	13	16
Like local candidate	10	10
Like their platform	8	8
Will handle economy better	7	7
Do more for farmers, common people, West (5% each)	15	15
Miscellaneous: good opposition party; things couldn't be worse; would do a good job; do more for elderly; other mentions	10	18
No reasons given	3	

[Peter Regenstreif, "PC, Liberal Voters' Intentions Linked Directly to Appeal of Party Leaders", *Toronto Daily Star,* October 18, 1972]

Guidelines for Inquiry

1. Which appear to be the most important factors in determining voters' intentions in regard to each party—leadership, platform, or traditional allegiance?

2. How do you account for differences in emphasis from party to party in regard to the above factors? Which do you regard as the most healthy political pattern? Why?

2. After the Election

(a) Results of 1968 and 1972 Federal Elections

Province	Liberals		P.C.		N.D.P.		S.Cr. (R.C.)		Ind.	
	1968	1972	1968	1972	1968	1972	1968	1972	1968	1972
Alberta	4		15	19						
British Columbia	16	4		8	7	11				
Manitoba	5	2	5	8	3	3				
New Brunswick	5	5	5	5						
Newfoundland	1	3	6	4						
Nova Scotia	1	1	10	10						
Ontario	64	36	17	40	6	11			1	1
Prince Edward Island		1	4	3						
Quebec	56	56	4	2			14	15		1
Saskatchewan	2	1	5	7	6	5				
Northwest Territories and Yukon Territory	1		1	1		1				
Totals	155	109	72	107	22	31	14	15	1	2

(b) I Am the Prime Minister . . .
    I Am the Prime Minister . . .
    I Am the Prime Minister . . .

WOULD THE *REAL* PRIME MINISTER PLEASE STAND UP...

Blaine, *The Spectator*, Hamilton

Guidelines for Inquiry

1. Compare the actual 1972 election results with earlier indications in Regenstreif's poll. How do you explain differences?
2. How does the cartoonist interpret the leaders' reaction to the election? How do the statistical results warrant such an interpretation?

3. What Happened?

(a) Liberals Behaved As If Issues Didn't Matter, Pollster Says

Once a slide begins, there seems to be no stopping it.

This is one important lesson of yesterday's election.

The Liberals entered the campaign with a solid lead in popular support and then lost it. The polls—both the Gallup of Sept. 20 and the Toronto Star's of Sept. 30—showed the Liberals with around 45 per cent and the Conservatives with 31 per cent.

But the Gallup Poll of Oct. 23—published last Saturday—showed the Liberals down six percentage points to 39 per cent while the Conservatives had 33 per cent, the New Democratic Party 21 per cent and Social Credit and others 7 per cent.

Yesterday's vote gave the Liberals only 38 per cent while the Conservatives had 35½ per cent, the NDP 17½ per cent and Social Credit and others 9 per cent.

The problem with popular vote standings in polls is that it is difficult to translate them into the number of seats the parties will win.

The surveys showed the Liberals exceptionally strong in Quebec but running barely ahead—if that—of the Conservatives in Ontario and beaten elsewhere.

So the Liberals figured to do well in Quebec perhaps winning over 60 seats out of 74. They didn't quite make it.

Ontario—a bastion for the Liberals in 1968 and a province where they had done extremely well since 1963—was a disaster for them this time. They emerged with fewer seats than the Conservatives for the first time since 1958. British Columbia and the Prairies also brought substantial losses from 1968.

The Atlantic region was the only bright spot as the Liberals gained three seats on a substantial popular vote improvement over four years ago.

The major question is why the Liberals slid so far and so fast.

The Liberals had one advantage in the election—Pierre Trudeau. He was the public's overwhelming favorite for prime minister over the other party leaders, party considerations aside. The Star's poll also showed that the most important factor motivating Liberal voters was simply that they liked Trudeau.

Against this, the Conservatives mounted an intensive issue-oriented campaign. They focussed on the problems people felt were most important: unemployment, the high cost of living, taxes and welfare. In other words, they used polls as vital instruments of political intelligence.

The NDP, too, took off after the Liberals, concentrating on the urban working class and those in primary producing areas.

The Liberals seemed to behave as if issues were not important. They campaigned as if Trudeau was going to have another coronation like the one in 1968. To many voters, the Prime Minister seemed unwilling to even bother explaining his government's activities in the last four years, or to project a program for the future.

Moreover, the Liberals were completely out-organized by the Conservatives everywhere in English Canada. The Conservatives not only dealt with issues people were interested in, they also used every device available to communicate with voters:

television, radio, print and door-to-door canvassing.

The only possible Conservative miscalculation was Quebec, where the party hoped Liberal defector Claude Wagner could convince Quebeckers to elect a few Conservatives. It turned out he was lucky to get in himself in Ste. Hyacinthe.

So in the five elections since 1962, the Liberals have started a campaign flying high and then faded. From 1963 on, it scarcely mattered that much because the opposition didn't have the organization to take advantage of Liberal weaknesses. It was an entirely different story this time.

[Peter Regenstreif, "Liberals Behaved As If Issues Didn't Matter, Pollster Says", *Toronto Daily Star,* October 31, 1972]

(b) Should Trudeau Be on Diving Board or Riding a Camel?

From a transcript of Prime Minister Pierre Trudeau's interview on the Judy LaMarsh open-line radio show in Vancouver.

Q: Look, one of the things that was so great in '68 and what the people just loved about you was your insouciance, your diving off things and pressing the flesh with people, being around. Have you changed so much, because we didn't see that in the last campaign? Don't you like people any more, don't you get turned on by them, because your advisers seem to keep you so far away from everybody? You know, it's almost as if you were passing by Olympus . . .

A: No, that's not quite true. I still enjoy people. I still enjoy meeting people. What did happen, I think, is the kind of . . .

Q: You got to be an old, married man in a hurry. That's the trouble.

A: No, when you talk about diving off diving boards, I certainly still dive off diving boards but what my staff tries to ensure is

that the press won't be around photographing me.

Q: Why? People like that.

A: Oh, I don't think . . . Half of the accusations against me, if I can judge by my mail and so on, are that I am not serious. I'm travelling all the time, I'm always off skiing, I'm always diving off diving boards or something.

Q: Well, if you'll forgive me, Prime Minister, you were so serious in the election you bored us all to death. It was the dullest election I've ever listened to.

A: Well, would you have been less bored if you had seen pictures of me on a diving board or riding a camel?

Q: Yes.

A: Well, I must say that I don't think you are typical of the average voter who wants to make sure that you are working 24 hours a day for him; after all that's what you're paid for . . .

Q: But, look, the first time you swept the country because they liked that and when you came back to them this time you were almost a different man and it puzzled everybody.

A: Well, you were around, Judy, for at least the last two years. There has been very severe criticism. Look, we made a poll and we know that one of the things that people accused me of most is of not being serious because I was always travelling, which isn't true. You know, I would go off to India to see Mrs. Gandhi, or attend the Commonwealth Conference in Singapore, and pictures that would be on the front pages would be of me riding a camel. So people would say, what the hell, he's not paid to ride a camel. This would be the news of going to Singapore to save the Commonwealth, quote unquote.

Q: Sure but they knew that you were there and we didn't have too many Prime Ministers who went to Singapore for anything. I think they like that: they maybe were a little leery about the yachts in the Baltic kind of thing, you know, because they couldn't tie that in so much. But I think the Russian visit was something that everybody is pretty proud about.

A: I've never been in a yacht in the Baltic.

[*Globe and Mail,* Toronto, February 24, 1973]

(c) The Country That Wouldn't Be Conned

The electorate knew its mind very well. Canadians had had enough of manipulation, of fancy theories, meaningless slogans, election goodies and all the other nonsense that goes with image-making and the engineering of consent. . . .

The message of this collective wisdom, expressed in the minority situation we're now enduring, was that the politicians should concern themselves with real problems that confront real people; the terrifyingly high cost of living, the lack of jobs even for the skilled and educated, and a tax structure that gives free rides to the corporate rich and the plainly lazy.

The roots of power still lie close to the ground in this country. The candidates who won their ridings were mainly those who ran on their own merits, the men and women most aware of local issues, most attuned to the changes that will be required to make our economy and society perform for the benefit of the greatest number of people. It was such an eccentric election because the official campaign seemed to touch so few voters. It was fought in rented arenas, aboard chartered jets, inside the echoing confines of open-line radio shows and in the backs of limousines escorted by sleek police outriders waving them through intersections. The campaign became a tumble of events that savaged the leaders' composures.

As they were being pushed and pummeled in and out of the howling halls, where they promised everything except a federal subsidy for motherhood (which we already have), the party leaders seemed, curiously, to become even further removed from the real concerns of the voters. In the last onrushing days of October they drew into themselves, and when they smiled it was only by pulling in their cheek muscles. Nothing danced in their eyes.

As Pierre Trudeau wearily proclaimed his second coming, he appeared to freeze in the aspic of his self-esteem. Robert Stanfield stolidly pushed himself across the land, reminding the blinking natives that he stood squarely in the creative centre of Canadian politics, making legions of reluctant converts. David Lewis, giving off the cold breeze of digested facts, found an issue that caught the headlines. But he didn't make any really dramatic breakthrough with the people because he tends to create a good first impression and a lousy seventeenth. . . .

Nobody went into a polling booth on October 30 and voted for the kind of parliament we've got. What most of us felt was a variation of a plague on all your houses, and the commons we now have is an expression of that discontent.

[Peter Newman, "The Country That Wouldn't Be Conned", *Maclean's*, November, 1972]

Guidelines for Inquiry

1. According to Regenstreif, LaMarsh, and Newman, how important was leadership in determining the election outcome?
2. How important was the issue of national leadership, as opposed to all the other issues, in deciding the outcome of the 1972 election? Support your view by using all the data you have been given.

C. THE PRIME MINISTER: EXERCISING AND MAINTAINING POWER

Political leaders at all levels are mainly concerned with making decisions. Secretaries, aides, civil servants, and executive assistants may carry them out, but it is the leader who makes the decisions on which action (or absence of action) is based. What kinds of decisions is a Canadian Prime Minister called upon to make? How does he or she make these decisions? How do pressure groups, laws, institutions, the nature of our society, and the personality of the leader affect the decision-making process? Does he or she have other functions besides making decisions? How many roles does a Prime Minister have?

A meeting of the Diefenbaker cabinet in 1958.

The Canadian Press

1. What Rules Govern the Office?

(a) How Did the Office Evolve?

. . . Sir Robert Walpole more than two centuries ago was the first authentic Prime Minister in the modern sense. Up to his time the Sovereign had regarded the ministers of the cabinet as his personal representatives. The practice of the Sovereign's being present at the cabinet meetings ended in the reign of George I who, not understanding English, regarded his presence in the cabinet as unfruitful and unnecessary.

However, it was not until the middle of the eighteenth century that the expression "Prime Minister" came into use. It is worthy of note that the office of prime minister is not mentioned in the British North America Act, which embodies Canada's written constitution.

To achieve the prime ministership in the United Kingdom, the person so chosen must have been in the House of Commons for fifteen years on an average and have passed through the fires of political controversy. It is often said that a young man could be prime minister in these days. Legally he could but it would be difficult for him because he would lack the experience in the atmosphere of the House of Commons.

A prime minister's private life must be an open book. Privacy ends when he accepts the seals of office. It has been said that "the political star performer leads the actor's life", and is liable to the discipline of the clergy. With the franchise being made universal, the elections since have been largely personality contests between leaders, with two alternative prime ministers before the public. Politics have become personalized.

Political leaders depend on the information media. This was best expressed by Lord Esher in referring to Lloyd George: "He lived by the press and by the press he shall die."

The powers of the prime minister include control of the agenda for all cabinet sessions. Generally speaking nothing can be dealt with in the cabinet unless the prime minister so decides. . . .

The prime minister used to be regarded as a first among equals in the cabinet but since the First World War there are no equals. His powers are now so wide and general, there seems little question that a prime minister today in the British parliamentary tradition has greater power than the president of the United States.

[John Diefenbaker, *Those Things We Treasure*, Macmillan of Canada, 1972]

(b) The Functions of the Prime Minister

This is the only legal definition which exists of the Prime Minister's powers in our system of government. In this article, the Privy Council means the Cabinet.

The Committee of the Privy Council, on the recommendation of the Right Honourable W. L. Mackenzie King, Prime Minister, submits the following memorandum regarding certain of the functions of the Prime Minister—

(1) A Meeting of the Privy Council is at the call of the Minister and, in his absence, of that of the senior Privy Councillor, if the President of the Council be absent;

(2) A quorum of the Council being four, no submission, for approval to the Governor General, can be made with a less number than quorum;

(3) A Minister cannot make recommendations to the Council affecting the discipline of the Department of another Minister;

(4) The following recommendations are the special prerogative of the Prime Minister:

Dissolution and Convocation of Parliament;

Appointment of Privy Councillors;

Cabinet Ministers;

Lieutenant-Governors (including leave of absence to same);

Provincial Administrators;

Speaker of the Senate;

Chief Justice of all the Courts;

Senators;

Sub-Committees of Council;

Treasury Board;

Committee of Internal Economy, House of Commons;

Deputy Heads of Departments;

Librarians of Parliament;

Crown Appointments in both Houses of Parliament;

Governor-General's Secretary's Staff;

Recommendations in any Department.

The Committee advises that this Minute be issued under the Privy Seal, and that a certified copy thereof be attached, under the Grand Seal of Canada, to the Commission of each Minister.

[Minute of the Privy Council, P.C. 3374, October 25, 1935]

(c) The Prime Minister's Stay in Office

Not long ago a well-known Canadian writer observed that Pierre Trudeau was well into the second half of his "first term" as prime minister. By that he presumably meant that the life of the Parliament which had been elected in 1968, which was Mr. Trudeau's first election while prime minister, had passed its half way mark. Under the British North America Act, a Parliament in Canada has a maximum life of five years, so that one elected in 1968 automatically finishes its course in 1973. Parliaments do not in fact often go a full five years, but that of 1891-6 did, while that of 1930-5 came within two days of it. On the other hand, Parliaments elected in 1925, 1957 and 1962 lasted only a few months.

But the maximum life of a Parliament has nothing to do with the period that a prime minister spends in office, and the notion that Mr. Trudeau was at any time in the second half of his first term is wrong on two counts. In the first place, even if one confuses the life of a Parliament with any term, Mr. Trudeau in 1971 was serving in his second Parliament as prime minister, not his first. He became prime minister on April 20, 1968, and he himself advised the dissolution of the twenty-seventh Parliament on April 23. By the time the twenty-eighth Parliament was elected on June 25, Mr. Trudeau had been prime minister for over two months, so no "term" started with the election.

That may sound like a quibble, but it isn't: the notion that a Canadian prime minister serves a term at all is wrong, and so wrong as to reflect a serious misunderstanding of our system of government. A Canadian prime minister obtains his position by being asked to form a government by the Governor General. If he accepts, he is appointed prime minister; and then, barring retirement or death, he serves for as long as a majority of the House of Commons will support him. Neither the beginning nor the end of his prime ministership has any necessary connection with an election.

He may become prime minister months after an election, as Alexander Mackenzie, the first Liberal prime minister, did on November 7, 1873; the last election had been strung out over three months in 1872 (elections did not take place all on one day in those primitive times), and won by the Conservatives under Sir John A. Macdonald, who was prime minister until November 5, 1873. Any single Parliament may include two or more prime ministers; several have seen two men successively in office, and that of 1891-6 had four: Macdonald, Abbott, Thompson and Bowell. Abbott and Bowell were both members of the Senate, and thus their seats in Parliament would not have been affected by any elections for the House of Commons; for surprising as it may sound, there is nothing in the constitution to prevent a senator from being prime minister. Sir Charles Tupper set a Canadian record by not sitting in either House of Parliament while prime minister: he took office on May 1, 1896, just after a dissolution of Parliament, his party lost the ensuing election, and he had resigned before the new Parliament met on August 19.

As the short administrations of Abbott, Thompson, Bowell and Tupper show, elections and prime ministerships are two separate things. The same point is demonstrated by those who enjoyed a long tenure of office. Sir John A. Macdonald became prime minister for the second time in 1878 and served, without interruption, through the elections of 1882, 1887 and 1891, until his death. Sir Wilfrid Laurier was appointed prime minister in 1896, and served without interruption through the elections of 1900, 1904 and 1908, until after that of 1911, when he was defeated. W. L. Mackenzie King became prime minister (for the third time) just after the election of 1935, and

survived through those of 1940 and 1945, until his retirement in 1948; and Mr. St. Laurent, taking over from King, served through the elections of 1949 and 1953, resigning after the defeat of his party at the polls in 1957.

The word "term", which is defined in the *Dictionary of Canadian English* as "a set period of time; the length of time that a thing lasts: a president's term of office", is clearly inappropriate when applied to the Canadian prime minister, and not least because (as the dictionary example shows) it confuses the office with that of the American president, who really does have a term. The confusion no doubt arises because in a democracy it is easy to assume that in an election those elected must include the head of the government. As the foregoing shows, a Canadian prime minister is not elected as such at all. It is true that he is ordinarily elected as an MP, but so are over two hundred other people; but he could be defeated as an MP and remain prime minister until he was able to get a seat (as Mackenzie King did twice), and, as the record shows, two of our prime ministers were not elected MPs at all, but Senators.

Now does it matter that a simple word like "term" should be wrongly used? If it misleads Canadians into misunderstanding their own form of government, or confusing it with a foreign government that is quite different, it seems to me that it does, particularly when one considers all the other Americanisms Canada is exposed to. And unfortunately the inaccurate use of "term", which is widespread, is not the only example. When a government is defeated in Canada, at either the federal or provincial level, it is common for the press to refer to the leader of the winning party as "prime minister elect" or "premier elect". Since neither a prime minister nor a premier is elected, the office of "prime minister elect" could hardly exist in Canada; yet it is quite accurate to refer to the winner of an American presidential election as the "president elect".

[Norman Ward, "Talk Canadian", *Quarterly of Canadian Studies,* Winter, 1972]

(d) How Strong Is a Canadian Prime Minister?

There is something marvelously Canadian, sneaky and indirect in the way power is vested in a Prime Minister. If you look at the British North America Act, which is the most important part of our written constitution, you will find no reference to him at all. Instead, you will keep stumbling across the Governor General, a potentate who sees all, knows all, does all, with the advice and consent of something called "The Queen's Privy Council for Canada". Its members "shall be from Time to Time chosen and summoned by the Governor General and sworn in as Privy Councillors, and Members thereof may be from Time to Time removed by the Governor General."

Got that? The Governor General does everything, but he has a gang of advisers, whom he appoints, and disappoints, from "Time to Time". Anything the Governor General doesn't look after is up to the Queen. Every act of law begins, "Her Majesty, by and with the advice and consent of the Senate and the House of Commons of Canada . . . "

The catch is that neither the Governor General nor the Queen makes a move in the name of Canada without direction from the politicians. The Privy Council, so potent on paper, has never met. Instead, its active members get together in the federal Cabinet, and the Cabinet is appointed, planned and run by the Prime Minister, who has the power not only to hire and fire its members, but also to advise the Queen on the appointment of the Governor General himself. There are a great many historical reasons why we operate this way; the most important boils down to that old stand-by, "Well, that's the way we do it, and it works. Now eat your soup."

The result of all this indirection is that power for a Prime Minister is pretty well what he is able to make of it. A strong Prime Minister may become a one-man band, playing all government tunes; a weak one may become a thin voice rising occasionally from the surrounding babble. Our first Prime Minister, Sir John A. Macdonald, was a strong man who laid down both the Canadian Pacific Railway and the National Policy—our first tariff system—in the teeth of entrenched opposition. Our fifth Prime Minister, Sir Mackenzie Bowell, was a weak man who was forced out of office by his own Cabinet.

In recent years, we have had both strong and weak men at the helm. John Diefenbaker is generally conceded to have been an overpowering figure; Louis St. Laurent, in his later years, is generally conceded to have been secondary to his minister of Trade, C. D. Howe; Lester Pearson was not known for his resolute control of government, Pierre Elliott Trudeau is.

The Prime Minister's power comes from his position as leader of the strongest party in the House of Commons, the party which has the confidence of the House. The post is won at a party convention (in the Bad Old Days, the leader was simply picked by party elders), rather than in a general election; but voters normally vote for or against the Diefenbaker government, the Pearson government, the Trudeau government.

So one source of the Prime Minister's power is his general acceptance as the man who *should* be in charge. A second comes from the fact that only he can advise the Governor General to dissolve Parliament. When a Cabinet Minister resigns, the government reforms around the gap; when a Prime Minister resigns (unless he is simply retiring), an election normally follows. If fractious ministers or discontented MPs push the Prime Minister too hard, they may be out next morning on the campaign trail, a fact that produces a wonderfully soothing effect on rebels and rivals alike.

The Prime Minister also has the right to make important appointments, including Privy Councillors, Cabinet Ministers, Lieutenant Governors, Senators, Chief Justices and such senior civil servants as deputy ministers (normally in consultation with the Cabinet Minister), ambassadors and the heads of important government bodies, like the CBC. He has an enormous amount of patronage to distribute, and that helps. Today's smart-aleck critic is not going to be tomorrow's senator; everybody knows it and acts accordingly.

His most important power, however, comes from his mastery of the Cabinet, that essential body which sets policy and presents legislation to the House of Commons. We can see how the system works with an example. When President Richard Nixon imposed a surcharge on imports to the United States in August 1971, Canada was drastically affected, because we depend heavily on exports to the U.S. Prime Minister Trudeau, who was abroad at the time, returned to Canada and summoned his Cabinet. The ministers of the responsible departments— Industry, Finance and External Affairs—

told him what they had learned from their experts and suggested a number of possible steps Canada could take.

A decision was made to spend $80 million to help companies affected by the import surcharge. No vote was taken on that decision—Cabinet never votes—the Prime Minister simply polled the views of his colleagues and accepted one proffered course of action. (In this case, there was general agreement on the action, but there need not have been; the only recourse for a discontented minister would be to resign.) Legislation was then framed and presented to the House of Commons and Senate where it was passed and became law.

In that example, a weak Prime Minister would accept whatever advice was advanced by his ministers and their civil service advisers; a strong one would make his own decision and make it stick.

So you can see that power, for a Prime Minister, is very much his own to frame, and that the key to its exercise lies in his handling of the Cabinet, which in turn controls the legislature.

In the U.S., matters are arranged quite differently. There, the executive, judicial and legislative branches are separate. Cabinet Ministers do not sit in the legislature and do not control it. Many Presidents have had their proposals amended, emasculated or defeated by Congress. A Canadian Prime Minister whose measures are defeated must resign; had Mr. Trudeau's $80 million plan been rejected, we would have had an election. In theory, this means that the Prime Minister is responsible to the Commons, but in practice it works the other way. An unwieldy body of 264* Members of Parliament (MPs) cannot possibly propose legislative action; it can only support or reject the decisions of the Cabinet with the understanding that rejection may mean ejection for every MP. For this reason, most authorities contend that a Canadian Prime Minister is more powerful than an American President.

Just the same, there are some very real checks on a Prime Minister; Mr. Trudeau calls them "counter-vailing forces". One of these is the Cabinet itself. A government leader who loses the respect of his colleagues is in trouble. John Diefenbaker was defeated, in part, by a Cabinet revolt. Another check is provided by the political party to which the leader belongs; if he strays too far from its wishes, he may find himself short of funds and campaign workers for the next election. The opposition provides another check. Opposition MPs are always quick to critize a government, and if they are simply brushed aside, they may win public sympathy. The defeat of the Liberal government in 1957 came, in part, because of the arrogance with which the opposition was treated in the earlier Pipeline Debate. Finally, an entrenched bureaucracy which believes the government is on the wrong track can find a million ways to balk it. John Diefenbaker complained that the civil service frustrated some of his proposals, and there is evidence to support his claim.

What all these checks mean is that the Prime Minister must use his power with discretion; he cannot move too quickly, for fear of losing his followers, or too slowly, for fear of being overrun by events. He must, in effect, follow in front—no easy task.

In recent years, because we live in a complex, demanding society, there has been a tendency to lodge more and more power in the Prime Minister's office and to downgrade the "counter-vailing forces". Statistics show the trend; in 1964, there were 15 employees in the Prime Minister's office; the estimates for next year call for 92.

Some observers have decried this development, and contend that the Prime Minister is becoming much too powerful; others argue that the only way to meet the swift challenges of today's society is to give the government leader the power and personnel he needs to make crucial decisions quickly.

The argument between these two schools of thought will be one of the most important issues we face over the next few years. It is a quarrel, really, over that most precious of all commodities: Power.

*After the most recent redistribution there are 282 seats in the House of Commons.

[Walter Stewart, "How Strong Is a Canadian Prime Minister?" *Canada & the World,* December 1971]

Guidelines for Inquiry

1. What are the origins and changing roles of the Prime Minister's office according to John Diefenbaker?
2. The Heeney excerpt lists the powers assigned exclusively to the Prime Minister. Which of them do you regard as most important? Why?
3. According to Ward, how do you distinguish between the life of a Parliament and a Prime Minister's tenure of office? How does this make a Canadian Prime Minister different from an American President?
4. How do you explain the differences between the powers of a Prime Minister listed by Heeney and the powers mentioned by Stewart?
5. To what extent do you think that, "in order to meet the swift challenge of today's society", we should assign more power to the office of Prime Minister?

2. How Has It Been Done?

(a) The Roles of a Prime Minister

On the basis of these pictures, hypothesize about the various roles a Prime Minister fulfils in our political system. Test your hypotheses by using the readings which follow.

The Canadian Press

The Canadian Press

The Canadian Press

The Canadian Press

(b) Differing Leadership Styles: Mackenzie King and Arthur Meighen

This excerpt is taken from a biography of William Lyon Mackenzie King, who was leader of the Liberal Party and Prime Minister of Canada from 1921 to 1948, with the exception of a few weeks in 1926 and the years 1930-5. Arthur Meighen, a former leader of the Conservative Party, was Prime Minister, briefly, in 1920-1 and in 1926.

. . . [The] attitude of Mackenzie King to political questions cannot be fully understood until one has grasped his conception of the role which the political party should perform in a democracy, and particularly in the Canadian democracy. He considered that the parties in Canada had two major functions: the [spreading] and carrying out of ideas and policies, and the bringing together of diverse and even conflicting groups and interests so as to secure a working agreement and a measure of common action. The second function was in his eyes even more important than the first; indeed its operation might necessitate party principles being temporarily shelved or substantially modified in order to secure the necessary consent among the rival forces within the party—the highest common factor on which all could unite. Such a conciliatory . . . influence was indispensable in a country like Canada where the bonds of national unity were weak and the [disrupting] forces of race, religion, geography, economic interests, etc. were unusually strong; these, if not held in some restraint, might quite conceivably disrupt the state itself.

King's belief in the party system and his conviction that the party was the necessary means for achieving popular consent thus led him at times to make enormous concessions to preserve the unity of the Liberal party. It seemed to him short-sighted indeed to push a much needed reform through Parliament and into the statute books at the price of a divided support and the virtual paralysis of that party for years to come. . . . The danger of pursuing King's policy is, of course, obvious, for the party leader may well confuse the retention of office with the necessity of maintaining party unity, and [throw away] all principles in a frantic effort to stay in power at any cost. . . .

King did not believe that it was his job as the leader of the party to become the passionate advocate of new causes, however admirable, but to bring together, consolidate and make operative a common will on all public questions when such a result was possible. . . . What King perceived in his early days as leader and what succeeding years confirmed, was that the Canadian people wanted no more commitments to and for the League of Nations [forerunner of the United Nations] than the minimum which was consistent with the maintenance of national self-respect. King gave them that minimum, or even, at times, a little less.

The difference between Meighen's approach to a political issue and that of Mackenzie King was drawn by Meighen himself over a decade later at a gathering of the Conservative party which was held to bid farewell to R. B. Bennett. In the course of his remarks Meighen touched on the subject of political leadership in terms which not only provided a clue to his own ideas but also quite clearly indicated Mackenzie King as the villain of the Canadian scene:

In our Dominion where sections abound, a Dominion of races, of classes and of creeds, of many languages and many origins, there are times when no Prime Minister can be true to his trust to the nation he has sworn to serve, save at the temporary sacrifice of the party he is appointed to lead. . . . If anyone tells me that fidelity [loyalty] to party and fidelity to country are always compatible, or that the wisdom of mere numbers is the wisdom of heaven, then I tell him that he loves applause far more than he loves truth. Loyalty to the ballot box is not necessarily loyalty to the nation; it is not even loyalty to the multitude. Democracy has failed and fallen in many lands, and political captains in Canada must have courage to lead rather than servility to follow, if our institutions are going to survive. There must be something better than an ambition to be re-elected, or democracy will fall, even in this Dominion.

It is interesting that King and Meighen each advanced the [diversity] of the Canadian people as a major justification of his special form of leadership. To Meighen the challenge had to be met by the [creation] of some broad concept of the national interest which would transcend this diversity and in large measure obliterate it. Having formulated this concept, Meighen then invoked all the arts of rational persuasion to secure its popular acceptance. His confidence in the product of his own judgment was so profound and his advocacy so determined that the policy was open to little or no discussion; still less could it be recast or toned down in any way to meet the demands or soothe the feelings of dissenting groups or interests.

Mackenzie King also perceived in this diversity of population a challenge, but a different kind of opportunity. Opposing views, as he saw it, should not be expected to undergo any rapid conversion. . . .

Meighen's excessive self-confidence inclined him to be somewhat contemptuous of and superior to public opinion. King's excessive caution and search for common ground tended to make him too acquiescent and too sensitive to that opinion. Yet King was able to accomplish infinitely more. His method was the necessary approach to office, although admittedly a stronger realization of his duty to take the initiative

would have added to his effectiveness. It was, of course, King's sensitivity to existing conflicts of belief and his search for existing areas of agreement which led to Meighen's taunts of loyalty to the ballot box and servility to public opinion. King might well reply that the best hockey player in the world is no use off the ice; that a party leader who cannot get elected and stay elected cannot govern and in due course will destroy the party he is supposed to lead. A condition [necessary] to the exercise of power in a democracy as elsewhere is to gain a place in the seats of the mighty.

Political leadership, in short, must always meet two tests: the ability to gain and stay in power, and the ability to use power once it has been gained. King's technique in bringing conflicting groups together made him a master in passing the first ordeal, though he allowed the same talent to undermine his effectiveness after he was in office. Meighen's technique never got him over the first barrier. He showed some ability to meet the second of the requirements of democratic leadership, but he was given little opportunity to demonstrate this capacity. There is, moreover, no escaping the fact that the same difficulties which prevented him from obtaining office would have been equally operative in preventing his staying there. In point' of fact, they did exactly that, for on the two occasions when Meighen attained the Primer Ministership, he was unable to secure confirmation from the electorate.

[R. MacGregor Dawson, *William Lyon Mackenzie King: A Political Biography,* University of Toronto Press, 1958]

Guidelines for Inquiry

1. What are the conflicting views of the leader's role represented by King and Meighen, according to Dawson?
2. Meighen is quoted as saying "Political

captains in Canada must have the courage to lead rather than the servility to follow, if our institutions are going to survive." How important to democracy is it to have leaders who will propose policies and reforms which a large portion of the people are not willing to support? Are you prepared to accept the proposition that a policy which you personally disagree with can still be good for the country as a whole? Why or why not?

3. Which of the two leaders described in this excerpt appeals more to you? Why?

4. **To what extent did our former Prime Minister, Pierre Trudeau, follow either one of these roles?**

(c) The Pearson Experience

The following passage is an excerpt from an interview with former Prime Minister Lester Pearson, quoted in *Apex of Power* by Thomas A. Hockin.

MR. HOCKIN: To shift from federal-provincial relations. Can I ask you some questions on how you would characterize the different kind of leadership required from you to set the tone and the direction of your administration in the parliamentary party, in the Parliament, before the public and in the Cabinet?

MR. PEARSON: Well, I can say something about this, though it is not easy to go into detail. There are different kinds of leadership involved, as the nature of your question indicates. Leadership in the party has to be established first with party members; and in the parliamentary caucus. I used to take caucus meetings very seriously and I was always available to members of the caucus for discussion. I never missed a caucus meeting if it was possible to be there. Not all of my predecessors or all my colleagues felt that way.

MR. HOCKIN: Did you ever chair caucus as Prime Minister?

MR. PEARSON: No, a private member is chairman of the caucus, but I was always there and I used to subject myself—as my colleagues did—to every kind of examination. I used to encourage the frankest kind of questioning, however critical. That helped, I hope, to establish and maintain a leader's position with his parliamentary colleagues. I tried to do this in the country by travelling and meetings. I did more travelling than most previous leaders, I think; that is travelling on party affairs and having party leaders come to Ottawa to discuss matters with me.

As for Parliament, you can't really establish leadership there as Prime Minister unless—I don't want to be too dogmatic about this—you have a deep and genuine feeling for parliamentary institutions. For this, it is a great help to have had a long parliamentary experience; to have risen from the ranks in Parliament where you can acquire, if you have not had it instinctively, a feeling for Parliament, of its importance and its traditions. I always had a feeling of deep respect for Parliament (after all I had been a constitutional historian!) but I entered at the top, on the front benches. I had been in civil service for many years before being elected and I had never done any parliamentary apprenticeship. And I confess I never had any great love for parliamentary battles and rows. I could get worried up about issues as much as anybody else, as a competitive human being, but I always thought debates which were repetitive and prolonged and too violent wasted much time. I used to get impatient because you couldn't get things done quickly enough because of those struggles in Parliament that other people may have loved. I was anxious to improve parliamentary procedure; make it more effective by improving its rules. I was very keen about this. I hope I gave some leadership in that sense. I could have done much more if I had had a majority of, say, thirty; I think then I would have been able to do a lot more about parliamentary reform, without destroying or weakening the reality of parliamentary work, and the importance of parliamentary opposition.

As for leadership in the country at large, you do this primarily by the impression you create, and by the action you take, the measures you put through Parliament. This requires speeches and appearances across the country, as well as speeches and, more important, action in Parliament.

A television image seems now to be very important—too much so I think. One can appear to be a leader on television if he is a good performer, a good actor. I always found this very difficult. I had no liking or aptitude for this kind of performance and always found it difficult to pretend that I was somebody else on television; or act a part. Indeed, I found it very difficult to be other than myself in my public appearances; too bad. I have been told I was only effective on television when I got excited about something—the flag resolution for example —that I could be forceful on such occasions and effective on television or in speaking. But generally I think you have to be a good "performer" even if you are not all worked up about the subject of the performance, if you are to impress masses of people as a political leader.

THE PRIME MINISTER AND MEETINGS
WITH OTHER HEADS OF GOVERNMENT

MR. HOCKIN: A key leadership role only a Prime Minister can exercise is in meetings of heads of governments in international affairs. For example, when you were Prime Minister, you visited the President of the

United States, and the Prime Ministers and Presidents of other countries. What were your perceptions of the use of these gatherings? Often the press seems to give the impression—by recording a rather empty communique—that meetings of heads of government are more symbolic activities than anything else, that they do not have a great deal of importance for solid policy.

MR. PEARSON: Well, I think to some extent that's true. I can give you one example. Right after I became Prime Minister I visited London. I don't remember anything very important being settled or even discussed there, but I felt the trip was of symbolic and political importance because some people were saying that we were dominated by the United States in everything; that I, especially, was too pro-American. So I thought it was wise to try to off-set that impression by not making my first trip as Prime Minister to the United States but to the U.K.; which I preferred to do in any event.

I won't name names but there are leaders of government who, quite frankly, seem to use many of their trips abroad mostly for domestic political purposes, in order to receive publicity and attention with political benefit back home.

Of course I don't think these visits are always merely symbolic. They can be very useful, and important, in putting to your opposite number a point of view which you wish him to have on certain policy matters that are being considered—by your government or his.

I remember that when I went to see Lyndon Johnson, that although it was difficult on occasion to discuss many things in depth and in detail (he was rather a busy man!— with interruptions even in the midst of meals or conversations) I was able to give him a Canadian viewpoint on issues that were not directly Canadian, but which might be of help to him even if it did not always harmonize with his own. It might give him a different perspective.

MR. HOCKIN: What do you mean "different perspective"? For example—with the U.S. —when you talked to the President did you talk about tough continental problems like oil imports or energy problems?

MR. PEARSON: Well, that's a good example. On discussing oil for example, when Washington was thinking of cutting back on the import of oil from our country, I could give the Canadian point of view first hand to the leader of the U.S. government. I could point out, for instance, that if they cut down on imports of Canadian oil, the Government of Canada would quickly be forced for economic and political reasons to build a pipeline to the East and this could mean the end of shipments of Venezuelan oil into the eastern part of Canada. I could tell the President, "You know who owns the Venezuelan oil companies?—your own people." Mr. Johnson might be struck by this argument so I would be able to bring him a "different point of view" than that which might have been put to him by those lobbying on behalf of the U.S. independent oil producers.

THE PRIME MINISTER, HIS CABINET AND THE PUBLIC SERVICE

MR. HOCKIN: Could you characterize the style of your operation with the Cabinet compared with Mackenzie King or St. Laurent?

MR. PEARSON: It is my impression that Mackenzie King was a better listener and analyser of points of view than a reader of documents beforehand. He operated more on intuition and impressions received from listening and discussing rather than by conclusions from examining briefs. Mr. St. Laurent's operation of Cabinet—I had firsthand experience of this—was very businesslike; he always had read his documents very carefully. He was well briefed as a law-

yer would want to be. As for me, I am a reader and examiner of briefs and memos dealing with points coming up. So I was well informed on the subjects under discussion. But I always encouraged Cabinet Ministers to speak up, argue their case to their colleagues, who were also encouraged to speak. My philosophy was to let a Cabinet Minister, as far as possible, run his own show and that it was not my job to be interfering in details. I felt that I should, in most cases, let Cabinet Ministers take the initiative in policy discussion in their areas and defend their initiatives in Cabinet. I would then have to make the decision if there was a division of opinion. I often met with Cabinet members individually to talk to them about policies in their fields and give them advice when necessary; but basically, I tried to let them run their own departments. My style of conducting cabinet meetings was relaxed, and informal; more so, I believe, than was the case with my predecessors. Mackenzie King, you know, never allowed anyone to smoke in Cabinet or have a coffee or any kind of break. He was the headmaster! Mr. St. Laurent's Cabinet was more formal than mine, but he was always a very considerate and courteous chairman, and anxious to encourage the widest participation in discussions.

MR. HOCKIN: As far as your control over policy generally, did you find that often policies were firmed up at the middle to deputy minister level and that often decisions were taken that at that level left the Prime Minister surprisingly little control?

MR. PEARSON: I must say in the case of the budget I often felt this. The budget—as was customary—would come to my desk about a week or so before it was to be brought before the full Cabinet and, really, that is pretty late for even a Prime Minister to have very much influence on it, though I may have had talks previously with the Minister of Finance on general policy matters underlying the budget. Other members of the Cabinet had even less time to examine the budget. I could, of course, have major influence on the broad lines of policy in a budget; but in accord with parliamentary practice, the other Cabinet Ministers really had little or nothing to do with the budget itself.

MR. HOCKIN: This might be more of an American than a Canadian question but there is a great problem American Presidents have of getting Government departments to respond to their wishes. Did you ever feel the public service did not respond to your wishes or the wishes of the Cabinet?

MR. PEARSON: Oh, I don't think this is a real problem in our system. Mr. Diefenbaker complained, I've heard, of what he called the "Pearsonalities" in the Department of External Affairs, when he was Prime Minister. But I've found that public servants are loyal to the government of the day as they should be. For example on unification of the armed forces, nearly all of the top military men were against it or doubtful about its wisdom but they got in line when the Cabinet laid down the policy; with only one or two exceptions.

I was a civil servant myself for many years. I admit that I can remember when the minister would decide (for instance) to open an Embassy somewhere and we in External thought we knew better than the minister on the subject; we might try to delay action hoping to convince the Minister that he should change his mind. But that would really be the extent of it and even that wasn't frequent. He made the decision, and if he didn't change it, we carried it out. I served both Mr. Bennett's and Mr. King's government and tried to be 100% loyal to both. Our civil service maintains and is proud of that tradition.

MR. HOCKIN: What about your control over Ministers on policy? Did you always leave

general initiatives to the Cabinet or to individual Ministers?

MR. PEARSON: There were occasions, of course, when I took initiatives of my own, aside from what other Ministers might wish to do, or not to do. For example in Medicare, as to carrying out our electoral commitments at a particular time. The same with the Canadian flag. The caucus and the Cabinet were divided on both issues. I heard arguments on both sides and then decided. There was also the nuclear weapons issue, though this was when we were in opposition. I talked to one or two of my senior colleagues about the matter, but I knew that if I talked to too many and we had too much discussion, any decision would leak out prematurely and I didn't want that.

[Thomas A. Hockin, *Apex of Power,* Prentice-Hall of Canada Limited, 1971]

Guidelines for Inquiry

1. Briefly summarize Pearson's view of the Prime Minister's leadership role in the following areas:
   (i) Caucus (the caucus consists of all the elected representatives of the party in Parliament)
   (ii) Parliament
   (iii) Country at large
   (iv) International conferences
   (v) Cabinet
   (vi) Public service
2. Mr. Pearson's views represent the opinions of only one leader. How might other Prime Ministers view these leadership roles differently?
3. Why is Pearson's statement that "one can appear to be a leader on television if he is a good performer, a good actor" somewhat frightening?

(d) Trudeau—New Style P.M., Power and Politics

Two years after being sworn into office Pierre Trudeau has gathered more power into his own hands than any previous prime minister.

He has built a personal political staff on a scale never before seen in Ottawa and centralized control of the federal bureaucracy in his own executive suite.

Trudeau tells his cabinet, "I shan't be around long," so that his ministers keep in line for the succession, and he stands above their battles so that they vie for his support.

His backbenchers regard his intellect with awe and sometimes fear the lash of his sarcasm when they question his policies.

He refuses to play Parliament's game of petty politics and his relations with the Governor-General are no closer than correct, as his compelling personality upstages a vice-regal couple who have made little impact on the public.

Trudeau's skill at communication overcomes normal political liabilities, and he easily tops the polls.

His frustrated opponents cry "president", meaning it as a protest against his power. Trudeau smiles, and his image-makers accept it as a compliment because they believe Canadians are conditioned by the memory of U.S. president John F. Kennedy to want a presidential leader.

But Trudeau's political philosophy is to create counterweights to power. The checks and balances to his own authority are appearing, sometimes with his encouragement . . . Parliament changes its role and new political forms emerge to challenge the presidential power.

POWER CENTRE—THE PMO

The command post of every Canadian government is in the towered, turreted and gargoyled East Block on Parliament Hill.

The East Block, in fact, is the closest Canadian equivalent to Washington's White House as the headquarters of the executive arm of government.

Prime Minister Pierre Elliott Trudeau has accepted this more readily than his predecessors and enlarged his personal staff to give him greater effective power and control over the entire operations of government.

NUMBER ON STAFF

His office establishment is 77 persons, including confidential aides on private contract down to $5,000-a-year civil service stenos. At the most recent count, 73 posts were filled.

This compares with Lester Pearson's establishment of 44 in 1967, his last year as prime minister, and far fewer in the time of John Diefenbaker.

The fact that Trudeau's staff is larger than that of his predecessors is not necessarily a criticism.

Pearson's aides were grossly overworked and hardly knew what it meant to take a day off at weekends. They fired decisions from the hip and the office was sometimes in a state of barely controlled chaos which was reflected in the image of the government.

Diefenbaker was destroyed partly by the absence of an effective machine for making decisions and exercising executive authority.

Trudeau has learned the lesson of these mistakes because his staff is based on veterans of the Pearson years, and even earlier.

Contrary to widespread impression, he has not brought in a whole new team, but taken over the existing East Block establishment and enlarged it by recruiting, in the main, young men who were already working around the government.

PRINCIPAL AIDES

His principal aide, for example, is Marc Lalonde, who first came to Ottawa to work for

Conservative minister Davie Fulton in the Diefenbaker era and later returned as policy secretary to Pearson. One of Lalonde's first pieces of advice to Trudeau was to enlarge the private staff so that aides would have time to think and to organize. . . .

. . . Many of the people who regularly deplored the disasters and crises of the Pearson and Diefenbaker years now look back upon them with affection as somehow more reassuring and comfortable than the smooth hum of Trudeau's computer.

But the fact is that Trudeau is running a different style of government and of politics.

The speed and pressure of government administration is constantly increasing. To use only one East Block index, the number of papers going before the cabinet doubled from an average of 383 a year in 1957-59 to about 800 a year 10 years later. . . .

Trudeau also uses his personal staff to develop information and advice from outside the cabinet and the regular channels of civil service organization, so that he has policy options before him when he makes final decisions.

While all this explains why Trudeau has increased his private staff, it does not change the fact that, for better or for worse, he has drawn more of the reins of power into his own hands than any recent prime minister.

THE MAIL FLOWS IN—AND OUT

In the TV age, when the Prime Minister talks directly to the people, more and more Canadians want to communicate back to him. They write to Pierre Trudeau in unprecedented and increasing numbers.

The Prime Minister's office received 17,-000 pieces of mail during February, but the average is 450 a day. This compares with 185 letters a day when Lester Pearson was prime minister.

The flow of answers has risen even more dramatically. While previous prime ministers were content merely to acknowledge many communications, Trudeau and his staff provide long informative answers.

During the Pearson period there were 21 employees in his correspondence section. Trudeau now has 37.

The increase of 16 accounts for more than half the total and much-criticized increase in the Prime Minister's personal establishment.

When Trudeau came to office and the mail began to pour in, attracted by his power of communication, government management experts and IBM experts helped set up a system to handle it.

Mail from ministers, members of Parliament, provincial premiers, heads of federal agencies, Liberal party leaders and other VIPs is routed to Trudeau's desk.

Other letters which are for any reason distinguished—they may be wise or witty or of special human interest—are submitted to Trudeau together with a reply ready for his approval and personal signature.

The mass of the mail, some 300 pieces a day, is handled by the correspondence office. A research unit provides standard answers to standard queries, and these are coded into special cards.

By selecting the right combination of cards, a letter writer can compose an appropriate answer to most correspondents seeking information from the Prime Minister.

The cards activate an automatic typewriter which produces an individualized reply, leaving space for the name and any additional information to be typed in. . . .

[The Correspondence Secretary] provides Trudeau each month with a detailed statistical analysis of the mail, complete with a narrative commentary and a selection of typical letters.

The correspondence division and its enlarged staff is an increasingly important channel of communication between Trudeau and the public. He takes in a broad sample of public opinion which yields a sophisticated understanding of the moods and concerns of the nation, and he sends out his personal explanations to tens of thousand of Canadians every year.

REGIONAL DESK MEN

Another way in which Trudeau has increased his staff and his personal political reach is by the appointment of four regional desk officers.

Prime ministers who come to office after long political experience have friends and contacts to call in Halifax or Vancouver or Toronto when they need private intelligence. But Trudeau's roots in the Liberal party are shallow and his political background limited to Quebec.

(A current and possibly apocryphal story relates that when Denison mine owner Steve Roman opened a recent talk with Trudeau with the familiar refrain of favor seekers, "I've been a Liberal for years . . . ", Trudeau put him down by saying pointedly, "I haven't been.")

The desk officers partly make up for this deficiency by keeping Trudeau alert to issues and opinion in the West, the Maritimes and Quebec. They also serve as a direct channel to provincial premiers and community leaders, supplementing and sometimes bypassing the provincial representation offered by cabinet ministers and members of Parliament. . . .

Trudeau likes to make maximum use of every trip out of Ottawa and his regional officers move ahead of him, programming every minute of his time. . . . *All* the implications of an invitation are weighed in advance, and one or more staff officers go ahead to inspect the ground and lay out the program to obtain the maximum benefit.

APPOINTMENTS MADE FROM "TALENT BANK"

A third area in which Trudeau has extended personal control is in making several hundred senior appointments each year to the Senate, crown corporations, federal agencies, and departments, and so on. Choosing the right men is a vital part of administration—and of patronage.

Most prime ministers have relied on personal knowledge or on recommendations from ministers and bureaucrats. Trudeau insists on an alternative source of advice and information in his own office. . . .

THE PCO—ADMINISTRATIVE CENTRE

When Prime Minister Mackenzie King sat down with his ministers for a cabinet meeting, he had two boxes before him on the table.

In the first box, the cabinet secretary placed papers requiring attention, and then discreetly withdrew. He returned after the private meeting to see which papers had been shifted into the second box, meaning they were approved for action.

The cabinet gave no explanations, had no written agenda and kept no minutes.

That was just 30 years ago when government was smaller and problems less complex.

The cabinet secretariat in the Privy Council Office has been growing steadily ever since, and today it is an elite staff encouraged by Prime Minister Pierre Trudeau to exercise a subtle, centralizing influence over the entire federal administration. . . .

INFLUENCE OF MANDARINS

The first source [of influence] is access to the Prime Minister, [controlled by] Cabinet Secretary Robertson, Ottawa's senior mandarin and a reserved but pleasant man with graying hair and the deep tanned face of a skier, who attends Trudeau's morning staff meetings and supplies him with all the official information and briefings he requires.

The second source of influence is control of the cabinet agenda and paperwork. When a departmental minister wants to take a proposal to cabinet, the Privy Council Office decides which committee to send it to, if the supporting documents are in order and, occasionally, when to bring it forward to the full cabinet.

Since Trudeau reorganized and rationalized the system of cabinet committees, this control of routine has become more rigid and important. . . .

DECLINE OF PARLIAMENT

The decline of the Commons had been apparent for years, of course, and the subject of much anxious comment. . . . Instead of a national forum, the Commons had become for many Canadians a theatre of the absurd in which mock battles were fought with wooden swords, the members were all actors, and nothing really changed.

As the backdrop to disenchantment, there was the intuitive understanding—still only half-formed today and of uncertain final shape—that representative democracy may be of passing relevance.

. . . Now that the people are in constant communication with the PM and the government, they are less willing to delegate their judgment to MPs. . . .

Trudeau . . . is a poor performer in the Commons and controls largely by refusing to recognize it as very important.

This is not to say he is autocratic or contemptuous. . . . Trudeau himself is a more faithful attender at the question time than most prime ministers have been, and reasonable queries usually get courteous replies. . . .

But the Commons is not primarily for the serious business of eliciting information or engaging in constructive comparison of ideas. It is for scoring party points, and Trudeau can hardly be bothered with that sort of battle, in which he is not very good anyway.

He answers partisan points with a quip or shrugs them off with disdain. Then, when he chooses, he strolls out of the House to make his case directly to the public by TV.

In the House debate, Trudeau is often put down by Opposition Leader Robert Stanfield, who has trained himself to be an effective parliamentarian.

On TV, Trudeau is, in a CBC man's admiring phrase, "better than Laugh-In", while Stanfield "looks like yesterday".

Stanfield can only express his frustration by attacking Trudeau for arrogance and blaming him for the decline of Parliament. But having said that, the Tory leader has to face reality by being absent more and more from the Commons as he goes out into the country to make public speeches.

"If we stay in the House we're dead," he remarked recently to an aide.

TRUDEAU STRENGTHENING PARLIAMENT

Prime Minister Pierre Trudeau may scandalize the critics by preferring television to the Commons as a channel of communication to the public, and by showing more interest in dialogue with students and farmers and protest groups than in answering opposition members at question time.

But he is also encouraging Parliament to be a more effective auditor and scrutineer of his government, and he has done more than any prime minister for years to assist his backbenchers.

The centre of parliamentary activity has shifted from the Commons chamber to the committees which are flourishing as never before.

INCREASED COMMITTEE WORK

. . . In the 1964-65 session, Commons committees reported on 36 matters; in the last session there were 122 reports.

Last year, committees held 339 meetings and spent 451 hours reviewing spending estimates, far more time than the full House could have devoted to the task.

This session, the committees have heard 397 witnesses so far, an unprecedented input of information and expertise from outside the government.

Last week, the verbatim record of the committees totalled 9,029 pages, compared with 5,268 pages in the Hansard record of the full House.

Nobody claims the committee system is anywhere near perfect. MPs who can lurk in decent obscurity in the full Commons are exposed as incompetents by the less formal, more demanding work of small committees.

There are probably too many committee sessions, particularly for members of minor parties who have to spread time and expertise too thin.

The government's own attitude is sometimes ambiguous; while encouraging committees with one hand, it will occasionally use the other to slap down their sense of independence.

But the trend to reform and renewal is clear, and Liberal MPs as much as opposition members are pressing for more power and responsibility. . . .

RESEARCH FUNDS AND CAUCUS

[Trudeau] has [also] provided $195,000 a year to leaders of opposition parties to pay 22 full-time and five part-time researchers to document criticism of the government.

Under pressure from his own backbenchers, Trudeau is now granting them $130,000 for research by the Liberal caucus independently of the government.

The caucus meets in private and is an important forum in which Liberal MPs can criticize the government without appearing disloyal. The way in which a prime minister treats caucus and reacts to criticism is a significant test of his respect for democracy.

Trudeau is a regular attender at caucus but impatient with the meetings when they are merely steam-valve sessions for backbench complaints.

He can be cutting in his summing up at the end of each meeting, and some members are afraid to tackle him for fear of being made to appear fools.

But Trudeau has also encouraged caucus to be more effective in questioning and checking the cabinet. . . .

Trudeau [has] agreed not to give final consent to [a] finished bill until he is satisfied that caucus has been consulted.

Caucus has reorganized its committees to coincide with cabinet committees, and they alternate weekly with sessions of the full body. . . .

Parliament and its machinery are obviously adapting and changing, and are going to change a great deal more, to match the new tools of power in the hands of the Prime Minister. MPs should have more independence and greater latitude to check the government without destroying it.

The trend is in that direction, but not fast enough to satisfy the critics.

[Anthony Westell, "Trudeau—New Style PM., Power and Politics", *Toronto Daily Star*, April 11-17, 1970]

Guidelines for Inquiry

1. How is Trudeau attempting to combine democracy and efficiency in our parliamentary system? Make judgments about his policies in this regard and support your views with appropriate evidence.
2. By comparing data about the performances of several prime ministers, assess Westell's claim that Trudeau has "gathered more power into his own hands than any previous prime minister".
3. To what extent do you think the office of Prime Minister should be reformed in order to better meet the political needs of Canadians?

SOMETIMES THE EQUALITY OF MAN CAN BE MEASURED IN DEGREES.

Blaine, *The Spectator*, Hamilton

(e) Leaders at Play

Have you ever noticed how self-righteously prissy so many people are about the sight of their political leaders enjoying a little relaxation? Even the go-limp-and-to-hell-with-everything group seems to become quite puritanical about the idea that a political leader should knock off his office duties and enjoy himself a bit now and then. A classic example of this phenomenon in our country is, of course, the protests which are sounded when our own Prime Minister, Pierre Trudeau, goes wandering far afield from Ottawa. Personally, I think such views are not only hypocritical, to a great extent, but unrealistic and approaching the outright stupid. I think that whether the Prime Minister stays on duty twenty-four hours a day, sleeping in his office, or takes a break or two every few weeks, has very little to do with his capabilities as a leader of the country.

I'll go further and say that the Prime Minister who spends almost every waking hour at his desk might easily be an incompetent while the one who gets away from it fairly often might well be possessed of sterling leadership qualities. Even the late Henry Ford, who could hardly be classed as a leisure-loving playboy, once stated that he preferred to see his top executives sitting there with their feet up on their desks just thinking now and then, instead of constantly scurrying around in circles. There's a lot of difference between mere movement and real action.

I imagine . . . that Mr. Trudeau gets an occasional inspiration while out on the ski hills or swimming in Mexico.

My granddad used to have a saying about "all work and no play makes Jack a dull boy" and I believe there was some wisdom in it. I have seen a few politicians supposedly relaxing, while doing such things as a spot of fishing. And I have a hunch that those who carry heavy responsibility in these complex and trying times are never able to wholly relax, to the point where their minds are completely off their problems.

We are asking an awful lot of our politicians these days. Quite often you hear, "What's the Prime Minister going to do?" about this situation, or "What's the President going to do?" about that one. Often, if we were honest with ourselves, we would admit that no single man or, even, political party can really do anything much unless all of us join in the effort. Until we are all trying to do our own level best to settle national problems, I don't think we should adopt such a pecksniffian and holier-than-thy-politician attitude toward those who are, usually with very little thanks and a great deal of abuse.

[Bruce West, "Leaders at Play", *Globe and Mail*, Toronto, August 16, 1971]

Guideline for Inquiry

Bruce West maintains that, "The Prime Minister who spends every waking hour at his desk might easily be an incompetent while the one who gets away from it fairly often might well be possessed of sterling leadership qualities." To what extent do you agree or disagree with this point of view?

(f) Canada's New Prime Minister

In May 1979 Canadians elected Joe Clark as prime minister, ending the eleven-year government of Pierre Trudeau. How has Clark indicated that he wants to change some aspects of his role compared with Trudeau? How successful has he been?

Progressive Conservative Party of Canada

unit 2: Québec in Canada, or Québec and Canada?

by John Patton

INTRODUCTION: THE DILEMMA

Can English Canada and French Canada continue to co-exist? Do our present social and political institutions allow both groups to achieve their aspirations? *Should* English Canada and French Canada continue to co-exist? If they were to separate, what might be the consequences? Where do you stand on the issue of Québec *in* Canada, or Québec *and* Canada? Here are a range of views on the question:

(a) We are going to need a system of republicanism which would be Canadian. . . . Is it not possible to have a President of the Republic at the top, who will see that those two Prime Ministers of the two nations [French Canada and English Canada] can in common determine their special needs, united at the top by a common monetary system, a common communications system, common customs regulations, a common army?

SOLANGE CHAPUT ROLLAND

(b) How many times have we heard complaints that "Quebec is running the country," that "what we need is national unity," and that "we're going to have to show them where to get off"? Quebec is a thorn in our flesh. . . .

If he is at all logical, the English Canadian who holds such views will have to admit the justice of the Quebec separatist point of view and accept the break-up of Confederation.

THOMAS SLOAN

(c) What confronts us is either the break-up of our country or its continuation as a fragmented, decentralized nation, firmly integrated in the U.S. economic and military empire. . . .

Our only hope of deliverance from this fate lies in the reassertion of Canadian nationalism in its first and integral form. The vain and perilous pursuit of dualism, which was not an original object of Confederation and has nearly brought about its undoing, must be abandoned. One nation, not two nations in one, can alone maintain an effective defense of Canada.

DONALD CREIGHTON

(d) An independent Québec and an independent Canada can be friendly neighbours respecting each other as equals. Anything else will only perpetuate misery and hatred.

LÉANDRE BERGERON

(e) I propose that we start with [the idea] . . . that the safest token of progress for Canada is a strong and dynamic French Canada, sure of itself, freed from fear, and thoroughly involved in all aspects of Canadian life. Equally, the safest way of building up a solid country, prosperous and free, on the borders of the United States, is for English Canada to play thoroughly the game of honest collaboration with the French element of the country.

PIERRE ELLIOTT TRUDEAU

(f) There is a widespread presumption, even among some learned experts, that there is only one "real" federal state and that Canada is its most magnificent and perfect expression. They fail to see that Canada may have to depart quite substantially from the present formula and move toward a new one. In defining the "national" Canadian interest, the pre-eminence of the central government may have to be greatly diminished to make way for a complex scheme in which the provinces, enjoying greater [autonomy] than they do now, may have to reach agreement among themselves, at the same time as they deal as more or less equals with the federal government.

JOHN MEISEL

Guidelines for Inquiry

1. Which viewpoints seem farthest apart? Which viewpoints seem closest together? Why?
2. With which viewpoint do you most agree? Why?
3. What types of evidence will you need to test the validity of your viewpoint?

Part One: Young Canadians in the Making?

1. The Two Solitudes: Canadian Students, 1966-67

This is a brief excerpt from the report of the National History Project, entitled *What Culture? What Heritage?* The evidence for the report was gathered by questionnaires, interviews, and open-ended essays, and the purpose of it was to investigate the teaching of history, social studies, and civics in Canadian schools.

French- and English-speaking students raised on radically opposed views of Canadian history cannot possibly understand each other fully. Perhaps enough has already been written to establish this point but some further evidence is so revealing that it should be brought forward here.

In naming artists, poets, and writers, for instance, the French-Canadian respondents to our Questionnaire invariably listed only those of their own ethnic group. Likewise, English-speaking students completely neglected French Canadians and named only standard textbook figures from their own ethnic group. As writers, French-Canadian students—showing greater variety and perhaps a greater knowledge of their culture—named Gabrielle Roy, Marie-Claire Blais, Yves Thériault, Roger Lemelin, Anne Hébert, Louis Hémon, and many others, all French Canadians. English-speaking respondents struggled to name Stephen Leacock, Farley Mowat, Hugh MacLennan, and a few others—all English Canadians. An analysis of the poets and artists mentioned reveals precisely the same situation. In literary, artistic, and other cultural areas, where so much could be done to foster mutual understanding, French-speaking students in Quebec, and English-speaking students from the rest of Canada, are living in two different worlds.

Again, in listing five important Canadians of the past hundred years, French-Canadian respondents identified exclusively with historical figures of their own nationality, almost totally neglecting any others. English-speaking students relied on Macdonald, Borden, King, Pearson and other well-known, mainly political, textbook names that may or may not have any real meaning for them and that reveal the overemphasis on constitutional and political history. Except for mutually acceptable names like Laurier and Vanier and occasional references to Louis Riel, respondents from the rest of Canada failed to list anyone outside the main Anglo-Saxon stream of textbook history.

Answers to the question on sources of pride or interest in Canadian history reveal other fundamental differences. As we have already noted in another context, English-speaking respondents, to the extent that they had any real interest at all in the past, named Canada's part in wars, Confederation and very little else. It is perhaps a strange commentary on the kind of history being taught in English-speaking Canada to note that the major source of pride, far outweighing any others, was Canada's part in the War of 1812, World War I and World War II. French-Canadian students could find no reason for pride in either wars or Confederation. The main answer from more than 75 percent of the Quebec respondents was pride in "our forefathers who fought to preserve our language, customs and religion", or in the early colonists who struggled against the elements "to build a French-Canadian land". Results like this were to be expected and serve to emphasize the basic differences already described in course outlines, textbooks, statements of aims, classroom materials and practices.

Our evidence reveals that these differences in approach to Canadian studies foster feelings of indifference, prejudice, misunderstanding and even hostility between the two linguistic communities. The indifference, or lack of sympathy and awareness among English-speaking students toward Quebec, was shown in their answers to the question asking for five important Canadian developments in the past year or so. Eighty-four percent of all respondents from English Canada made no references of any kind to Quebec. As far as most of them were concerned, things like the Truscott case, strikes, inflation, wheat deals with China and other materialistic developments were far more noteworthy than Daniel Johnson's election victory, the Quiet Revolution, separatism or anything else in French-speaking Canada. The same lack of interest also was revealed in the question on sources of worry about present-day Canada. Anything to do with Quebec or with French-English relations was a cause of concern for only 14 percent of the English-speaking students. The great majority were much more aware of such things as poor government in Ottawa, labor disputes, scandals and high taxes.

When asked to identify "two or three differences between French Canadians and other Canadians", 19 percent of the English-speaking respondents said there were no differences; 9 percent were unable or unwilling to think of any; and the best that 42 percent could manage was single-word references to religion and language—surely signs of a lack of attention in the Canadian studies classroom or of plain indifference. But of all the others who did have definite ideas to which a value judgment could be attached, the great majority expressed unsympathetic, critical and at times hostile feelings toward French Canadians. Fewer than 6 percent of all English-speaking respondents said anything complimentary about French Canadians or defended Quebec's stand on any current issues. . . .

French-Canadian responses to some of these same questions further emphasize the enormous gap between the young people of our two linguistic communities and show that French-Canadian students have their own deep-seated prejudices. Although Canadian human interest stories caught their youthful fancy too, their major interests in current affairs and their main worries about present-day Canada were directed inward to their own province. Declining birth rates, the threat of immigration to their survival, foreign domination of their resources, the failure of French Canadians outside Quebec to stand up for their rights or protect their language, and other problems never mentioned by the English-speaking students were among their primary concerns.

"LET US FLY ON OUR OWN WINGS"

These ingrown interests were very clearly revealed in 300 randomly selected Open-ended Essays written by Grade 11 French Canadians. Writing about what they thought of Canada, these students almost without exception dwelt on such things as the Conquest, the constant struggle to survive, the compulsion to speak a "foreign" language, their domination by the English and their need to stand together to maintain their homeland and the rights of French Canadians. (As an interesting aside, the great majority of these young students showed a much better command of their own language and a greater sense of historical perspective than did the English-speaking students who also wrote this Essay.) Ninety-three percent of these 300 Essays contained passages similar in tenor to the following direct translations.

"For me, Canada is a homeland, but one which is limited to the Province of Quebec. Although we have been conquered by the English, in Quebec we are still united, incessantly demanding the right of language. In effect, in order to hold a good job today, we must be able to speak English. I know we have been conquered and the English have every right over us; but why do we not return to our ancient traditions? We have perhaps been conquered but I believe that all that is history, is past."

"Canada is a country which results from a union of provinces which have made a pact and have ceded a certain part of their power to an organism, the federal government. I find unjustifiable the reasons given by this government for taking over the country and for withdrawing all powers, all responsibilities from the provinces."

"I think Canada ought to remain united but that in Quebec one ought to be able to speak French and especially that French remain the first language in Quebec. I think that the French Canadians in Quebec should not be obliged to learn English but that the English Canadians in Quebec should be obliged to learn French. . . . In Quebec, which is more than 80 percent French Canadian, I wish the remaining 20 percent would learn French without further delay. . . . Why do the English of Quebec oblige the French to learn English?"

"For me, Canada is a great, a beautiful country, but one which I don't know well enough to appreciate. Given the fact that I live in the 'State of Quebec', I want our fine province to be free of all the gear imposed on it by the federal government and old British traditions. I would like to see the separation of our dear province from the others. . . . I want us to be 'maître chez nous' and I believe we are capable of this."

"I think we have given enough to England. If only the English would let us fly on our own wings. . . . Canada, my relatives; Quebec, my parents!"

[A. B. Hodgetts, *What Culture? What Heritage?* Ontario Institute for Studies in Education, 1968.]

The issue of instruction in French and English at Elliot Lake Secondary School (Ontario) in 1973 led to the above demonstration.

2. Youthful Definitions of Canadian Society

These charts, compiled for the Royal Commission on Bilingualism and Bicultur-alism, give information about the attitudes of Canadians, between the ages of thirteen and twenty, from various regions and ethnic groups. Their answers were compiled according to the language spoken in the home.

(a) How Does a Person Get Ahead in Canada?

Per cent who said each factor was very important in helping a young person get ahead in Canadian life

Factor	English				French			
	13-14	15-16	17-18	19-20	13-14	15-16	17-18	19-20
(1) Get good grades in school	97	94	96	91	76	69	62	69
(2) Work hard	95	92	92	98	52	45	41	55
(3) Have a nice personality	88	86	82	81	63	71	65	79
(4) Get a university education	84	76	79	79	55	38	51	54
(5) Know the right people	56	43	52	50	50	46	53	57
(6) Be able to speak both French and English	44	40	35	29	69	74	78	82
(7) Come from the right family	28	23	18	24	32	23	32	22
(8) Come from the right religious group	14	7	12	10	50	31	27	18
(9) Be born in Canada	12	10	10	4	27	23	16	26
(10) Have parents with a lot of money	4	8	6	4	13	12	9	9

(b) Government Preferences

Question: Which government would you say does the *most* for people?

Response	English	French	Other
	%	%	%
The government of your city, town, or township	23	23	37
The government of your province	33	40	39
The government of Canada	32	22	22
I'm not sure	13	15	2
Total	101	100	100

Question: Which one would you say does the least for people?

	English	French	Other
	%	%	%
The government of your city, town, or township	30	21	14
The government of your province	12	13	19
The government of Canada	26	34	25
I'm not sure	31	32	42
Total	99	100	100

Question: Which government would be best to work for — if the salary was the same on each job?

	English	French	Other
	%	%	%
The government of your city, town, or township	28	27	27
The government of your province	22	34	19
The government of Canada	39	28	38
I'm not sure	11	11	16
Total	100	100	100

(c) What Groups in North America Have Most in Common?

Question: Who would you say have more in common — English-speaking Canadians and Americans or English-speaking Canadians and French-speaking Canadians?

Response	English	French	Other
	%	%	%
English-speaking Canadians and Americans	68	41	69
English-speaking Canadians and French-speaking Canadians	20	39	9
I'm not sure	12	20	22
Total	100	100	100

Question: Who have more in common — French-Canadians and Americans or French-Canadians and English-Canadians?

	%	%	%
French-Canadians and Americans	8	21	10
French-Canadians and English-Canadians	70	60	63
I'm not sure	21	19	27
Total	99	100	100

[John J. Johnstone, *Young People's Images of Canadian Society*, Queen's Printer, 1969]

Guidelines for Inquiry

1. Are there any differences in the way Canadian students look at their country? If so, what accounts for the differences?
2. Would it be a good idea, in your opinion, if schools across the country gave students a common, universally accepted view of Canada? Cite evidence to support your position.
3. How do you react to the views expressed by the French-speaking students?
4. How would you have responded to the questions asked by Hodgetts: e.g., name as many Canadian artists, poets, and writers as you can think of; list five important Canadians of the past hundred years; what is the major source of pride for you, as a Canadian; list five important developments in Canada in the past year; identify two or three differences between French Canadians and other Canadians; what do you think of Canada? Analyse your own answers in light of Hodgetts' comments.
5. What differences among English- and French-speaking youth are indicated in Johnstone's tables of statistics? Compare Hodgetts' and Johnstone's findings.

Part Two: Perspectives on Nationalism: Which Nationalism? Whose Perspective?

1. O Canada!

O Ca - na - da, we stand on guard for thee!
Pro - té - ge - ra nos foy - ers et nos droits.

2. O Canada! Where pines and maples grow,
    Great prairies spread and lordly rivers flow,
How dear to us thy broad domain,
    From East to Western Sea,
Thou land of hope for all who toil!
    Thou True North, strong and free!
O Canada, glorious and free!
    We stand on guard, we stand on guard for thee.
O Canada, we stand on guard for thee!

3. O Canada! Beneath thy shining skies
    May stalwart sons and gentle maidens rise,
To keep thee steadfast through the years
    From East to Western Sea,
Our own beloved native land!
    Our True North, strong and free!
O Canada, glorious and free!
    We stand on guard, we stand on guard for thee.
O Canada, we stand on guard for thee!

2. Sous l'œil de Dieu, près du fleuve géant,
    Le Canadien grandit en espérant.
Il est né d'une race fière,
    Béni fut son berceau;
Le ciel a marqué sa carrière
    Dans ce monde nouveau,
Toujours guidé par sa lumière
    Il gardera l'honneur de son drapeau,
Il gardera l'honneur de son drapeau.

3. De son patron, précurseur du vrai Dieu,
    Il porte au front l'auréole de feu,
Ennemi de la tyrannie,
    Mais plein de loyauté,
Il veut garder dans l'harmonie
    Sa fière liberté,
Et par l'effort de son génie,
    Sur notre sol asseoir la vérité,
Sur notre sol asseoir la vérité.

Alternate Wording

O Canada! Our home and native land!
    True patriot love in all thy sons command.
With glowing hearts we see thee rise,
    The True North strong and free!
From far and wide, O Canada,
    We stand on guard for thee.
God keep our land glorious and free
    O Canada, we stand on guard for thee.
O Canada, we stand on guard for thee.

Guideline for Inquiry

To what extent are the French and English versions of "O Canada!" similar? In what respects do they differ? Why?

2. The View from B.C.?

"We'd adore motoring through Quebec . . . doing our bit, so to speak, to knit Confederation."

[Norris, *Vancouver Sun*]

3. The National Outlook of English-speaking Canadians

Probably because the alternative is so clumsy, the terms "English-Canadian" or "English" are used interchangeably in Quebec to signify those people in the rest of Canada who do not speak French or who are not of French descent. Yet these terms are wildly misleading. They imply the existence in Canada of only two races, and thus that any revision of Confederation must be based upon a dialogue or bargaining process between these two races. Each term also carries the suggestion that the words "Canada" and "Canadian" have come to mean "English Canada" and "English Canadian". Thus the problem in Quebec eyes concerns the relations between the "two nations"; and it is a striking fact that "nation" and "race" are virtually interchangeable terms in Quebec.

The most striking facts about the English-speaking view of Canada are that it rejects racial nationalism and is the product of a deep commitment to slowly evolved historical tradition. There are good reasons why both these aspects of the English-speaking view are less well publicized and less widely discussed than the racial nationalism of French-Canadian spokesmen. There are even better reasons why the English-speaking view should be much more precisely understood at the present time. For that view, in the developing crisis of Confederation, will assert itself with increasing vigour.

I have said that English-speaking Canadians take a non-racial view of nationality. This will astonish the spokesmen of French-Canadian nationalism, and may surprise some others who have unreflectively accepted the French-Canadian version. Fingers will point to such historical expressions of English-Canadian racialism as the United Empire Loyalist tradition, the Imperial Federation movement, the Protestant Protective Association, the Ontario and Manitoba schools questions and the conscription crises of two world wars. Specialists in this argument will even resurrect Louis Riel. In each of these instances (with the probable exception of Riel) there was undoubtedly, on the part of Canadians of British descent, a feeling of racial identification. But one would have to be blind not to recognize that the racial component in the English-speaking view has steadily grown less significant. Not only that, the English-speaking view has always anticipated a Canadian nationality in which the significance of racial origin will diminish rather than increase.

At the time of Confederation, indeed, all the supporters of the movement, French- and English-speaking alike, talked of the founding of a new nationality. No amount of quibbling about the different meanings attached by "English" and "French" to the word "nation" can obscure the fact that in the 1860's a political nationality was being founded. The debate and conferences leave absolutely no room for doubt on the matter. Nor is there room to doubt that English-speaking Canadians, then and even more now, thought of Canadian nationality as something that included people of French, British and other origins and which would move steadily toward its own sense of identity. That identity was not to be homogeneous in the American sense, but diverse. It would [guarantee], and has guaranteed, to various minorities (especially the French-speaking minority) particular rights with respect to language, religion, land-holding, military service, hunting and fishing.

Yet while local differences of culture and law were to be guaranteed (especially in Quebec), there was never any question of an "equality of two founding races". The "races" were, in fact, not equal. A central purpose of Confederation was to recognize this fact and to avoid the frictions which the "two nations" idea had created during the unhappy political evolution under the 1841 Act of Union.

In order to maintain minority rights within Quebec and the other provinces, without at the same time permitting Quebec to become a state within a state, the predominance of Ottawa and the rights of the Canadian majority there (however it might be composed) had to be accepted. As *Le Canadien* of Quebec put it in 1864: "Il faut que nous nous résignions à n'être dans le congrès fédéral qu'une minorité comme il faut que de son côté la population anglaise du Bas-Canada se résigne à n'être qu'une minorité dans le législature provinciale."

Any survey of Canadian political history reveals that the idea of two "founding races" (each with the expectation of its own developing nationality) has been and must be destructive of the idea of Canada. Moreover, even if one wishes to call the political settlement of 1867 a "compact" or "entente", it is still crystal clear that the "entente" is being broken today by the leaders of the Quiet Revolution and not by any "English-Canadian" view of Confederation. Strange, because of all Canadians the Quebeckers refer most frequently to history as their master.

[Kenneth McNaught, "The National Outlook of English-Speaking Canadians", in *Nationalism in Canada,* ed. Peter Russell, McGraw-Hill Ryerson Limited, 1966]

Guideline for Inquiry

McNaught sees a real difference between English- and French-Canadian nationalisms. What is it? To what extent do you support his position?

4. English-Canadian Nationalism and the French Canadians

[In 1763] the English were already the most nationalist of nationalists. The whole country, proud of its political and economic superiority, unanimously favoured the planting of the flag in the most far-flung lands. This nationalism was necessarily cultural, too; to English eyes they bestowed a priceless favour on the undeserving countries they colonized: the right to share the Anglo-Saxon language and customs. And then, despite having so effectively and admirably built up the cult of civil liberties at home in England, they gave not the slightest thought to the protection of minority rights for others.

From the moment of delivery of the Royal Proclamation of 1763, the intention was obvious: the French Canadian was to be completely assimilated. In 1840 Durham, while "far from wishing to encourage indiscriminately [these] pretentions to superiority on the part of any particular race", none the less considered that assimilation was simply "a question of time and mode".

Throughout this period, Canadians of British origin would have considered it an indignity to be in any inferior position. So they invented all kinds of stratagems by which democracy was made to mean government by the minority.

Generations passed. Hopes of assimilating the French Canadians dimmed to a flicker (although right up to 1948, immigration laws continued to favour immigrants from the British Isles over those from France). But English-speaking Canadians have never given up their condescending attitude to their French-speaking fellows, even to this day.

At Ottawa and in provinces other than ours, this nationalism could wear the pious mask of democracy. Because, as English-speaking Canadians became proportionately more numerous, they took to hiding their intolerance behind acts of majority rule; that was how they quashed bilingualism in the Manitoba legislature, violated rights acquired by separate schools in various provinces, savagely imposed conscription in 1917, and broke a solemn promise in 1942.

In Quebec, "where they had the money if not the numbers, our Anglo-Canadian fellow-citizens have often yielded to the temptation of using without restraint the means at their command." This was how, in politics, Anglo-Canadian nationalism took on the form of what André Laurendeau has so admirably named the "cannibal-king theory" (*théorie du roi-nègre*). Economically, this nationalism has been expressed essentially in treating the French Canadian as *un cochon de payant*. Sometimes, magnanimously, they would go as far as putting a few straw men on boards of directors. These men invariably had two things in common: first, they were never bright enough or strong enough to rise to the top, and second, they were always sufficiently "representative" to grovel for the cannibal-king's favours and flatter the vanity of their fellow-tribesmen. Finally, in social and cultural matters, Anglo-Canadian nationalism has expressed itself quite simply by disdain. Generation after generation of Anglo-Saxons have lived in Quebec without getting around to learning three sentences of French. When these insular people insist, with much gravity, that their jaws and ears aren't made for it and can't adapt themselves to French, what they really want to get across to you is that they will not sully these organs, and their small minds, by submitting them to a barbarous idiom.

Anglo-Canadian nationalism produced,

inevitably, French-Canadian nationalism. As I have said before, speaking of the roots of our nationalism and the futility of its tendencies:

> Defeated, occupied, leaderless, banished from commercial enterprise, poked away outside the cities, little by little reduced to a minority and left with very little influence in a country which, after all, he discovered, explored and colonized, the French Canadian had little alternative for the frame of mind he would have to assume in order to preserve what remained of his own. So he set up a system of defense-mechanisms which soon assumed such overgrown proportions that he came to regard as priceless anything which distinguished him from other people; and any change whatever (be it for the better or not) he would regard with hostility if it originated from outside.

"Alas," I added, "the nationalists' idealism itself has been their downfall. 'They loved not wisely but too well.'"

THE CONFLICT OF NATIONALISMS IN CANADA

We must accept the facts of history as they are. However outworn and absurd it may be, the nation-state image spurred the political thinking of the British, and subsequently of Canadians of British descent in the "Dominion of Canada". Broadly speaking, this meant identifying the Canadian state with themselves to the greatest degree possible.

Since the French Canadians had the bad grace to decline assimilation, such an identification was beyond being completely realizable. So the Anglo-Canadians built themselves an illusion of it by fencing off the French Canadians in their Quebec ghetto and then nibbling at its constitutional powers and carrying them off bit by bit to Ottawa. Outside Quebec they fought, with staggering ferocity, against anything that might intrude upon that illusion: the use of French on stamps, money, cheques, in the civil service, the railroads, and the whole works.

In the face of such aggressive nationalism, what choice lay before the French Canadians over, say, the last century? On the one hand they could respond to the vision of an overbearing Anglo-Canadian nation-state with a rival vision of a French-Canadian nation-state; on the other hand they could scrap the very idea of nation-state once and for all and lead the way toward making Canada a multi-national state. . . .

In actual fact, Anglo-Canadian nationalism has never had much of an edge. Those among French Canadians who have had the acumen to realize it—the Constitutionalists, as I call them—have naturally wagered on the multi-national State, and have exhorted their compatriots to work for it boldly and eagerly. But those who could not see it have never ceased in their fear of a largely imaginary adversary. Among these are, first, the assimilated converts and boot-lickers who have given in to the idea that French Canada is already dead, and that the Anglo-Canadian nation-state is rising triumphant over its remains; these, though, are insignificant in number and even more so in influence, so I am writing them off as a force to be reckoned with. Secondly, there are Separatists and nationalists of all shapes and sizes baying after independence, who devote all their courage and capabilities to stirring up French-Canadian nationalism in defiance of the Anglo-Canadian variety. These are incessantly promoting what Gérard Pelletier has very aptly called "the state-of-siege mentality". Now, recalling something I once wrote, "the siege was lifted long ago and humanity has marched ever onward, while we remain stewing steadily in our own juice without daring even once to peek over the edge of the pot."

THE SORRY TALE OF FRENCH-CANADIAN
NATIONALISM

We have expended a great deal of time and energy proclaiming the rights due our nationality, invoking our divine mission, trumpeting our virtues, bewailing our misfortunes, denouncing our enemies, and avowing our independence; and for all that not one of our workmen is the more skilled, nor a civil servant the more efficient, a financier the richer, a doctor the more advanced, a bishop the more learned, nor a single solitary politician the less ignorant. Now, except for a few stubborn eccentrics, there is probably not one French-Canadian intellectual who has not spent at least four hours a week over the last year discussing separatism. That makes how many thousand times two hundred hours spent just flapping our arms? And can any one of them honestly say he has heard a single argument not already expounded *ad nauseam* twenty, forty, and even sixty years ago? I am not even sure we have exorcised any of our original bogey men in sixty years. The Separatists of 1962 that I have met really are, in general, genuinely earnest and nice people; but the few times I have had the opportunity of talking with them at any length, I have almost always been astounded by the totalitarian outlook of some, the anti-Semitism of others, and the complete ignorance of basic economics of all of them. . . .

It goes without saying that if, in the face of Anglo-Canadian nationalism, French Canadians retreat into their own nationalistic shell, they will condemn themselves to the same stagnation. And Canada will become a sterile soil for the minds of her people, a barren waste prey to every wandering host and conquering horde.

[P. E. Trudeau, *Federalism and the French Canadians,* Macmillan of Canada, 1968]

Guidelines for Inquiry

1. Explain the "cannibal-king" aspect of Anglo-Canadian nationalism.
2. Trudeau says of Canadian nationalists: "They loved not wisely but too well."

What does he mean? What is your position on this matter?
3. Compare Trudeau's views with those of McNaught.

5. Towards the Liberation of the Québécois

Our elite has told us stories about our past but has not set our past in the context of History. The stories they told us were conceived to keep us, the Québécois, outside History.

The elite who collaborated with the English colonizer after the defeat of the Rebellion of 1837-38 behaved like the elites of all colonized peoples. Instead of fighting to rid Québec of the colonizer, they turned back to a "heroic" past to avoid facing the present. They went about glorifying the exploits of figures like Champlain, Madeleine de Verchères and martyred missionaries to make us believe that at a certain epoch we too were great colonizers and nation builders. Since we were colonized by the English we could find compensation in the fact that we had colonized the Red man. Our elite had us dreaming about the great French Empire of America of Frontenac's time, to save us from the real humiliation of being a conquered people imprisoned in Confederation. Generations of Québécois were indoctrinated in this reactionary nationalism that defined us as a chosen people whose mission was to evangelize the world and spread French Catholic civilization throughout America.

With the American-capitalist industrialization of Québec, a more "enlightened" and secular elite undertook to revise our past. Under the guise of "objectivity" and of scientific research of "historical facts", historians in our universities accumulated many facts and documents. But there the work ended. This kind of historian places himself outside history. He is like an angel of knowledge rummaging through humanity's garbage dumps to extract material for neat obituary notices. In these terms our history is a long disinterment confirming, without admitting it, our defeat and subjection. In borrowing the Americans' research methods, these historians also borrowed their point of view; according to which American capitalism sets the supreme order, and the small nations, relics of another era, are marginal.

Recently, a few of our historians have been daring to interpret the facts, daring to orient their historical work within the context of Québécois life, and daring to set themselves within the framework of the evolution of the people of Québec toward their liberation.

We Québécois are an imprisoned people subjected to colonialism. To change our situation we must first understand it. To understand it well, we must analyze the historical forces that brought it about. Once we have defined the forces that reduced us to colonial status, and those that keep us there today, we can identify our enemies correctly, study the relationships of forces carefully and engage in struggle more effectively. . . .

. . . Our history can be divided into three parts:

The French Regime,[1] which dates from the first French explorations at the beginning of the sixteenth century to 1760, date of the Conquest of New France by Great Britain.

The English Regime, which begins with the Conquest of New France and continues until the beginning of the twentieth century when it gives way to the American Regime.

The American Regime, which begins with the invasion of American capital[2] at the beginning of the twentieth century and follows with an increasingly greater hold by American capitalists,[3] first on our econo-my,[4] then on our politics,[5] and finally on our culture.[6]

We can see that there has not yet been a *Québécois Regime,* that is, a Regime in which the Québécois would be masters of their destiny. It has always been the Regime of *the Others.* We, the Québécois, have always been under the domination of these "others". We have been colonized[7] in the past and are still being colonized. Yet one senses during the last few years a movement taking shape in Québec which is demanding that we make it a *Québécois Regime,* that our economy belong to us, the Québécois, that Québec become a sovereign[8] state, and that the Québécois themselves direct the politics of their own country.

1. *regime:* structure or organization of a society and its government at a given period of time.
2. *capital:* money invested in a business or enterprise which yields interest based on the exploitation of the labour power of the workers in the enterprise.
3. *capitalists:* individuals who have capital to invest in different enterprises in order to extract a maximum profit without concerning themselves with the interests of the workers.
4. *economy:* all human activity concerned with the transformation of material resources in order to satisfy the needs of the group, class or people that controls the resources.
5. *politics:* the general administration of a country; political power is the control exercised on society by those who have the country's administration in their hands.
6. *culture:* the personal characteristics of a people; a particular way for a people to express itself, to act on reality and to view the world. A nation's culture depends on its political and economic situation.
7. *colonized:* the condition of a people who have been conquered by a foreign power and who are maintained in position of economic, political and cultural inferiority. The relationship between colonized and colonizer is the same as that between slave and master.
   The colonizer manipulates the colonized to serve his own interests. The colonized, defeated, stripped of his human dignity, submits to slavery and searches for escape in dreams, religion, or intoxicants, until the day when he realizes that he too has a right to personal freedom, and takes the steps necessary to rid his country of the colonizer.
8. *sovereign:* state of liberty and independence that allows a country to govern in the way it sees best, to

make appropriate laws, and to deal with other countries on an equal footing.

[Léandre Bergeron, *History of Québec: A Patriot's Handbook,* New Canada Publications, 1971]

6. Responsible Government Is Dead

This letter to Premier Davis of Ontario appeared as an advertisement in the *Ottawa Citizen*, December 6, 1971.

Dear Mr. Davis:

... The Quebec Revolution was many years in the planning stage, timing, and the use of terror related to L. B. Pearson's permissive Government, and in the opinion of many students of Canadian affairs, a deliberate set-up to encourage the Quebecoise radicals to launch their plan of conquest of Canada. The radicals are only a front, and dupes, for the super planners and intellectuals in State and University circles.

The B & B Commission was made up of left wing radicals who were appointed and paid handsomely to "impose" French on to Canada, not only language, but to accomplish two goals, to put the control of Canadian affairs into the hands of the Quebec French and English speaking left wingers, dedicated to creating a Republic and to make the French language No. 1 in Canada, and thereby take control of Parliament and the Civil Service, since most of the "bilingual" people are the French who speak English for economic reasons.

The late Andre Laurendeau, co-chairman of the B & B Commission, Jean Louis Gagnon, later appointed B & B chairman, and B & B Commissioner Frank Scott, dean of McGill Law School, were all known for their sympathies in Communist fronts, as was Lester B. Pearson who created the "Company of Young Canadians". ....

The intent of the "enforcers" re our Federal Civil Service is not to promote bilingual people. The promotions now go to French people who speak some sort of English. Proof of this is to be found in the 1969 report of the Public Service Commission. Quote: "Distribution of enrolment in Commission courses, by location and language: National Capital Region—French courses, 2,256, English courses, 272."

The heat is on the English speaking Civil Servants to take the course or else. Read the letters to the editors, and newspaper articles of discrimination and firing of English speaking Civil Servants. This take-over is a war of nerves with a time schedule before the next election, all of this aided and abetted by a limp and dormant Conservative Opposition, who are incapable of opposing.

Meanwhile action comes from the people. Judge J. T. Thorson is typical, a most distinguished Canadian, former Chief Justice of Canada's Exchequer Court, and former Liberal Cabinet member and President of the World Council of Jurists, at age 82, is now stumping Western Canada, giving addresses to large audiences on the Trudeau Government's arrogance in pushing through Bill 130 to impose the French language on all Canada, illegally contravening the B.N.A. Act, and he challenges this Bill through Canada's highest courts. This is a Man! He intends to stump central and southern Ontario on his return to arouse Liberals to vote against Trudeau and his Government.

Meanwhile to silence opposition and to intimidate Canadians, Trudeau and his French group, aided and abetted by his cowed and voiceless minions in Parliament, imposed a War Measures Act, on all of Canada, to defend freedom they tell us! How do we find freedom when freedom is usurped by Parliament and dies in the very place it was born—the House of Commons —which once barred a dictatorial king. Canadians are unrepresented in Parliament. ....

Ottawa is the battleground for the take-over of Canada by Quebecois, substituting French Canadians for English speaking Canadians, placing the French Canadians in key posts, illegally including Hull, P.Q. in the Federal seat of Parliament which again proves Trudeau's scorn for the Constitution and putting 150 Million dollars in Government buildings in Hull, P.Q. to house French Canadian Civil Servants, and we are now told English speaking workers from Ottawa and Ontario cannot get a work permit in Quebec.

Let us not be unmindful of the erosion of influence of English speaking Canadians in Canadian affairs when, over the past fifteen years all the "media" of Public and National Information has been transferred from Ontario and Canada to Quebec province. The dialogue of Government today is between Quebec City and Ottawa, not between Ottawa and Canada. Examples:

A. C.B.C. Radio and Television for Canada —now in Montreal. Bulk of the tax money and live broadcasts going to Quebec, and controlled by French ministers. Our air waves are saturated with French.

B. National Printing Bureau—formerly Ottawa, now Hull, P.Q. where the employees were once 50% and more English speaking, now of 850 employees, less than 10% are English speaking and none soon.

C. National Film Board—Studios and offices in Montreal, formerly in Ottawa.

D. Secretary of State—Gerard Pelletier, who controls all embassies, protocol, citizenship, elections, re-zoning of boundary lines, the Monarchy, to encourage or destroy, all broadcasting, granting of licenses, etc. for radio and T.V. and cable, all the Civil Servants of Canada, including the R.C.M.P.

Thus we can assume that Quebecoise have almost complete control of all the media and contact, and control of Canada's publicity at home and abroad, its Civil Service, and communications systems, its control over Foreign Affairs, and the emphasis is always "French" thus to impress foreigners that Canada is a French country first, by filling all possible air channels for radio, T.V. with French stations in Quebec, the Maritimes, and Ottawa. The dominance of the Francophone over the English point of view is safely locked in to Quebec. This unequal control affects the life, welfare, and purse of everyone in Canada.

To further rub in the French fact, 22,000 Civil Servants have been impelled to take French courses. Hopeless for most from the start, some have suffered heart attacks, only 5% graduated as qualified to dialogue in French. To humiliate the English speaking Civil Servants and to intimidate is part of the grand plan to complete the take-over of Canada by controlling the Government and the Civil Service. . . .

We must be "Unusual Conservatives" standing firm for Christian Democracy and individual responsibility, a united English speaking Canada coast to coast, encouragement of private enterprise, and every man and woman a responsible Capitalist, conscious of his neighbour's need. Clean up the minds and morals of the Nation. Maybe the churches will try Christianity for a change.

Throw all this eyewash of French Canadian control of Canadian affairs, with a Republic plus socialism, and flirting with Communism down the sewer. The ecology of Canada cannot absorb any more of this nationalistic garbage. . . .

To "Voice of Canada" members or supporters. Your membership dues of $5.00 and contributions help defray the costs of these messages. Please mail to P.O. Box 3250, Station C, Ottawa.

[Voice of Canada, "Responsible Government Is Dead", 1971]

Guidelines for Inquiry

1. Compare Bergeron's historical analysis of Québec's position with that of Trudeau.
2. (a) What evidence of emotional appeal can you find in the articles by Bergeron and the writer for "Voice of Canada".
   (b) On what basis could each one be considered a patriot?
   (c) Look carefully at both articles and list the "enemies of the people" that each writer discovers. Even though the writers take opposite viewpoints, to what extent are there similarities in the kinds of "enemies" they speak of?
   (d) Which writer seems to be in greater command of his facts? Defend your view.
3. Discuss the following quotation in the light of the above articles: "By a historical accident, Canada has found itself approximately 75 years ahead of the rest of the world in the formation of a multi-national state and I happen to believe that the hope of mankind lies in multi-nationalism . . . " [Pierre Elliott Trudeau].

7. Nationalism in Canada: A Virtue or a Vice?

(a) GERTRUDE: . . . I don't know all the reasons for the upsurge of nationalism in the world today, but I think the sense of alienation induced by technology must be part of it. As people become smaller and smaller cogs in bigger and bigger wheels, as their environment stretches out over the whole world and beyond into outer space, there is a need to be reassured that they are not alone, that they can relate to a human society in which they feel valuable and fulfilled.

SOLANGE: In Canada, and in French Canada especially, there are two kinds of nationalism. One is positive. I am first a Québecer; it doesn't make me into someone who hates Canada. It doesn't make me into a separatist. It makes me a positive nationalist. (When somebody is afraid of the word "nationalism", I suspect that person of being afraid of himself and of refusing to accept himself as he is, with his limitations, his richness, his quality.) The second kind includes the people who are strident nationalists, and whose nationalism is coloured by terrorism, racism, fanaticism. They are trying to enlarge their identity by imposing it on other people. Well, this is not my kind of nationalism. I don't want to impose French on Calgary, but I don't want Calgary to impose English on me. I respect your English if you respect my French. This, to me, is an aspect of nationalism, and probably the only one to which I relate.

GERTRUDE: I feel very much the same way regarding my Canadian identity vis-à-vis the United States. . . .

[Solange Chaput Rolland and Gertrude Laing, *Face to Face,* New Press, 1972]

(b) The point, however, is that Canadians who expend their energies in search of the national soul really do know what it is that they are looking for. Indeed, they often have a very precise idea of what the Canadian identity will be, once uncovered. That such people know what the Canadian identity should be is what sends them on the search, for the very essence of nationalism is that it is an ideology which exists in the minds of men who wish to change their society from its present condition into some better, future condition. Nationalism in Canada, as elsewhere, is very often the doctrine of the discontented. Indeed, it might be argued that while a patriot is a man who loves his

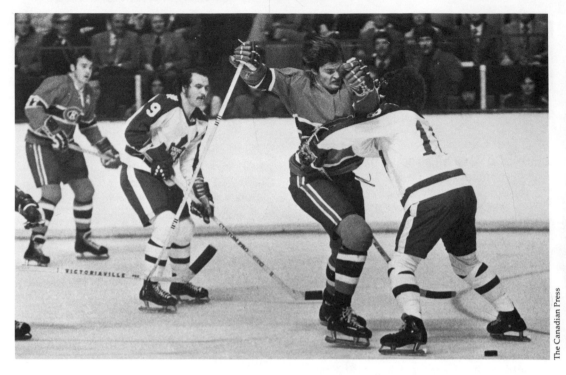

A Montreal-Toronto game in 1972. Do sports activities such as this tend to unite or divide us? Why?

country, a nationalist is a man who hates it.

The clash of nationalisms in Canada, then, is a clash that has taken the place of genuine political thought. It has provided the ideological means whereby contenders for political power, parties, classes, sections, even individuals, have attempted to generalize and legitimize their interests. "Nationalism," George Orwell noted in his matter-of-fact fashion, "is power hunger tempered by self-delusion." What nationalists in Canada have wanted is power to alter the fact of the country to shape its spirit, to make it over in their own image. But in the end the ideologists' success is limited, for the country stubbornly refuses to exchange its occasionally anarchic pluralism for a strait-jacket identity.

[Ramsay Cook, *The Maple Leaf Forever*, Macmillan of Canada, 1971]

Guideline for Inquiry

Where do you stand in the argument that nationalism tends to be dangerously emotional, rather than logical?

Part Three: Are the Issues Basically Economic?

1. Bigots and Jobs

IT SEEMS TO ME THAT, FOR YEARS AND YEARS, MANAGEMENT IN THIS COUNTRY HAS BEEN VERY AWARE OF CANADA'S FRENCH-SPEAKING POPULATION

A YOUNG FRENCH-CANADIAN WITH PROPER QUALIFICATIONS WAS ALWAYS WELCOMED WITH OPEN ARMS BY ANY ORGANIZATION DOING BUSINESS NATIONALLY

THE REASON THERE WERE SO FEW OF THEM WAS - THEY DIDN'T HAVE THE EDUCATION AND SO LACKED THE KNOW-HOW AND EXPERIENCE OF THE BETTER JOBS

BUT QUEBEC IS, AT LAST, UP-DATING ITS SCHOOLS AND SOON THERE WILL BE PLENTY OF YOUNG QUEBECERS WITH TECHNICAL EDUCATIONS

BUT POLITICIANS WON'T WAIT, THEY WANT THE VOTES **NOW**, AND POLITICAL PRESSURE CAN STAMPEDE PRIVATE INDUSTRY, CROWN CORPORATIONS AND GOVERNMENT DEPARTMENTS

I HATE TO SEE INDIVIDUALS PROMOTED BECAUSE OF THEIR LANGUAGE OR ETHNIC ORIGIN OR FOR ANY REASON EXCEPT PURE ABILITY! DOES THAT MAKE ME A BIGOT?

DOUG WRIGHT

The Spectator-Hamilton

Doug Wright, *The Spectator*, Hamilton

[*Hamilton Spectator*, October 16, 1972]

2. Economic Colonialism?

In 1969, the third volume of the *Report of the Royal Commission on Bilingualism and Biculturalism* was published. It contained a study of the economic position of French Canadians, based on 1961 census statistics. Some Quebeckers drew what they considered to be damning conclusions from them, and what follows is a series of quotations which contain these conclusions, followed by pertinent statistics. Do the statistics support the conclusions drawn?

(a) Main Hypothesis

Economic arguments are so popular with federalists, you'd almost think the French Canadians really benefited from Confederation, that their economic situation would be threatened if they withdrew from it. Oddly enough, statistics published by the federalists themselves tell us a very different story.

[Marcel Rioux, *Québec in Question,* James Lewis and Samuel Publishers, 1971]

(b) Do the Statistics Support the Main Hypothesis?

(i) Managers and Workers

Within the big Canadian manufacturing industries, French-Canadian personnel become less and less numerous as one goes up the corporate hierarchy; in passing from the category of hourly wage-earners to that of management, the proportion of French Canadians dropped by two-thirds. To each "majority" there corresponds a different "minority".

[*La Presse*, October 23, 1968]

OCCUPATION AND ETHNIC ORIGIN—QUEBEC, 1961
(PERCENTAGES)

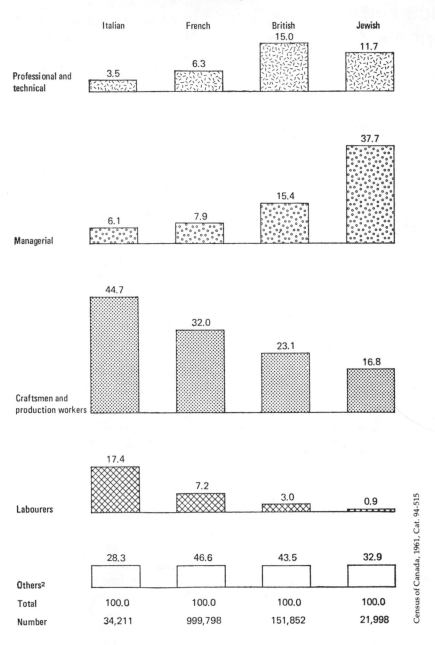

[*Report of the Royal Commission on Bilingualism and
Biculturalism,* Volume 3A, 1969]

(ii) Income

The table below brutally exposes the economic conditions of French-speaking Quebeckers.

[Marcel Rioux, *Québec in Question,* James Lewis and Samuel Publishers, 1971]

LABOUR INCOME

Average labour income of male salary- and wage-earners, by ethnic origin—Quebec, 1961

	Labour income	
	Dollars	*Index*
All origins	$3,469	100.0
British	4,940	142.4
Scandinavian	4,939	142.4
Dutch	4,891	140.9
Jewish	4,851	139.8
Russian	4,828	139.1
German	4,254	122.6
Polish	3,984	114.8
Asiatic	3,734	107.6
Ukrainian	3,733	107.6
Other European	3,547	102.4
Hungarian	3,537	101.9
French	3,185	91.8
Italian	2,938	84.6
Indian	2,112	60.8

SOURCE: Raynauld, Marion, and Béland, "La répartition des revenus".

[*Report of the Royal Commission on Bilingualism and Biculturalism,* Volume 3A, 1969]

(iii) Education and Income

French Canadians benefit the least from education. They obtain even fewer economic advantages than the Italians in their progress from elementary school to high school to university. . . . The French Canadians would be perfectly justified in showing less enthusiasm for education than other ethnic groups.

[*La Presse,* October 25, 1968]

INCOME OF ENGINEERS

Labour income of male engineers, by ethnic origin, employment status, and age group—Montreal metropolitan census area, 1961

		Ethnic origin		
Employment status and age	Average	British	French	Other
Number	1,731	824	420	487
Overall average labour income	$8,084	$8,508	$7,919	$7,150
Salaried				
Number	1,667	805	395	467
Average labour income	$7,801	$8,465	$6,961	$7,367
Age 15-24	3,246	3,372	3,113	3,257
group 25-34	6,715	7,168	6,540	6,233
35-44	8,719	9,054	8,262	8,375
45-54	9,394	10,319	8,216	8,483
55-64	10,049	10,688	9,244	9,182
65 and over	7,083	7,288	7,055	4,300
Self-employed				
Number	64	19	25	20
Average labour income	$15,471	$10,336	$23,060	$10,865
Age 15-24	4,000	—	—	4,000
group 25-34	11,500	8,500	15,500	9,000
35-44	14,765	6,616	25,416	12,887
45-54	13,316	12,500	15,211	10,560
55-64	23,042	15,640	41,000	9,850
65 and over	11,850	6,666	17,033	—

SOURCE: Raynauld, Marion, and Béland, "La répartition des revenus".

INCOME OF ARCHITECTS

Labour income of male architects, by ethnic origin, employment status, and age group — Montreal metropolitan census area, 1961

		Ethnic origin		
Employment status and age	Average	British	French	Other
Number	106	23	44	39
Overall average labour income	$9,157	$12,339	$8,500	$8,023
Salaried				
Number	72	16	25	31
Average labour income	$7,036	$8,675	$7,456	$5,851
Age 15-24	2,666	3,550	—	900
group 25-34	5,385	6,066	5,910	4,900

35-44	8,777	8,966	10,312	6,942
45-54	8,723	10,660	7,600	7,483
55-64	6,850	11,000	5,533	6,750
65 and over	8,825	11,500	6,500	—

Self-employed[1]
| Number | 34 | 7 | 19 | 8 |
| Average labour income | $13,650 | $20,714 | $9,873 | $16,437 |

SOURCE: Raynauld, Marion, and Béland, "La répartition des revenus".

[1] The income of self-employed architects is not given by age group because their numbers are too small to be statistically significant.

INCOME OF PHYSICIANS AND SURGEONS

Labour income of male physicians and surgeons, by ethnic origin, employment status, and age group — Montreal metropolitan census area, 1961

| Employment status and age | Average | Ethnic origin | | |
		British	French	Other
Number	650	147	348	155
Overall average labour income	$12,728	$15,206	$12,770	$10,283
Salaried				
Number	293	74	135	84
Average labour income	$7,527	$10,232	$6,985	$6,017
Age 15-24	1,666	1,180	2,000	1,700
group 25-34	4,302	4,593	4,767	3,362
35-44	10,878	13,136	9,922	10,004
45-54	15,765	23,000	9,966	10,550
55-64	13,189	16,100	13,271	8,250
65 and over	11,342	3,700	13,933	15,100
Self-employed				
Number	357	73	213	71
Average labour income	$16,996	$20,247	$16,437	$15,329
Age 15-24	—	—	—	—
group 25-34	12,012	12,000	11,310	15,320
35-44	18,334	21,860	18,079	16,213
45-54	20,734	20,800	20,720	20,681
55-64	16,153	22,420	16,067	8,583
65 and over	11,815	15,175	8,900	7,775

SOURCE: Raynauld, Marion, and Béland, "La répartition des revenus".

[Report of the Royal Commission on Bilingualism and Biculturalism, Vol. 3A, 1969]

Guidelines for Inquiry

1. (a) Compare the distribution of occupational levels among Italians and French in Québec in 1961. In what sense does the comparison become less significant when total population figures for Italian and French in Québec are considered?
   (b) To what extent is the quotation in (b)(i) supported by the diagram labelled "Occupation and Ethnic Origin"?
   (c) Which group would appear to have greater economic power in Québec at the moment, British or French? What might this mean politically?
2. (a) Does the chart "Labour Income" support the quotation in (b)(ii)? Prove your contention.
   (b) In what sense can the chart "Labour Income" be called "Political dynamite"?
3. To what extent do the charts "Income of Engineers", "Income of Architects", and "Income of Physicians and Surgeons" support the quotation in (b)(iii)?
4. Do the statistics given here support or refute the main hypothesis? Support your view with specific references to the statistics, and make sure you consider all the statistics, not just those that happen to support your view.
5. Imagine yourself to be a young French Canadian in Québec looking for a job. How would you react to these statistics?
6. Research the extent to which there have been changes since 1961.

3. Are Dollars in Flight from Québec?

(a) They Are

"... INDUSTRIALISTS ... INVESTORS ... MERCHANTS ... DEVELOPERS ..."

M. R. Tingley, courtesy of *London Free Press*

[*Ting Cartoons,* London Free Press, 1970]

(b) . . . Or Are They?

. . . Who knows what secret thoughts about Quebec lurk in the minds of business executives? Who knows whether economics or emotion dominates, whether profits or prejudice guides decision? Not even the businessmen themselves know.

At last June's annual meeting of the Canadian Manufacturers' Association an Ontario textile manufacturer talked to reporters about "an overall feeling that people in business would rather stay out of Quebec when it comes to building plants or investing heavily. Of course, no one minds just selling there.

"I have heard people say that we outside of Quebec are not properly informed, that the picture we get is often distorted. Well I say that whether or not we're properly informed is not really the question—what's important is how we feel and what action, or lack of it, will result." . . .

[A] new [Quebec] industry and trade commission in Toronto will be largely concerned with reaching American subsidiary companies, which are often consulted by their parents when investment in Quebec is being considered. These are some of the facts that will underpin its economic promotions:

• Total investment, largely assisted by public funds, rose by more than 11.5 per cent in the province last year, compared with 8 per cent for Ontario and just under 10 per cent for Canada as a whole;

• Capital expenditure in the manufacturing sector was down 7.5 per cent in 1971, but this was more than a full percentage point better than the drop in Ontario;

• Only about 52,000 new jobs were created in the province last year, far short of the Bourassa goal of 100,000. But this was still a remarkable performance in the circumstances. Business confidence was not high anywhere in Canada last year, and Quebec had just come through the kidnap-murder crisis of October 1970. Job creation in 1971 was at a rate four times better than the year before;

• Gross provincial product was up by 8.4 per cent last year, and another 9 per cent is forecast for this year;

• Personal incomes increased 8.7 per cent in the province (8.9 per cent for Canada as a whole), and retail sales were up by 8 per cent (Canada, 8.7 per cent).

• Investment in housing was up almost 20 per cent last year, slightly above the increase for all of Canada.

There are, moreover, some encouraging signs in recent decisions by the private sector.

Magnasonic opened a million-dollar headquarters building in Montreal in June. Union Carbide announced a new $5 million plant. Canadian Hoechst is putting $3 million into plants in a Montreal suburb. B.C. Packers is investing $1.5 million in the Gaspé. Canadian Johns-Manville, Asbestos Corp., Control Data Corp., I.B.M. Canada, Quebec Cartier Mines, Northern Electric, United Aircraft and Wabasso are among more than 150 companies who announced new or expanded investment in the province during a recent nine-month period. Their combined outlay will be more than $1.3 billion. This doesn't include the Canadian Pacific real estate development now underway around the site of Montreal's Windsor Station, which will cost about $250 million.

There is even a mini-boom in British investment in Quebec. Carrington Viyella has bought sixty-five per cent of Montreal's Consolidated Textile Mills, which had sales of $24 million last year; Marks and Spencers is into a joint venture with Peoples Department Stores; Raleigh will be manufacturing its top-quality bicycles at Waterloo, Que.; Norton Villiers is building a plant to assemble motorcycles; and British candy-maker Trebor Sharps Ltd. is producing hard candies and toffees in a new factory in Granby.

Even if the business and economic picture is not all gloom—and it is not—the problem remains to convince businessmen of this fact. Not only businessmen in Ontario, but the jittery executives on the scene whose knowledge of Quebec can often be measured in the straight line between their air-conditioned offices on Dorchester and their homes in Westmount and the Town of Mount Royal. Service industries in particular, which have nothing to move but their people, are on the run. . . . Quebec's share of commercial and financial services has dropped from nearly thirty per cent of the Canadian total in 1965 to just over seventeen per cent.

The flight of advertising agencies is also indicative because, as one account executive puts it, "We don't lead the way. We just follow the client."

In 1965, the ten largest ad agencies in Canada serviced sixty per cent of their accounts from Toronto and forty per cent from Montreal. Last year, the division was seventy-two per cent to twenty-eight per cent. Not one of these agencies currently has its chief executive in Montreal.

Defections from Quebec, or reluctance to invest there, cannot really be explained without reference to emotional and psychological factors. The provincial economy is not booming, but it is certainly not falling apart. Labour relations are no more unstable than those in the rest of the country. Even the economic uncertainties posed by a potential separatist government have been fairly defused with the publication of René Lévesque's economic manifesto—*Quand Nous Serons Vraiment Chez Nous.* There is scarcely a word in it that hasn't been uttered at one time or another by the most conventional Liberal.

[Anthony J. Patterson, "Can Bourassa Stop Them From Sneaking Away?" *Saturday Night,* September 1972]

Guidelines for Inquiry

1. (a) Is business "on the run" from Québec or is such a situation a myth?
   (b) Who might be interested in spreading such a myth? Is there any evidence to substantiate this?
2. Did the "October Crisis" of 1970 appear to have any appreciable impact on the Québec economy? Explain.
3. To what extent do economic issues appear to be a factor in analysing the issue: Québec in Canada or Québec and Canada?

Part Four:
In the Sweet Bi and Bi

1. The Language of Defeat

This is a selection from *The Impertinences of Brother Anonymous*, originally published in 1960. It was an irreverent commentary on major problems facing **French Canada and became an instant best-seller.**

> We are proud of being vanquished, we play and work as vanquished men. We laugh, we weep, we love, we write, we sing as the vanquished. All our moral and intellectual life can be explained by this single fact, that we are cowardly and dishonoured vanquished men.
> LEON BLOY

In October, 1959, André Laurendeau published a short column in *Le Devoir* in which he qualified the speech of French-Canadian students as "joual talk". He, not I, invented the name. It was well chosen. The thing and the name are alike, both hateful. The word joual is a summary description of what it is like to talk joual, to say *joual* instead of *cheval,* horse. It is to talk as horses would talk. . . .

Joual, this absence of language, is a symptom of our non-existence as French Canadians. No one can ever study language enough, for it is the home of all meanings. Our inability to assert ourselves, our refusal to accept the future, our obsession with the past, are all reflected in joual, our real language. Witness the abundance of negative turns of speech in our talk. Instead of saying that a woman is beautiful, we say she's not bad-looking; instead of saying that a pupil is intelligent, we say he's not stupid; instead of saying that we feel well, we say we're not too bad. . . .

. . . We live joual because our souls are impoverished, and so we speak it. I am convinced there is no substantial difference between the degradation of our language and the slackness of our attitude to the fundamental liberties which a *Maclean's* survey revealed in October, 1959. When our youth has surrendered those liberties, as they seem to have done in practice if not in theory— the word liberty is still respectable—they easily give up grammar. The apostles of democracy, like the apostles of good speech, appear like gentle madmen. Our people keep their admiration for machines and technique. They are impressed by nothing but money and luxury; the graces of syntax do not interest them. I flatter myself that I speak correct French—not elegant, but correct. My pupils nonetheless speak joual; I make no impression on them. Indeed I fancy that they sometimes do not understand me. To be understood, I often must have recourse to one or another joual expression. We speak two different languages, my class and I, and I am the only one who speaks both. What can we do? The whole French-Canadian society is foundering. Our merchants show off their English company names, the billboards along our roads are all in English. We are a servile race; our loins were broken two hundred years ago, and it shows. . . .

I hear talk of a Provincial Office of Linguistics. I am all for it. The language is public property and the State should protect it as such. It protects moose and trout, it protects the national parks, and it does well; those are all public property. The State ought to protect the language just as strictly. An idiom is as good as a moose; a word is worth as much as a trout.

The Quebec Government ought to require respect by law for the French language, in the names of companies and in their advertising. I understand that manufacturers and big trading companies must at some time or other appear before the Government to be registered or be legally recognized. That's the time the Government should lie in wait for them. "Give yourselves French names, advertise in French, or we don't know you," it can say. Then we would have no more Thivierge Electric, or Chicoutimi Moving, or Turcotte Tire Service. If these two spheres, titles and advertising, were watched as closely as Laurentide Park, the language would be saved right there.

[Brother Pierre Jérôme, *The Impertinences of Brother Anonymous*, Harvest House Limited, 1962]

2. Language and Cultural Identity

The French Canadian today is saying: "I do not like what I am and where I am going: now that I am beginning to understand the forces that make me so, I want to change the structures in order to become what I want to be." The sixty-four dollar question is, of course, is it too late? René Lévesque's new Parti Québécois does not think so, although it certainly emphasizes the extreme urgency of the situation. It is now or never, they say. It is a huge gamble, they recognize, but, they hasten to add, who has ever rejected a great risk when his very life is at stake? The independence movement in Quebec springs from one prime malaise, and it is not essentially economic, as most people believe. The independence movement in Quebec is aimed, first and foremost, at saving the French culture, language and personality on the North American continent. In essence, it is a linguistic-cultural revolution.

[Raymond Gagné, "Cultures in Conflict: The Imperative of Language", *Canadian Dimensions Kit # 6: Quebec (1)*, August 1971]

Guidelines for Inquiry

1. According to Brother Jérôme, what is the relationship between "joual" and the problems of French Canada?
2. Brother Jérôme contends that "language is public property and the State should protect it as such." Why does he say that? To what extent do you agree with his position?
3. Compare Gagné's views with those of Brother Jérôme.
4. How are the issues of language and economics interwoven?

3. Montreal Italians Choose English

It is evident that the chief medium of communication and thus contact between the Italian community and the rest of Canadian society is language. The educational process by which young immigrants and those born in Canada acquire a formal knowledge of language is through the school system. But in Quebec, and especially in Montreal, education is a complex matter. There are English schools and French schools, Protestant ones and Roman Catholic ones. . . . As the table shows, three out of four Italian Canadians send their children to English schools. The proportion who do so has increased annually, having risen in the last 20 years from just over 50 per cent to 75 per cent.

Pupils of Italian origin attending French-speaking and English-speaking Roman Catholic schools, various years

Year	English schools	French schools	Total number
	%	%	
1941-42	55	45	3263
1950-51	51	49	3633

Canada Wide Feature Service Limited

In 1969, a meeting was held in the suburb of St. Léonard, in Montreal, to discuss the proposal of the Québec government to create an English-language school for the children of Italian Canadians. The picture shows the outbreak of a chair-throwing battle between pro-English and pro-French groups over the issue.

1955-56	61	39	7434
1960-61	70	30	13,800
1962-63	75	25	16,556

[SOURCE: Bureau de la Statistique, Commission des Écoles Catholiques de Montréal.]

What accounts for the popularity of English as opposed to French schools? This is a question which we asked many informants. Their answers were usually unequivocal. They told us that it was only natural for immigrants to send their children to English schools because if they knew English it would be easier for them to get jobs. Moreover by knowing English they could more easily move to other parts of Canada, or to the United States for that matter, in their search for better jobs. One immigrant said: "We have left our friends and family and our country behind. We have come all the way to Canada in order to better ourselves and provide for the future of our children. It just simply wouldn't make sense for us to limit the range of jobs open to our children by educating them in French, for French is only spoken in the province of Quebec. English is the language of North America."

[Joseph Boissevain, *The Italians of Montreal*, Queen's Printer, 1970]

Guidelines for Inquiry

1. What reasons did Italian immigrants in Montreal give for choosing to speak English?
2. If Gagné's assessment is correct—that it's now or never for the survival of the French language—should immigrants in Québec be permitted to speak English? What criteria would you set up in order to determine a person's right to speak the language of his or her choice?

4. One, Two, or Twenty Languages?

This is an excerpt from the memoirs of André Laurendeau, who was an outstanding French-Canadian journalist and co-chairperson of the Royal Commission on Bilingualism and Biculturalism. He is recounting details of a trip he made to the Canadian West in 1955.

"You know," he says to me, "there's a French radio station in Edmonton that plays great music."

He's a nice guy, a chance acquaintance, but chance and travel go well together. I was on my way to meet a group of artists when I suddenly found myself talking to this business man, a little rough at the edges, who bombarded me with questions about Quebec.

"That radio station is right down my alley," he added. "I like the music and since I don't know any French to speak of, I don't hear the commercials."

But he really made me sit up when he asked abruptly with a kind of friendly aggressiveness, "Tell me, will you, what do the French Canadians out here want with their own radio station?"

I stared at him incredulously. What inspired this question, which I couldn't help associating with a kind of secret fanaticism? Up till now the man's behaviour had suggested nothing but warmth and friendship.

"I really don't follow you," I replied. "You tell me that the music on the French station is excellent and that you like music. And if you don't like French you can always switch to three or four English programs, so why should one little French station bother you?"

"No, no," he says stoutly, "you're not answering my question. I'm not talking about my own preferences. I'm asking why you French Canadians, who are a long way from being the largest minority in Alberta, think they have got to have a radio station all their own when the Ukrainians and the Germans haven't got one."

I was ready to get angry. This way of treating us like a minority the same as all the rest is an interpretation of history that we consider false and offensive. We don't look down on the other minorities, but when an immigrant lands in Canada he should know that he is entering a bilingual country where there are two basic language groups. He can choose between them. The fact that there are French schools and radio stations doesn't give the other language groups the right to have them too. To maintain the contrary is to deny the existence of French Canada and to consider Canada a country with a single language.

But I keep my temper and manage to reply coldly, "Perhaps you can tell me why French Canadians should *not* have a French station here?"

"Why?" he replied without the slightest hesitation. "Because when they do, they show they want to stay a separate group and that gets our goat. In places like this you either speak one language or you speak twenty." . . .

I tried to explain my point of view to my new friend. "When you state your dissatis-

Toronto Star Syndicate

This is what happened to a bilingual stop sign put up by a suburban borough of Toronto. As a result of the incident, the experiment with bilingual stop signs was ended. Should traffic signs in large Canadian urban centres be worded bilingually? Why?

faction with the existence of French radio in the West, do you know what you're doing? You're working for the separatist cause in Quebec."

"I don't see how that is."

"Well, you're saying that French Canadians can't live *as French Canadians* in other parts of the country."

"But that's not true," he says, "I like French Canadians."

"Yes, I know you're not prejudiced. You're ready to welcome us warmly as long as we speak English."

"Come on, don't exaggerate. We let French Canadians speak their own lan-

guage. Only it's irritating. . . . "

"That's just it. You don't really accept French Canadians as they are. It's enough to convince many people in my province that despite all the hypocritical clichés about national collaboration, the only place that a French Canadian can really feel at home is in Quebec. And if Quebec is the only possible place to live, why should a French Canadian be interested in the rest of Canada! Why shouldn't he want to make Quebec his true home, for himself alone?"

[André Laurendeau, *Witness for Quebec*, Macmillan of Canada, 1973]

5. Prime Minister Trudeau Introduces the Official Languages Act

These are the comments made by Pierre Trudeau on October 17, 1968, on introducing the Official Languages Act to the House of Commons.

TRANSLATION

Mr. Chairman, many of the bills which are placed before the House are concerned with a specific problem, or a single occupation, or one region of the country. The measure now before us, concerning the official languages, is a reflection of the nature of this country as a whole, and of a conscious choice we are making about our future.

Canada is an immense country, but it is not an easy country to know. Even under modern conditions, it is a long and expensive trip from St. John's to Vancouver, or from Windsor to Inuvik. The great differences of geography, history and economics within our country have produced a rich diversity of temperament, viewpoint and culture.

This is easy to state, Mr. Chairman, and it has been repeated in hundreds of patriotic speeches; but without the direct experience which has not been available to most Canadians, it is difficult to appreciate it fully.

The most important example of this diversity is undoubtedly the existence of the two major language groups, both of which are strong enough in numbers and in material and intellectual resources to resist the forces of assimilation. In the past this underlying reality of our country has not been adequately reflected in many of our public institutions.

ENGLISH

Much of our political theory and tradition, Mr. Chairman, has been inherited from the major countries of western Europe. It so happens that the majority of these countries are relatively [uniform] in language and culture. It has been practical for many of them to operate on the principle of one state, one language. For Canadian descendants of west Europeans this has often appeared to be the normal situation, subject to a few unimportant exceptions. Even today, it is not unknown for a European statesman to offer advice on the future of this country based on such old world ideas.

Looked at from a contemporary world viewpoint, it is the apparently [uniform] states of western Europe which are the exception. Many eastern European, Asian and African states contain within a single political unit a great variety of languages, religions and cultures. In many of them this diversity is reflected in a federal system of government and in two or more official languages. In the past, multi-cultural states have often resulted from conquest or colonialism. In the modern world, many are based on a conscious appreciation of the facts of history, geography and economics.

This latter case is the case of Canada, a country blessed with more prosperity and political stability than most other countries, and where we are making our choices methodically and democratically. In all parts of the country, within both language groups, there are those who call for uniformity. It will be simpler and cheaper, they argue. In the case of the French minority, isolation is prescribed as necessary for survival. We must never underestimate the strength or the durability of these appeals to profound human emotions. But surely these arguments are based on fear, on a narrow view of human nature, and on a defeatist appraisal of our capacity to adapt our society and its institutions to the demands of its citizens.

Those who argue for separation, in whatever form, are prisoners of past injustice, blind to the possibilities of the future.

We in this House, we who have chosen to sit in the federal parliament, have rejected this view of our country. We believe in two official languages and in a pluralist society, not merely as a political necessity but as an enrichment. We want to live in a country in which French Canadians can choose to live among English Canadians, and English Canadians can choose to live among French Canadians, without abandoning their cultural heritage.

Those of us who have some experience of the difficulties and opportunities of this course are conscious of the risk. But we are convinced that, as a country and as in-dividuals, we must take it. French Canada can survive, not by turning in on itself, but by reaching out to claim its full share of every aspect of Canadian life. English Canada ought to attempt to understand this, and I believe it is doing so to an increasing degree. English Canada should not, of course, attempt to absorb French Canada. All Canadians should capitalize on the advantages of living in a country which has learned to speak in two great world languages.

[P. E. Trudeau, Speech in the House of Commons, October 17, 1968]

6.

[Published in the *Ottawa Citizen*, November 21, 1970]

IN THE SWEET **BI** AND **BI**

DANS LE **BI** ET **BI** DOUCE

M. R. Tingley, courtesy of *London Free Press*

Guidelines for Inquiry

1. What view of the nature of Canada is behind Trudeau's speech on the Official Languages Bill?
2. What view of the nature of Canada is behind the arguments of the Canadian Loyalists Association?
3. For each of the questions in the following chart, two opposing positions are identified. Between these positions there are many possible points of view. Where exactly would you place yourself? At one end or somewhere in between? Why?

How do you feel about instruction in the French language in schools?

It should be compulsory from Grade 1 to the completion of secondary school.

It should be optional in secondary school.

Where do you stand on the issue of bilingual public broadcasting?

Major radio and television stations should broadcast in both French and English in each province.

Radio and television stations broadcasting in French should be confined to the province of Québec.

What are your opinions about bilingualism in federal government agencies?

All services of the federal government should be available in both French and English.					Federal government services should be available only in English outside of Québec.

How do you feel about official bilingualism versus official multilingualism?

All major languages in Canada should be accorded official recognition.					Only two major language groups, French and English, should receive official recognition.

Is bilingualism essential to the political leadership of this country?

A person who aspires to be Prime Minister of Canada must be fluently bilingual.					Ability to speak both languages is an unnecessary qualification for a potential Canadian Prime Minister.

Is bilingualism essential to Canadian unity?

Québec should be forced to leave Confederation if it insists on some measure of official bilingualism in Canada.					The existence of two major language groups must be encouraged by our government as essential to Canadian unity.

Pilsworth, *Saturday Night*

7. A New Challenge to Québec's Survival?

Odd things happen in this country: While Anglo-Canadians worry about the consequences of the Federal government's policy on bilingualism, French-speaking Quebeckers harp on the theme of survival. Moreover, with figures to support them, they wonder whether they will reach the year 2000. To understand the situation, we must backtrack into history, destroy a few myths, and stick to facts.

There are those who still dream of a Canada which is bilingual from coast to coast. This is not only Utopian, it is the cause of a mass of misunderstandings. Even though Ottawa makes laudable attempts to offer services in the two official languages, Canada is not a country where French and English have the same chances of expanding. This is a fact now admitted by most Quebec francophones.

Quebec's position is becoming clearer and clearer. Outside Quebec, there are a million francophones in the rest of Canada, half of whom have already been assimilated into the majority group. Moreover, the others still have to earn their living in English. Anyone who has travelled outside Quebec is aware that [in fact] English is the official language. Only the Acadians in New Brunswick have a community life which is coherent, to some extent.

French Canadians living outside Quebec have few illusions as to their chances of survival. Even if some provinces show sympathy towards them today, it is unlikely that francophones will be able to form groups which are strong enough to resist assimilation. Why bother when it is so easy to learn English?

There is no sense going back to the historical reasons for the progressive and irreversible integration of francophones into the anglophone majority. It is useless by now. It might be possible to artificially create a sort of French mystique in some parts of Canada. But it appears very unlikely that the course of history can be changed.

So the province of Quebec remains the only area where the majority of francophones in this country is concentrated. Thanks to an exceptionally high birth-rate which lasted for 200 years, they now form 80 per cent of the population. It was mainly their isolation in the country which allowed them to avoid assimilation and, all in all, to form a race which was self-sufficient.

As long as Quebec francophones lived by themselves and were satisfied with their own customs as a means of asserting their existence, anglophones in Quebec—and in the rest of Canada—could rest easy. And this is what they did, since the French-Canadian "elite" was not too greedy in its demands. There were a few revolts, but they were put down harshly. English Canadians have become accustomed to regarding the French-speaking Quebecker as a charming fellow, rather a chatterbox perhaps, but who could be made to appreciate common sense. Representing a majority in Canada, the anglophones considered the francophones as a minority, and sometimes as one minority among others. There was eventually going to be a rude awakening.

The "What does Quebec want?" of the '60s was mainly due to the fact that Anglo-Canadians did not understand, or refused to admit, that French-speaking Quebeckers no longer regarded themselves as a minority but as a majority in their own province. Reality was advancing much faster than English Canada realized.

But in this ever-evolving Quebec, there has arisen in 1971 a problem which everybody thought was forgotten. Even though they regard themselves as a majority in their own province, francophones are no less worried about their collective future. The fact is that the birth-rate has been falling for fifteen years, and immigrants are assimilating themselves more and more into the English-speaking community.

The way things are going, Montreal will have an English majority in 10 years at the most. Since 40 per cent of Quebec's citizens live in the metropolitan area, what will become of French Quebec when this plateau has been passed? This is the agonizing question which confronts the "urbanized" francophone during this decade, but traditional defence reflexes cannot be counted upon for survival. . . .

The question of the status of French in Quebec must be settled quickly if we do not want future generations of francophones to be forced to concentrate on an exhausting fight for survival. Having constantly retreated in other provinces, francophones want to be sure that they will be able to go on living in Quebec. But pragmatic anglophones must realize this, instead of poisoning the social atmosphere with dreary [predictions].

[Claude Gravel, "The New Survival", *La Presse,* March 11, 1971]

Guidelines for Inquiry

1. What is the main point which Claude Gravel is making in the *La Presse* editorial? Does this mean that French-speaking Canadians, too, are unimpressed by or hostile to the policy of bilingualism?
2. What are the possible implications of the situation which Gravel is describing?

Part Five: Terror, Murder, and Panic in the "Peaceable Kingdom"

1. The Grim Days

At 8.30 a.m. on October 5, 1970, James Richard Cross, Senior British Trade Commissioner in Montreal, was kidnapped. At 11.45 a.m., radio station CKAC in Montreal received a communiqué that Cross was in the hands of a cell of the Front de Libération du Québec. Some of the chief demands of the communiqué were: (a) that the political manifesto of the F.L.Q. be made known to the Canadian people through the major media, (b) that 23 "political" prisoners be freed and flown to either Algeria or Cuba, (c) that the police cease searching for the kidnappers. The communiqué ended by threatening Cross's life unless the conditions were met in 48 hours.

Prime Minister Trudeau and Québec Premier Bourassa quickly consulted. The federal government was responsible for the safety of foreign diplomats; the provincial government was responsible for civil and criminal law. Both governments delayed their decision, but further communiqués from the F.L.Q. insisted that the F.L.Q. manifesto be broadcast as a minimum condition for sparing Cross's life.

On the evening of October 8, the manifesto was read over the radio and television network of Radio-Canada, the French-language service of the Canadian Broadcasting Corporation.

The Front de Libération du Québec is not a messiah, nor a modern-day Robin Hood. It is a group of Québec workers who have decided to use all means to make sure that the people of Québec take control of their destiny.

The Front de Libération du Québec wants the total independence of Quebeckers, united in a free society, purged forever of the clique of voracious sharks, the patronizing "big bosses" and their henchmen who have made Québec their hunting preserve for "cheap labour" and unscrupulous exploitation.

The Front de Libération du Québec is not a movement of aggression organized by high finance and the puppet governments in Ottawa and Québec (the Brinks "show", Bill 63, the electoral map, the so-called social progress tax, Power Corporation, "doctors insurance", the Lapalme boys . . .).

The Front de Libération du Québec is self-financed by "voluntary taxes" taken from the same enterprises that exploit the workers (banks, finance companies, etc. . . .).

"The money power of the status quo, the majority of the traditional teachers of our people, have obtained the reaction they hoped for: A backward step rather than the change for which we have worked as never before, for which we will continue to work."—René Lévesque, April 29, 1970.

We once believed that perhaps it would be worth it to channel our energy and our impatience, as René Lévesque said so well, in the Parti Québécois, but the Liberal victory showed us clearly that that which we call democracy in Québec is nothing but the democracy of the rich. The Liberal party's victory was nothing but the victory of the election riggers. . . .

As a result, the British parliamentary system is finished and the Front de Libération du Québec will never allow itself to be distracted by the pseudo-election that the Anglo-Saxon capitalists toss to the people of Québec every four years.

A number of Quebeckers have understood and will act. In the coming year, [Premier] Bourassa will have to face reality: 100,000 revolutionary workers, armed and organized . . . .

Yes, there are reasons that you, Mr. Tremblay of Panet St., and you, Mr. Cloutier, who work in construction in St. Jérôme, that you cannot pay for "vaisseaux d'or" with all the "zizique" and the "fling-flang" as does Drapeau the aristocrat—who is so concerned with slums that he puts colored billboards in front of them to hide our misery from the tourists.

Yes, there are reasons that you, Mrs. Lemay of St. Hyacinthe, can't pay for little trips to Florida like our dirty judges and parliamentary members do with our money.

The brave workers for Vickers and Davie Ship who were thrown out and not given a reason know these reasons. And the Murdochville men, who were attacked for the simple and sole reason that they wanted to organize a union and who were forced to pay $2,000,000 by the dirty judges simply because they tried to exercise this basic right —they know justice and they know the reasons.

Yes, there are reasons that you, Mr. Lachance of St. Marguerite St., must go and drown your sorrows in a bottle of that dog's beer, Molson. And you, Lachance's son, with your marijuana cigarettes.

Yes, there are reasons that you, the welfare recipients, are kept from generation to generation on social welfare. . . .

We have had our fill of the system which exercises a policy of heavy importation while turning out into the street the low wage earners in the textile and shoe manufacturing trades in order to provide profits for a clutch of damned money-makers in their Cadillacs who rate the Québec nation on the same level as other ethnic minorities in Canada.

We have had our fill, as have more and

more Quebeckers, of a government which performs a thousand and one acrobatics to charm American millionaires into investing in Québec, La Belle Province, where thousands and thousands of square miles of forests, full of game and well-stocked lakes, are the exclusive preserve of the powerful 20th century seigneurs.

We have had our fill of the hypocrite Bourassa who reinforces himself with Brinks armor, the veritable symbol of the foreign occupation of Québec, to keep the poor natives of Québec in the fear of misery and unemployment in which they are accustomed to living.

We have had our fill of taxes which the Ottawa representative to Québec wants to give to the Anglophone bosses to incite them to speak French, to negotiate in French. Repeat after me: cheap labor means manpower in a healthy market.

We have had our fill of promises of jobs and prosperity while we always remain the cowering servants and boot lickers of the big shots who live in Westmount, Town of Mount Royal, Hampstead and Outremont, all the fortresses of high finance on St. James and Wall St., while we, the Quebeckers, have to use all our means, including arms and dynamite, to rid ourselves of these economic and political bosses who continue to oppress us. . . .

Production workers, miners, foresters, teachers, students and unemployed workers, take what belongs to you: your jobs, your determination and your liberty. And you, workers of General Electric, it's you who make your factories run, only you are capable of production. Without you General Electric is nothing.

Workers of Québec, start today to take back what is yours: take for yourselves what belongs to you. Only you know your factories, your machines, your hotels, your universities, your unions. Don't wait for an organization miracle.

Make your own revolution in your area, in your places of work. And if you do not make it yourselves, other usurpers, technocrats and others will replace the iron fist of the cigar smokers which we know now, and all will be the same again. Only you are able to build a free society.

We must fight, not one by one, but together. We must fight until victory is ours with all the means at our disposal as did the patriots of 1837-38 (those whom your sacred church excommunicated to sell out to the British interests).

From the four corners of Québec, those who have been treated with disdain, the lousy French, and the alcoholics will vigorously undertake combat against the destroyers of liberty and justice. We will banish from our state all the professional robbers, the bankers, the businessmen, the judges and the sold-out politicians.

We are the workers of Québec and we will go to the end. We want to replace the slave society with a free society, functioning by itself and for itself. A society open to the world.

Our struggle can only be victorious. You cannot hold back an awakening people. Long live free Québec.

Long live our comrades who are political prisoners.

Long live the Québec revolution.

Long live the Front de Libération du Québec.

[*F.L.Q. Manifesto*]

On October 9, the Québec Minister of Justice, Jérôme Choquette, publicly appealed to the kidnappers for proof that Mr. Cross was still alive. A note, in Cross's handwriting, was sent, along with further communiqués demanding the release of "political" prisoners for the life of the diplomat. The governments were given twenty-four hours to act.

At 6 p.m. on October 9, Choquette replied on television to these communiqués, affirming his government's belief in social justice, but rejecting the demand to release the prisoners. He did promise the kidnappers a safe conduct to a foreign country in return for the life of Mr. Cross.

A few minutes after the Minister had completed his address, Pierre Laporte, the forty-nine-year-old Minister of Labour in the Québec cabinet, was made a captive of the F.L.Q.'s Chénier cell. The new group threatened to kill Laporte unless the original demands of Cross's kidnappers were met. On October 11, just five minutes before the deadline stipulated by the Chénier cell, Premier Bourassa made the following statement on the air:

The stability of our political institutions is menaced by events which are exceptional and unprecedented in our province. What makes these actions both fundamentally unjust and extremely dangerous is the fact that we live in a place where freedom of expression and action is one of the greatest of all the countries of the world.

Even the political parties who question the political system itself have every liberty to express themselves. Moreover, in the last few years, people have not failed to use this freedom of expression to spread hatred and lies systematically.

The government cannot, must not and will not remain idle when the well-being of the individual is threatened at its very roots. I am too proud of being a Quebecker not to express to you my resolution and that of the government I lead to surmount this most serious crisis.

In this effort to safeguard the fundamental values of our civilization, I am sure that I have the support of all the elected representatives of the people, and I ask every-body to remain calm and confident in these difficult circumstances.

Are not, in fact, the merits of our people, their exceptional industriousness, their respect for others, their sense of liberty the best assurance of the victory of justice and peace?

This basic truth which, all things considered, should reassure us, must not make us forget, however, the extremely pressing difficulties confronting us, in which the lives of two persons are at stake: a typical Québec politician devoted to the progress of his community, and a distinguished diplomat who has no part in the tensions which afflict our society.

In this connection, the *Front de Libération du Québec* has issued a communiqué demanding the whole and complete acceptance of their seven demands. Moreover, the Minister of Labour has sent me a letter in which he deals with two problems, police searches and the liberation of political prisoners.

Need we mention that we all value the lives of Mr. Laporte and Mr. Cross? Fate, in a rare example of its cruelty, decreed that the maintenance of public order should place their lives in jeopardy. It is because we truly value the lives of Mr. Laporte and Mr. Cross that, before discussing the fulfillment of the demands that have been made, we wish to establish procedures which would guarantee, to take the example referred to by Mr. Pierre Laporte, that the liberation of political prisoners would save the lives of the two hostages.

This is a preliminary arrangement that simple good sense forces us to demand, and it is on these terms that we ask the kidnappers to enter into communication with us.

How indeed could we agree to these demands without being assured that the other half of the agreement be fulfilled? The government of Québec believes that it would be acting irresponsibly towards the State, and towards Mr. Laporte and Mr. Cross, if it did not insist on these precautions.

We wish to save the lives of Mr. Laporte and Mr. Cross. It is because we want this with all our heart that we make this offer.

My dear fellow-citizens; a great statesman once said: "To govern is to choose." We ourselves have chosen individual and collective justice.

As for myself, I will fight for this justice with all the means at my disposal, assuming all the risks, whatever they may be, that are necessary to assure the future of our people.

[Address by Premier Bourassa, October 11, 1970]

Le rendez-vous électronique

[*Le Devoir*, October 16, 1970]

On October 12 federal troops arrived in Ottawa to take up positions around important buildings and to provide an escort for important politicians. Further ominous communiqués were received from the F.L.Q. There were rumours, with no firm evidence, that Ottawa was pressuring Québec to take a hard line with the kidnappers. On October 14 sixteen leading Québécois released the following statement:

The Cross-Laporte affair is above all a Québec drama. One of the two hostages is a citizen of Québec, the other a diplomat whose function temporarily made him a citizen of this province, with the same rights to the respect of his life and of his human dignity as each one of us.

The FLQ people, on the other hand, are a group on the fringes of this same Québec society, but still constitute a part of our reality, for extremism belongs to the social organism, even if it indicates ill health and puts society in mortal danger.

We have reflected upon the fate of these two human lives, the collective reputation and honour of our society, and the real risk it is now running of social and political degradation. All these considerations make clear to us the fact that the primary responsibility for finding a solution and applying it must rest with Québec.

The attitudes of certain people outside Québec, of which the latest and most incredible is that of Premier Robarts of Ontario, have contributed to the atmosphere of rigidity, almost military already, which one perceives in Ottawa. This situation threatens to reduce Québec and its government to a tragic impotence. We must make a superhuman effort to agree to negotiate and to compromise. On this level, we believe that Québec and its government really have the moral mandate and the responsibility, the knowledge of the facts and of the political climate necessary to come to an informed decision.

We feel this urgency all the more strongly because we fear, from certain quarters outside Québec especially, the terrible temptation of embracing a political stance favouring the worst, i.e., the illusion that a chaotic and thoroughly ravaged Québec would at last be easy to control, by any means whatever.

Setting aside the differences of opinion we may have on a great variety of subjects, aware only of the fact that at this moment we are all Quebeckers and thus vitally involved in the matter, we insist on giving our entire support to the intentions expressed by the Bourassa government on Sunday night; essentially, we most urgently recommend negotiations to exchange the two hostages for political prisoners—these negotiations must be made in the teeth of all objections from those outside Québec, which necessarily will require the help of the federal government.

We urgently request all the citizens who share our point of view to make their opinions known publicly as soon as possible.

The signatories to the declaration are:

René Lévesque, president of the *Parti québécois*

Alfred Rouleau, president of the Desjardins Life Insurance Company

Marcel Pépin, president of the CSN (*Fédération canadienne des employés de services publics,* Canadian Federation of Government Employees)

Louis Laberge, president of the FTQ (*Fédération des travailleurs du Québec,* Québec Federation of Labour)

Jean-Marc Kirouac, president of the UCC (*Union Catholique des cultivateurs,* Catholic Farmers' Union)

Claude Ryan, editor of *Le Devoir*

Jacques Parizeau, president of the executive committee of the *Parti québécois*

Fernand Daoust, secretary of the *Parti québécois*

Yvon Charbonneau, president of the CEQ (*Corporation des enseignants du Québec*, Québec Teachers' Corporation)

Mathias Rioux, president of the *Alliance des professeurs de Montréal,* Montreal Teachers' Association

Camille Laurin, parliamentary leader of the *Parti québécois*

Guy Rocher, professor of sociology at the University of Montreal

Fernand Dumont, director of the *Institut supérieur des sciences humaines* (Institute of Humanities) at Laval University

Paul Bélanger, professor of political science at Laval University

Raymond Laliberté, ex-president of the CEQ

Marcel Rioux, professor of sociology at the University of Montreal

[Marcel Rioux, *Quebec in Question,* trans. James Boake, James Lewis and Samuel Publishers, 1971]

On October 15 groups of university students in Montreal held mass meetings to express sympathy with the F.L.Q. There had already been threats against the lives of relatives of the "political" prisoners and police were checking a large number of bomb threats. Premier Bourassa called the army into Montreal and Quebec City.

The Premier then outlined, via the media, the position of the Ottawa and Québec governments: (1) a recommendation that five of the "political" prisoners be paroled, (2) safe conduct out of the country for the kidnappers.

At 3 a.m. on October 16 the following letter was received by Prime Minister Trudeau:

GOVERNMENT OF QUEBEC
THE PRIME MINISTER

Québec City, October 16, 1970.

Mr. Prime Minister,

During the last few days the people of Québec have been greatly shocked by the kidnapping of Mr. James R. Cross, representative of the British Government in Montreal, and the Hon. Pierre Laporte, Minister of Labour and Manpower and Minister of Immigration of Québec, as well as by the threats to the security of the state and individuals expressed in communiqués issued by the Front de Libération du Québec or on its behalf, and finally by all the circumstances surrounding these events.

After consultation with authorities directly responsible for the administration of justice in Québec, the Québec Government is convinced that the law, as it stands now, is inadequate to meet this situation satisfactorily.

Under the circumstances, on behalf of the Government of Québec, I request that emergency powers be provided as soon as possible so that more effective steps may be taken. I request particularly that such powers encompass the authority to apprehend and keep in custody individuals who, the Attorney General of Québec has valid reasons to believe, are determined to overthrow the government through violence and illegal means. According to the information we have and which is available to you, we are facing a concerted effort to intimidate and overthrow the government and the democratic institutions of this province through planned and systematic illegal action, including insurrection. It is obvious that those participating in this concerted effort completely reject the principle of freedom under the rule of law.

The Québec Government is convinced that such powers are necessary to meet the present emergency. Not only are two completely innocent men threatened with death, but we are also faced with an attempt by a minority to destroy social order through criminal action; it is for those reasons that our government is making the present request.

The government is confident that, through such powers, it will be able to put an immediate stop to intimidation and terror and to ensure peace and security for all citizens.

Please accept, Mr. Prime Minister, my very best regards.

Robert Bourrassa

The Right Honourable Pierre Elliott
  Trudeau,
Prime Minister of Canada,
House of Commons,
Ottawa

[Letter from Premier Bourassa to Prime Minister Trudeau, October 16, 1970]

An hour after this letter was received the War Measures Act and other regulations were approved—the first time this had happened in Canada during peacetime. The Act made reference to a "real or apprehended insurrection". The legislation gave police wide powers to arrest, enter premises without warrants, and hold prisoners without bail. Membership in the F.L.Q. was declared illegal. By nightfall of October 16, two hundred and fifty suspected members of the F.L.Q. were arrested.

Prime Minister Trudeau said that use of the Act was "only an interim and . . . somewhat unsatisfactory measure". Some parliamentarians, in particular many N.D.P. members, protested what they felt was a serious suspension of civil liberties. On the evening of October 16 the Prime Minister made the following statement on national television:

I am speaking to you at a moment of grave crisis, when violent and fanatical men are attempting to destroy the unity and the freedom of Canada.

What has taken place in Montreal the past two weeks is not unprecedented. But Canadians have always assumed that it could not happen here. Our assumption may have been naïve, but it was understandable; understandable because democracy flourishes in Canada; understandable because individual liberty is cherished in Canada. Notwithstanding these conditions —partly because of them—it has been demonstrated now to us by a few misguided persons just how fragile a democratic society can be, if democracy is not prepared to defend itself, and just how vulnerable to blackmail are tolerant, compassionate people.

Every government in this country is well aware of the existence of deep and important social problems. And every government to the limit of its resources and ability is deeply committed to their solution. But not by kidnappings and bombings. By hard work. There is available everywhere in Canada an effective mechanism to change governments by peaceful means.

The kidnappers' purpose is to exploit the normal, human feelings of Canadians and to bend those feelings of sympathy into instruments for their own violent and revolutionary ends. To bow to the pressures of these kidnappers who demand that the prisoners be released would be not only an abdication of responsibility, it would lead to an increase in terrorist activities in Quebec. Should governments give in to this crude blackmail, we would be facing the breakdown of the legal system and its replacement by the law of the jungle.

If a democratic society is to continue to exist, it must be able to root out the cancer of an armed, revolutionary movement, that is bent on destroying the very basis of our freedom. For that reason the Government decided to proclaim the War Measures Act. The War Measures Act gives sweeping powers to the Government. It also suspends the operation of the Canadian Bill of Rights.

These are strong powers and I find them as distasteful as I am sure you do. In short, I assure you that the Government recognizes its grave responsibilities in interfering in certain cases with civil liberties, and that it remains answerable to the people of Canada for its actions. The Government will revoke this proclamation as soon as possible. It is my firm intention to discuss then with the leaders of the opposition parties the desirability of introducing legislation of a less comprehensive nature.

I recognize, as I hope do others, that this extreme position into which governments have been forced is in some respects a trap. It is a well-known technique of revolutionary groups, who attempt to destroy society by unjustified violence, to goad the authorities into inflexible attitudes. The revolutionaries then employ this evidence of alleged authoritarianism as justification for the need to use violence in their renewed attacks on the social structure.

Violence, unhappily, is no stranger to this decade. The Speech from the Throne, opening the current session of Parliament a few days ago, said that "we live in a period of tenseness and unease." This Government has pledged that it will introduce legislation which deals not only with symptoms but with the social causes which often underlie or serve as an excuse for crime and disorder. We shall ensure that the laws passed by Parliament are worthy of respect. We shall also ensure that those laws are respected.

Persons who invoke violence are raising deliberately the level of hate in Canada. They do so at a time when the country must eliminate hate, and must exhibit tolerance

and compassion in order to create the kind of society which we all desire. This Government is not acting out of fear. It is acting to prevent fear from spreading. It is acting to maintain the rule of law without which freedom is impossible. Those who gain power through terror rule through terror. The Government is acting, therefore, to protect your life and your liberty.

Canada remains one of the most wholesome and humane lands on this earth. If we stand firm, this current situation will soon pass. We will be able to say proudly, as we have for decades, that within Canada there is ample room for opposition and dissent, but none for intimidation and terror. There are very few times in the history of any country when all persons must take a stand on critical issues. This is one of those times; this is one of those issues. I am confident that those persons who unleashed this tragic sequence of events with the aim of destroying our society and dividing our country will find that the opposite will occur. The result of their acts will be a stronger society in a unified country. Those who would have divided us will have united us.

[Address by Prime Minister Trudeau, October 16, 1970]

Initial Canadian press reaction to the proclamation of the War Measures Act was as follows:

Canadian press comment on the use of the War Measures Act to battle the Quebec terrorists generally showed cautious approval. However, some editorial writers expressed concern that the Government was overreacting by taking extreme measures.

The *Montreal Star* said: "It is to state the obvious to say that this is a sad day for Quebec and for Canada, and indeed for any civilized community. But let it be emphasized where the responsibility lies. . . . It is not with those who suspend liberties but with those who violate them.

"Meanwhile, we must keep the action of the Government . . . in perspective. Its behaviour all along has been balanced and humane, and if it has invoked the Police Act and the War Measures Act it has done so on the basis of knowledge which it has accumulated and which no one outside government is yet in a position to challenge.

NO THREAT

"The War Measures Act itself is subject to scrutiny by Parliament and represents no long-range threat to individual rights."

La Presse of Montreal comments: "A society which has learned to protect itself is not necessarily a police state. A police state is one in which the police have all the powers and use them according to their own discretion or according to the orders of a totalitarian power . . . without being subjected to the law. A state in which there are no police is nothing at all. A state which has a strong police, but under a precise law understood by all, reinforces the very condition of its existence."

Other press comment:

Le Soleil of Quebec: "It had to be expected. The abuse of liberties by a few inevitably leads to the curtailment of the liberties of all. . . .

"The kidnapping of a British diplomat and of a Québec Cabinet minister, the menace of renewed violent actions, the more or less anarchical publication of communiqués from clandestine organizations, the danger in which organized terrorism which may become open and generalized violence has placed our institutions, have all called for a vigorous reaction from our governments. That reaction became fact when the War Measures Act became law. . . .

LESSON

"The lesson to be learned from these events as far as Government powers are concerned is that it would be best, in the near future, to adopt laws which would be a balance between the very radical War Measures Act, and our current laws which leave the Government with too few recourses against clandestine actions. . . . All's fair in war; terrorism, kidnappings and assassination threats call for corresponding repression measures. . . ."

Peterborough Examiner: "The proclamation of the War Measures Act by the Government of Canada signifies the end of an era in the history of this country. Never before has it been necessary for a Canadian government to resort to such a measure in peace time, but then, never before has the country faced such a serious threat to its democratic traditions.

"However repugnant it is to us, we must understand that extraordinary times require extraordinary actions. It's a fact of life that force creates force and that there are times when democracy has to resort to undemocratic methods to survive. Democracy has a right to defend itself."

REGRETTABLE

Welland Tribune: "The mass majority of Canadians will be found grimly commenting and it's about time. It's a most regrettable situation but one in which sensible people will stand by Prime Minister Trudeau and his Government in finally exercising the authority it ought to show in electing to go the limit on behalf of law and order which decent Canadians desire to be observed in all parts of the nation."

The *Hamilton Spectator:* "What else could the Government do in a situation when the entire nation is faced with the treasonable acts of young terrorists who have already used bombs, kidnappings and murder as weapons against the state—sit tight? A large number of Canadians will applaud Prime Minister Trudeau's decision. They will applaud him further if he brings back capital punishment for certain acts of treason such as kidnapping and blackmail."

Kingston Whig-Standard: "The Federal Government and the Government of Québec are obviously in possession of alarming information concerning a threat of some kind to the safety of this country. . . . There have been persistent rumors of a plot involving French insurrectionists who are joining with the FLQ, presumably to try to overthrow the Québec government. It may be that these rumors . . . combined with the anxiety aroused by the kidnappings have forced Ottawa and Québec to take this decisive action."

Edmonton Journal: "Many Canadians may be worried that the Federal Government is over-reacting by treating the kidnapping of two officials as a state of anticipated insurrection. But we do not have the information available to the Government.

"We can only take on faith, for the time being, that the further measures taken have been necessary for the peace, order and good government of Canada. Members of the Federal Cabinet know as well as other Canadians that the powers now invoked are tolerable only in times of genuine national emergency."

BLOW STRUCK

Brandon Sun, Manitoba: "Prime Minister Trudeau has struck a great blow for the FLQ. Not at them. No single action can do more to bring over to the side of violent separatism than the invoking by the prime minis-

ter of the War Measures Act, and the subsequent round-up of hundreds of Quebeckers, on suspicion of being associated with, or sympathetic to, the FLQ."

Brantford Expositor: "To the FLQ's ruthless use of bombing, killing, robbing and kidnapping only one answer is possible from a society determined to preserve majority rule and orderly change, and our Prime Minister has given it."

Victoria Times: "The reasons for such extreme measures—even considering the two kidnappings—are not clear. . . . By implication and by the Government's reaction to the events in Quebec, there may be a greater threat to Canada's democratic institutions than has yet been publicly aired. If this is the case the Government has the responsibility to communicate any such dangers to the Canadian people."

Vancouver Sun: " . . . at last government has armed itself to fight fire with fire and match ruthlessness with ruthlessness. Both the chance for the honorable release of the hostages of the FLQ and the chance for the Canadian nation to return to stability, law and order have been enhanced by this total rejection of the cowardly and self-destructive course of compromise."

Saint John Telegram-Journal: "Canada was patient long enough—too long, many of her citizens thought. . . . Proclamation of the War Measures Act giving extraordinary powers to the Federal Government is not the reaction to two kidnappings. It is the reaction to years of mounting provocation until all the forces of law and order were challenged by criminals whose aim is utter destruction of the nation."

[Toronto *Telegram,* October 17, 1970]

Photo *La Presse*

On Sunday, October 18, the body of Pierre Laporte was found in the trunk of a car at St. Hubert Airport in Montreal. A message from Mr. Cross on the same day indicated he was alive. On October 19 René Lévesque, leader of the Parti Québécois, spoke to a Montreal rally:

René Lévesque, leader of the separatist Parti Québécois, told a cheering crowd of 2,200 last night that Prime Minister Pierre Trudeau had "coldly gambled and lost the life of Pierre Laporte."

Laporte, Québec Labour Minister, was kidnapped on October 10 and strangled October 17 after the government refused to bow to ransom demands of the Front de Libération du Québec, which still holds British diplomat James Cross. . . .

Lévesque charged that Trudeau is "leaving Cross to die a slow death. . . . These are only minor obstacles on the course he is following."

He was the main speaker at a rally in Paul Sauvé Arena protesting the War Measures Act. The meeting was organized by the Québec Committee for the Defence of Liberties, formed after the act was invoked to combat further terrorism and kidnappings.

The FLQ says it will release Cross only if 24 "political prisoners"—convicted or accused terrorists—are freed and flown to Cuba. The government has agreed to let only the kidnappers fly there.

Lévesque called Trudeau a cynical, unscrupulous conservative who used the FLQ crisis "to bring Quebec back in step and scare the people back into docility."

The separatist leader said Trudeau had used Premier Robert Bourassa as "a miserable front" in "blowing alarm out of all proportion."

He accused Bourassa of lying when he said October 11 he wanted to negotiate the release of the two captives.

Lévesque claimed Bourassa lied again when he told the National Assembly he was prepared to exchange 11 convicted terrorists to save Laporte and Cross.

"And he also lied the day after Laporte died," Lévesque continued, "when he issued an appeal for reconciliation and unity after a long period of silence, betraying his complicity with the federal government.

"Either he agreed with Trudeau and is a hypocrite, or he was against Trudeau and is not worthy of being at the head of a party."

Lévesque predicted Quebec will sink into anarchy and repression within five years unless it unites behind his party.

"This is the hour of the last chance for a democratic change," he said.

[*Toronto Daily Star*, October 20, 1970]

Strong emotions were stirred by the crisis. On November 15 on C.T.V.'s program "W5", the results of a poll were announced which indicated that 87 per cent were in favour of and less than 6 per cent opposed to the introduction of the War Measures Act. The same survey indicated that 50 per cent were in favour of suppressing student militants; 43 per cent in favour of suppressing hippies; and 30 per cent in favour of suppressing labour and women's "lib" militants.

Duncan Macpherson; reprinted by permission of *Toronto Star*

[Macpherson, *Toronto Daily Star*, 1970]

George Bain, a *Globe and Mail* columnist, wondered out loud how the governments' actions during the crisis would appear "when everyone has a moment to think".

There is an electric current of alarm running through the country at the moment and, with it, a willingness to accept without serious question what those in authority say needs to be done. But what will be the reaction when everyone has a moment to think?

The question doesn't originate here but with a United States newsman relatively new on the scene. So what sort of answer do you give him? Something like this:

The Prime Minister can hardly miss being applauded by the bulk of Canadians, no matter what happens. If there are no more acts of terrorism in the Province of Québec for the next little while, then having put into effect severe restrictions on citizen freedoms—as, for instance, freedom from being picked up and summarily clapped in jail—will appear to have been an act of foresight and prudence.

It will have worked, won't it?

And if anything gets blown up in the Province of Québec in the next little while, as things have been getting blown up from time to time since before even Pierre Trudeau entered politics, the adoption of extraordinary powers under the War Measures Act will appear to have been an act of prudence, and foresight.

It will have been proved necessary, won't it?

But (another question) won't the Government some time be forced to state, in the minutest detail, the elements composing the state of apprehended insurrection in the name of which the War Measures Act was invoked? If the President of the United States had resorted to such powers, there would have been the damndest outcry in the (his) country and a wave of demands that the President prove, preferably on national television, with diagrams, if possible, that the emergency actually existed which warranted so drastic a departure from the normal.

Yes, to the last, and, no, to the first. Yes, there would have been an outcry because Americans, perhaps always, but certainly in the past 10 to 15 years—since the U-2 and the Bay of Pigs and other disclosures of a less than incorruptible regard for facts—are less inclined to take things on faith. This is partly good, partly bad; in any event, it's the case.

As for the, no, part: no, the Government won't necessarily be forced, ever, to state in any sort of detail the components of the state of apprehended insurrection which has been said to exist.

If any further act of terrorism occurs, even though it is no different in quality from dozens of others which have happened over the past several years, it will be taken as confirmation of the fact that a state of insurrection exists, and existed, which is beyond the ability of civilian authority with ordinary powers to control.

No one will think to ask the question in those circumstances.

And if nothing further happens, the whole issue will be forgotten. A month from now, the Government has promised to introduce specific legislation of less odious nature than the regulations under the Wartime Measures Act. By the time this has been debated, and perhaps amended, and passed, can anyone imagine Opposition Leader Robert Stanfield rising in his place to ask for an accounting of the Government's reasons for acting as it did in the first instance?

The country would yawn and say, "There's Stanfield being dull again. Why doesn't he get with what's going on today, not six weeks ago, for cripe's sake?"

End of issue.

But how can anyone ever know, then, whether there really was anything in all those hints and allusions to a perhaps plot to blow up Montreal, and perhaps plans to perhaps bring down other governments, and to perhaps assassinate a number of people— all of this with perhaps connivance from forces outside the country?

Answer: Well, that is the question, isn't it? How does one judge whether the Government availed itself of extraordinary powers justifiably, because it had to deal with a pervasive menace which could not be attacked with anything less, or unjustifiably, in frustration, unless the Government is made to state its case? OK, how?

[George Bain, "What Will Be the Reaction?", *Globe and Mail,* Toronto, October 22, 1970]

By late October the police had identified 6 wanted persons in connection with the kidnappings. By the end of December they had arrested 468 persons and had released 408 without laying charges. On November 3 the House of Commons approved a less sweeping act to replace the War Measures Act.

Early in the morning of December 3 police surrounded a Montreal apartment house where James Cross was being held. After hours of dramatic bargaining, the kidnappers were whisked away to be flown to Cuba in exchange for the freedom of the diplomat.

In the early hours of December 28 three men were apprehended in a tunnel beneath the basement of a farmhouse south of Montreal. All of them were charged in connection with the murder of Pierre Laporte. The crisis was over.

Difficult questions remained. Had the government officials involved been insensitive to the plight of the hostages? Did

Ottawa pressure Québec into a "tough" stand? Was there evidence of civil disorders in Montreal sufficiently serious to justify the passage of the War Measures Act? Did officials use the War Measures Act to intimidate legitimate nationalists and leftists? To what extent would the crisis contribute to a polarization of opinion between French and English Canada?

Public opinion polls registered Canadians' immediate reactions to the crisis:

(a) Any doubt that the War Measures Act was favoured by most voters is dispelled by the Liberal party's mighty leap in the past weeks, to a record figure of 59 per cent of voter support.

The significance of this figure, based on the Gallup Poll's regular national sampling of opinion, can be gauged when one realizes that in the 1968 election, the Liberal party was described as "sweeping the polls", when it obtained 46 per cent of the popular vote.

Poll figures show the shift present in all areas of the country, including Quebec, where the Liberal popularity is at a new high.

The question which Gallup interviewers put to an accurate cross-section of voting-age Canadians was the standard one:

"If a federal election were held today which party's candidate do you think you would favour?"

Highlights, since the last election, from Institute records show this pattern:

	Lib.	P.C.	N.D.P.	Soc. Credit & others
	%	%	%	%
CIPO pre-election report (June 1968)	47	29	18	6
Election, June 25, 1968	46	32	16	6
February 1970	43	27	19	11
April	40	28	22	10

August	47	27	19	7
October (pre-War Measures Act)	42	31	20	7
Today	59	22	13	6

In terms of opinion polling, the 17 percentage point jump is most dramatic and unusual. It will be even more unusual if subsequent studies show the Liberal party maintaining this lead, as one of the things one learns in polling is that what goes up may sometimes come down.

All the percentages shown above are based on those Canadians who have a preference. In the case of the latest poll, this represents about 61 per cent of the sample. The number of undecided voters, at 39 per cent, is slightly higher than usual.

[Canadian Institute of Public Opinion, December 16, 1970]

(b) Despite gloomy predictions, actions of the FLQ terrorists have made very little impact on the way French- and English-speaking Canadians feel about each other. Among the English, 81 per cent say they feel no differently today than they did about a year ago. Among the French 72 per cent say their attitudes towards the English have not changed.

Only a small segment of the English-speaking Canadians (9 per cent) say they feel less friendly—while 7 per cent are more friendly. In French Canada still fewer citizens are less friendly towards the English (6 per cent) while more (13 per cent) say they are friendlier toward them.

Reasons for feeling less cordial among the 9 per cent of English Canadians have to do partly with the FLQ actions—but about the same proportion speak in terms of opposition to separatism, and of the amount of attention paid to Quebec in general. A Westerner's explanation for his reaction sums up this feeling: "They are supposed to be Canadians, but they are clinging to France and the French."

The question asked of each race:

"Would you say you feel more friendly, or less friendly, towards the English- (French-) speaking Canadians than you did, say, a year ago?"

	More friendly	Less friendly	About the same	Un- decided
	%	%	%	%
English-Canadian attitudes	7	9	81	3
French-Canadian attitudes	13	6	72	9

[Canadian Institute of Public Opinion, December 23, 1970]

(c) Canadians approve the War Measures Act to a remarkably high degree—87 per cent. This represents a pinnacle of support for any government action as reported by the poll over many years.

The question:

"In general, do you approve or disapprove the government's action in bringing in the War Measures Act to handle the FLQ crises, with the promise that it would be replaced shortly with special legislation to give the government the temporary powers it needs?"

Here is the way Canada reacts as a nation, compared to viewpoints among the main racial backgrounds, and those with varying education.

	Approve	Dis- approve	Un- decided
	%	%	%
Canada	87	6	7
English-speaking	89	5	6
French-speaking	86	9	5
Other races	79	5	16
Public school education	81	5	14
High school, technical	89	6	5
University	89	7	4

[Canadian Institute of Public Opinion, December 12, 1970]

Guidelines for Inquiry

1. To whom was the F.L.Q. Manifesto directed? What was the basis of its appeal? What is the significance of its reference to 1837-8? What reason does it give for having rejected peaceful means?
2. How did Bourassa respond to the F.L.Q. demands? What reasons did he give for doing so?
3. What was the attitude of the "Sixteen" to suggestions from outside Québec as to how to deal with the crisis? Why did they feel that this was an internal matter for Québec? Do you agree? What course of action did they propose?
4. What course of action did Bourassa request the federal government to take? What reasons did he give?
5. How did Ottawa respond to this request? What justification did Prime Minister Trudeau give to the people of Canada for doing so? Do you feel this was the correct action to take?
6. (a) Judging from the press comments, how did Canadians view the government's action? Can you detect any common thread of uneasiness?
   (b) To what extent, if any, do you think this indicates a lack of vigilance in regard to civil liberties in Canada?
7. What was René Lévesque's interpretation of the federal government's actions? To what extent do you agree with him?
8. (a) What questions are raised by George Bain? How does he attempt to answer them? How would you answer them?
   (b) Are they important, given the circumstances at the time?
   (c) What is the significance of his analogy with the United States?

2. The Crisis in Perspective

(a) The Government Over-Reacted, But . . .

SOLANGE: It is so difficult to explain how we felt when the army was here. The army in Québec, for whatever reason, is a peculiar symbol. I felt reassured, and at the same time, I hated the army in Québec. It was the Redcoats again! I know that what I am saying will make our readers jump, but to me, *l'armée au Québec, c'est l'occupation!* I know we *asked* the soldiers to come, because at that time we really thought that a lot of people needed to be protected. But while I was physically reassured, at the same time I was psychologically hurt. *L'Armée est au Québec! Le Québec est occupé!*

GERTRUDE: I think I would have felt the same way if they had come to Alberta to protect me from my fellow-Albertans.

SOLANGE: Would you really? *Tiens!* I suppose you would, but I never thought of it that way. How self-centred we can be in Québec! To me, the army was a symbol of English Canada.

GERTRUDE: To me, it represents simply a force that I don't want. I realize that there are times when it is necessary, like taking medicine when you're ill, but I'm sure that psychologically I would have had the same reactions as you—minus the Redcoats!

SOLANGE: You know, the famous Habits-rouges, and the Patriotes, and the revolt of 1837 are very much alive today in Québec. We seem to be re-living history. Some of the FLQ militants in jail are beginning to sound like heroes for some of our youth. I have even heard that there are classrooms in Québec where huge posters of Paul Rose, who is accused of the murder of Pierre Laporte, hang on the walls. This is the part which I despise. But to come back to the army, I must say something: The army came once because the government of Québec asked for protection for some of its citizens. Now there are a number of people in Québec, and I think I am one of them, who believe that if tomorrow we were to vote massively for l'indépendance du Québec, the Canadian Government, backed by nine other provinces, would send the army back— not to keep us in Confederation because they want us, but so as not to disrupt the Canadian equilibrium.

GERTRUDE: Some Canadians have said quite openly that they would "send in the troops", but I wonder if they would if the time ever came. By the way, Solange, you equated the army with the Redcoats, and yet it was French-speaking soldiers who were sent in, not English!

SOLANGE: Well, this may sound foolish, but I have to say it: they were told not to speak! There they were, standing on the corners, in front of the houses, never smiling and never speaking, so whether they were French or English, we didn't know! All we could see was that they wore a uniform.

At the time that the Prime Minister of Canada proclaimed the War Measures Act, did he appear in the eyes of the whole country as the leader that the people had voted into power to put Québec in its place?

GERTRUDE: I want to be sure that I understand you correctly. If you are thinking that this was the logical result of the election to office of the man who many people expected would "put Québec in her place", I would say No.

SOLANGE: I say Yes, Yes, Yes!

GERTRUDE: I don't think this was the feeling of most Canadians. On the other hand, if you mean that at that moment he became the true leader of the country, at any rate of English-speaking Canada (and I think to a large extent of French-speaking Canada too), the leader who took the action that most of the people approved of, that most of the world approved of, then I would say Yes. I think he gained enormous prestige even in the eyes of Canadians who up to that point had not been convinced of his leadership. I have to say, however, that personally I found it hard to accept his action; I felt that we didn't need this extreme measure, although certainly I was in no better position than any one else to know that. I was also very much afraid of the long-term political consequences.

SOLANGE: You remember, Gertrude, that the day M. Laporte was kidnapped you were in my home at Lac Marois, and when I drove you to the airport we were in a state of near panic. After all, M. Laporte was somebody we both knew. The very first day that I met you we sat on either side of him at a banquet, so we were both very much distressed. On the way to the airport we saw helicopters and planes searching the area, which added to our feelings of apprehension. When the War Measures Act was proclaimed, I was in Winnipeg, and I was awakened that morning with words that still haunt me: "Ottawa has declared war on Québec!" You can imagine how I felt! For about ten minutes I really believed this, until by listening to the news, I began to understand that M. Bourassa had asked the troops to come to Québec.

There is no doubt that the War Measures Act was a very drastic act. We still don't possess all the facts surrounding the FLQ crisis, but we certainly know now that there was not an armed guerilla uprising planned, that there was not an "apprehended rebellion", that only thirty-two guns were found, and so on. I believe that our government over-reacted, but I think I would have done the same thing if I had been in their shoes. What I cannot accept is that the government has never given us the facts, nor admitted that it over-reacted. As a result, we live in a very uncertain atmosphere. If the government was sure that there was a possibility of open rebellion, they were right to take the steps they did, but since there is nothing to confirm this opinion, are we to suppose that we will once again be occupied if another crisis arises in Québec? The United States did not invoke any such extreme measures when there were riots in Chicago, riots all over the United States: the National Guard kept law and order. Great Britain has a special law that permits the government to send troops to Northern Ireland without mobilizing the whole of Great Britain. Is there something that the government could do or say that would ease our anxiety about the future?

GERTRUDE: It is not too realistic to expect governments to admit that they were wrong! I agree with you, by the way. I don't condemn their action because I don't know the facts, and I suspect that they didn't know the facts at the time. The important question, however, is the one you raise: what is going to happen the next time a situation like this occurs?

SOLANGE: *If* such a situation recurs.

GERTRUDE: Of course. I don't think you can really compare what happens in other countries with what happens here. Between England and Ireland there is the Irish Sea. As far as we know, the IRA have not been active in England, and the British institutions are not endangered on the mainland. On the other hand, it is possible to conceive of an attack from Québec on Ottawa, so we have to protect the central government of the country, as well as the citizens of Québec. As far as the riots in the United States are concerned, those solutions weren't very happy either. I wouldn't like to see our Canadian problems handled that way. So other countries have not found the perfect solution to these problems either.

[Solange Chaput Rolland and Gertrude Laing, *Face to Face*, New Press, 1972]

(b) A "Smash" Is Coming?

This is part of an interview with Roch Carrier, the novelist.

CARRIER: . . . That's sad. Another thing which is sad is that inevitable war between the French and the English. For me it's really a conviction, that, which I found in writing my novel—that it was impossible not to collide. In the novel, I put all those contrary forces and I let them free, and *ils se sont frappés.*

CAMERON: You think that will happen in reality?

CARRIER: Yes, it will come. When I hear the news from Ireland, it's so near Québec. We will have another October event, maybe in December this time, and the army will come back, and there will be little smashes, but—

CAMERON: —eventually you see a big smash?

CARRIER: Yes. Let's say, in a cold way, you don't accept that somebody takes what's yours. I think that for an English Canadian Québec is his property. Ontario is not the property of a Québécois but I think that Ontarians feel that Québec is their property because it's part of the country, and nobody wants to lose what belongs to him. Québec will leave Confederation under new legislation maybe, but it's not possible to imagine Québec leaving smoothly. That's what I discovered by writing that book too: the villagers have nothing against the soldiers, the soldiers have nothing against the villagers, they are doing their job. But things go on, and the machine is running. They have to smash. I don't want that smash, and I remember a sentence by Richler one year ago in a magazine: he was saying that Québec was going through the same sterility as Ireland. And I was quite surprised to read what I was thinking myself. I don't want that sterility, I don't want that smash. So I decided to work, to do something in Québec, to continue to participate in the building of a literature, participate more and more in what I know, the cultural life, and maybe to try to have friends outside the frontier. I try to know a little bit more what's happening there. Maybe it will be possible to have a kind of collaboration. Naturally I prefer to try to find something we have in common; that's better than an opposition. So that's what I'm working on. The Québécois is very much frustrated because he doesn't feel he has his real part in Canada. I think we have to go outside, we have to take part.

CAMERON: Something like touring the country with the English version of *La Guerre* might be tremendously useful.

CARRIER: I think it would be, because the first task we have is to tell the truth. You have to take some risk to tell the truth.

[Donald Cameron, *Conversations with Canadian Novelists,* Macmillan of Canada, 1973]

(c) It Is Difficult To Assess the Situation

The significance of the crisis can be interpreted in two distinct but related ways. It was, first, a crisis for Confederation and for French/English-Canadian relations. But even more, it was a crisis for Québec society itself. Once again, English Canadians were forced into awareness of the existence of forces prepared to go to desperate lengths to achieve independence. Many English Canadians blurred, if they did not obliterate, the distinction between moderate and violent separatists and were prepared to use the events as a signal to crack down on all forms of nationalism. Similarly, some French Canadians saw the sending of troops and the use of the War Measures Act as evidence that English Canada would use force rather than tolerate separation in any

form. But the crisis never did become a confrontation between the mass of English Canadians and the mass of French Canadians; it did not divide the country on ethnic lines. Revulsion against the kidnappings was as intense in Québec as elsewhere. The Gallup poll reported that 89 per cent of English Canadians supported the Government's use of the War Measures Act; so did 86 per cent of French Canadians. The federal Liberals gained in popularity all across Canada including Québec, where, said the Gallup poll, "the popularity of the Liberal party is at a new high." Furthermore, despite the disputes about who was really in charge and where the initiative came from, the drastic government efforts to deal with the FLQ were a *joint* effort of the Montreal, Québec, and federal Governments.

The FLQ terrorism and the reaction against it therefore involve much more than a crisis for federalism. The FLQ directed its attack not simply at the federal system, but at the whole social, economic and political make-up of Québec society. It did not so much endanger the federation, as it did public order, established authority, and the existing economic system. It was these aspects of the crisis that were stressed by leaders like Montreal Mayor Jean Drapeau, Québec Justice Minister Jérôme Choquette and others in their public statements. The sin of the Front d'Action Politique (FRAP), which was mounting a strong campaign in the Montreal municipal elections, and which was bitterly attacked as subversive by Mayor Drapeau, was not its separatism but its economic and social ideology and its mobilization of the dissatisfied.

It is hard to assess how much of a real threat the FLQ posed to Québec society or whether there was a real possibility of a massive insurrection. The evidence so far revealed suggests that the FLQ was not very large or well organized, though as a dedicated splinter group, it had—and still has—considerable capacity for disruption. The extreme reaction to the events both by government and citizens perhaps tells us more about them than it does about the FLQ. The most likely explanation for the response is that many groups felt threatened and insecure even before the October events. Many English Canadians had a sense of the fragility of Confederation and of the ease with which it could be destroyed. French Canadians feared the bewildering new climate of *contestation,* alienated students, militant workers and the decay of old values. In such an atmosphere of self-doubt, it takes little to trigger the feeling that the edifice is about to come tumbling down, and that all possible powers must be used to save it. The "party of order" triumphs—at least for a while.

Whether the autumn events will lead to the further growth of separatism is not clear. In the short run, separatist support may have weakened by the association, however unfair, with the use of violence. (The PQ candidate in the February by-election in Chambly did, however, increase his vote slightly.) The FLQ actions may have convinced some wavering federalists to support that option more firmly. On the other hand, the governmental reactions have probably led some wavering nationalists towards a firmer separatist stance.

The events produced a special agony for Québec intellectuals, appalled at the use of violence, but equally appalled at the sight of federal troops patrolling the streets, at the suspension of civil liberties, at the use of mass arrests often without much apparent reason, and at what appeared to many of them as federal intrusion into Québec's own crisis. For them, the events were not something to be assessed and analysed from afar. Instead they created an intense and complex personal crisis, in which they were pressed to make virtually impossible choices. How

these dilemmas were faced, and what choices were made, is not known, but in the long run they may be vital since the intellectuals play a central role in defining the alternatives and opportunities of the changing society.

The middle has become an increasingly uncomfortable place. There is likely to be a hardening of the lines and a decline in the influence of the moderates, whether they be separatists like René Lévesque or federalists like Claude Ryan of *Le Devoir.* Some committed separatists have become convinced that the English Canadians have demonstrated that they would not tolerate a Québec decision to separate and would use force to prevent it. If this feeling is widespread the future of the *democratic* separatist movement would be weaker. Some English Canadians may welcome this, on the assumption that a more militant movement would have less chance of building widespread support. But the price would probably be in the long run even more violence, and more repression. At any rate, separatism of whatever sense will remain a central factor in provincial politics, and electoral success of the PQ, especially if the Bourassa government fails to improve economic conditions, is by no means an impossibility.

It is still too early, however, to assess what the results will ultimately be. The issue of separation is now inextricably intertwined with all the other issues dividing Québec: questions about the relationship between generations, classes, and ethnic groups, about civil liberties, the economy, and all the rest. It is impossible any longer to discuss Separation versus Confederation as an abstract issue independent of the social and political context of Québec. The choices made on any of the other issues will decisively affect Québec's choices on the constitutional question.

Intense conflict and fragmentation, not

consensus, characterize Québec politics to-day, and will continue to do so. The election results and the FLQ kidnappings and their aftermath both reflect and will contribute to this pattern. Militant opposition will continue, as, perhaps, will correspondingly militant attemps to repress it. Widespread agreement on any constitutional option is therefore very unlikely to emerge in the near future. It is impossible to say how the complex political currents now flowing will resolve themselves. In any case, English Canadians have limited ability to influence the final outcome. But their goodwill and understanding, their willingness to meet Québec half-way or more than half-way, can provide a more reasonable climate of opinion for the continuing dialogue.

[Richard Simeon, "Postscript", in *One Country or Two?*, ed. R.M. Burns, McGill-Queen's University Press, 1971]

Guidelines for Inquiry

1. (a) On what points do Solange Chaput Rolland and Gertrude Laing agree? On what points do they disagree?
   (b) With which one do you find yourself in agreement? Why?
2. Carrier firmly believes that "ils se sont frappés". Do you? Why?
3. Why does Simeon suggest moderates in Québec might have been hurt by the October Crisis? What are the implications of such a development?

Part Six: Future Developments

1. Revitalized Federalism?

You will not be astonished if I affirm my faith in a form of government called federalism. I would like to state precisely that, as far as I am concerned, federalism is not an expedient, nor is it a compromise. Far less is it a makeshift as some people believe it to be. On the contrary, it is a forward-looking political formula, to which I would subscribe even outside the Canadian context.

Why?

The first priority, when we choose a political system, is the human person. Not the person as an abstract notion; what is of prime importance is concrete human beings, you, me, the farmers, the workers, the businessmen, the tenants on Delorimier Street and the residents of Lethbridge, the workers of Windsor and the fishermen of Gaspésie or Newfoundland. Politics, as we say here, is made "for the people", and not "the people" for politics. . . .

The great advantage of federalism is that it brings the State and the citizen closer, it allows for local legislation for local needs, regional for regional needs, and federal for confronting global problems.

I could express the second reason for my preference for federalism in a phrase so popular that it has become banal: "To govern is to foresee". I mean that any political formula worth the name is by definition oriented toward the future. Now the future will mean a greater understanding between peoples; it consists of pooling the wealth of the world; it is the march towards unity—or it is atomic warfare.

But [togetherness], pooling, unity, do not mean uniformity. Some people dream of an international society where everybody would speak the same language, would live in the same way, would eat the same meals, and would watch the same television programs. This type of world would have certain advantages, but chances are that we would die of boredom.

It remains certain that we are evolving toward a closer union among peoples. If there is an irresistible tendency in the modern world, that is the one.

Now, federalism is the *very* political system which allows for union in freedom and for unity in diversity. It is undoubtedly why hundreds of millions of men live within a federal framework, in India and the United States, in Brazil, in Germany and the U.S.S.R.; this is why hundreds of millions more are moving toward federalism, through stages that are called customs unions, common markets, or economic communities.

This is the basis for the attitude that I adopted and maintained for twenty years, in the constitutional debate which occupies a central place in Quebec and Canada.

I believe in a political formula centred on the person, a political formula whose prime consideration is to secure for the men and women of this country the greatest measure of welfare and freedom possible. . . .

THE FUNDAMENTAL OPTION: FEDERALISM OR RUPTURE

The first requirement, in my opinion, is precisely to put Canadian federalism to the test. But not only by criticism, intellectual speculations, the framing of abstract, theoretical solutions. No, we must test it through action, directly—that is, through active participation . . . in all aspects of federal politics.

This, of course, presupposes that we resolve certain contradictions . . . which stifle some minds. Some people assert that Quebec's progress is incompatible with Canada's—and vice versa that they would destroy one another if they went on living together.

I propose that we start with the contrary hypothesis, namely that the safest token of progress for Canada is a strong and dynamic French Canada, sure of itself, freed from fear, and thoroughly involved in all aspects of Canadian life. Equally, the safest way of building up a solid country, prosperous and free, on the border of the United States is for English Canada to play thoroughly the game of honest collaboration with the French element of the country.

We are facing a clear choice. The first hypothesis, that of incompatibility, whatever its name, leads to separation. . . . The second hypothesis is the federalist experience, approached with boldness, and with the new means and resources of modern Quebec.

We have to choose between the two. The worst attitude would be hesitation, to shift from the one to the other, and let the events decide for us.

[P. E. Trudeau, "Of Truth and Freedom in Politics: French Canadians and the Federal Challenge", in *Canadian Federalism: Myth or Reality?*, ed. J. P. Meekison, Methuen Publications, 1968]

2. A Sovereign Québec and a New Canadian Union?

A SOVEREIGN QUEBEC

For our own good, we must dare to seize for ourselves complete liberty in Québec, the right to all the essential components of independence, i.e., the complete mastery of every last area of basic collective decision-making.

The Financial Post

If you were a young French Canadian raised in Montreal, living in conditions similar to the situation suggested in this picture, would you agree with the views of Trudeau or with those of Lévesque? Explain.

This means that Québec must become sovereign as soon as possible.

Thus we finally would have within our grasp the security of our collective "being" which is so vital to us, a security which otherwise must remain uncertain and incomplete.

Then it will be up to us, and us alone, to establish calmly, without recrimination or discrimination, the priority for which we are now struggling feverishly but blindly: that of our language and our culture.

Only then will we have the opportunity

—and the obligation—to use our talents to the maximum in order to resolve without further excuses or evasions all the great problems that confront us, whether it be a negotiated protective system for our farmers, or decent treatment for our employees and workers in industry, or the form and evolution of the political structures we must create for ourselves.

In short, this is not for us simply the only solution to the present Canadian impasse; it also is the one and only common goal inspiring enough to bring us together with the kind of strength and unity we shall need to confront all possible futures—the supreme challenge of continuous progress within a society that has taken control of its own destiny.

As for the other Canadian majority, it will also find our solution to its advantage, for it will be set free at once from the constraints imposed on it by our presence; it will be at liberty in its own way to rebuild to its heart's desire the political institutions of English Canada and to prove to itself whether or not it really wants to maintain and develop on this continent an English-speaking society distinct from the United States.

—AND A NEW CANADIAN UNION

And if this is the case, there is no reason why we, as future neighbours, should not voluntarily remain associates and partners in a common enterprise; [this] would conform to the second great trend of our times: the new economic groups, customs unions, common markets, etc.

Here we are talking about something which already exists, for it is composed of the bonds, the complementary activities, the many forms of economic co-operation within which we have learned to live. Nothing says that we must throw these things away; on the contrary, there is every reason to maintain the framework. If we destroyed it, interdependent as we are, we would only be obliged sooner or later to build it up again, and then with doubtful success.

Such an association seems to us, in fact, made to measure for the purpose of allowing us, unfettered by obsolete constitutional forms, to [create whatever organizations] . . . would best serve our common economic interests: monetary union, common tariffs, postal union, administration of the national debt, co-ordination of policies, etc.

And nothing would prevent us from add-

ing certain matters which under the present system have never had the advantage of frank discussion between equals: the question of minorities, for one; and also the questions of equal participation in a defence policy in proportion to our means, and a foreign policy that might, if conceived jointly, regain some of the dignity and dynamism that it has lost almost completely.

We are not sailing off into uncharted seas. Leaving out the gigantic model furnished by the evolution of the Common Market, we can take our inspiration from countries comparable in size to our own—Benelux or Scandinavia—among whom co-operation is highly advanced, and where it has promoted unprecedented progress in the member states without preventing any of them from continuing to live according to their own tradition and preferences.

To sum up, we propose a system that would allow our two majorities to extricate themselves from an archaic federal framework in which our two very distinct "personalities" paralyze each other by . . . pretending to have a third personality common to both.

This new relationship of two nations, one with its homeland in Québec and another free to rearrange the rest of the country at will, would be freely associated in a new adaptation of the current "common-market" formula, making up an entity which could perhaps—and if so very precisely—be called a Canadian Union.

[René Lévesque, *Option for Québec,* McClelland and Stewart Limited, 1968]

Guidelines for Inquiry

1. What reasons does Pierre Trudeau give for favouring a federal political system? Why does he feel that Canada would be best served by a strong

and dynamic French Canada? Do you find these arguments convincing? Why?

2. Why does René Lévesque feel "that Québec must become sovereign as soon as possible"? Would it be possible for Québec to achieve these things while remaining in Canada? To what extent do you find this a reasonable aspiration?

3. Where do you think Canada is going—"One Nation", "One State—Two Nations", "Two States"? Where do you feel it should go? Why?

3. Constructing a Value Grid

Now that you have completed your study, you are asked to put forward a series of proposals regarding the central issue of the unit: Québec in Canada, or Québec and Canada? In devising these proposals, you should consider the problems related to such matters as language, education, history, and economics. But, because it is easy to propose solutions, and much more demanding to act on them, you will be asked to discover how much you personally *value* your proposals, and how far you would be willing to go in implementing them.

Get a large sheet of paper (the larger the better), and mark off eight columns. The columns should be wide enough to allow you to write complete answers in sentence form. Use the following headings for the columns:

Proposals for Resolving the Issue: Québec in Canada, or Québec and Canada?
A. *What alternatives have you considered?*
B. *What are the consequences of your proposals?*
C. *Would you be willing to spend $5 of your money to achieve this goal?*
D. *Would you be willing to spend several hours each week to work towards this goal?*
E. *Would you be willing to publicly advocate your proposals? If so, how?*
F. *In what way(s) have you acted on your proposal already?*
G. *What do your answers to A-F indicate about the nature of your commitment to your proposals?*

Here is a sketch of how you might set up your columns.

Proposals...	A	B	C	D	E	F	G
1.							
2.							
3.							
4.							
5.							

unit 3: The Americans and Us

by Cary Goulson

Duncan Macpherson; reprinted by permission of *Toronto Star*

INTRODUCTION

There are those who argue that in a brief period of time Canada may have moved from colony to nation and back to colony. In proof of this, they point to such factors as American direction of North American defence, American takeovers of Canadian businesses, and American dominance of the mass media. We have little time left, they warn, if we want Canada to survive as an independent political community.

How can Canada survive? You will be asked to take a tentative position on this dilemma. You will then be challenged with an array of economic, social, and political evidence in order to test, and quite possibly revise, your position.

Major sub-sections of this unit are entitled: One Economy? One Culture? and One Diplomacy? In each case you will be invited to weigh a variety of viewpoints under the heading "The Issues Joined"; then in a section entitled "Data and Debate" you will be given information and opinions that should assist you in clarifying your stance on the issues.

Part One: Canada: Is It All Over?

1. Your Profile

Prepare a chart of eight columns. List your *favourite* three choices for each of the following categories:

(a) Television Programs
(b) Movies (select from those you have seen during the past year)
(c) Singing Groups
(d) Athletes (each should represent a different sport)
(e) Magazines
(f) Historical Figures (name only those not living today)
(g) Holiday Locations
(h) Books

2. Underhill (1957)

In [1940] we passed from the British century of our history to the American century. We became dependent upon the United States for our security. We have, therefore, no choice but to follow American leadership.

[Frank Underhill, *In Search of Canadian Liberalism,* Macmillan of Canada, 1960]

3. Mowat (1959)

In short, I now conclude that the only solution to our trouble with the Americans is to jine 'em; from which it follows that I no longer believe we can lick 'em. . . . It is impossible for us to surmount the prime difficulty that, in order to do battle in any sphere with the United States, we would in effect have to do battle with ourselves since in almost every important social, intellectual and economic aspect we have already become pseudo-Americans.

[Farley Mowat, "Let's Apply for Admission as the 51st State", *Maclean's,* June 6, 1959]

4. Camp (1969)

Be realistic about America. Be realistic about Canada; we are a minority shareholder and we have the inevitable options of the minority shareholder—the limited powers of persuasion and the unfathomable powers of prayer.

[Dalton Camp, "Canadian-American Interdependence: How Much?", *Canadian Forum*, February 1969]

5. Horowitz (1970)

Our political and intellectual elites, true to the Canadian tradition, are moderately concerned about the impending demise of their country, and moderately determined to do something about it, on condition that whatever be done be moderately done. This moderation will be the death of us.

[Gad Horowitz, *Maclean's*, February 1970]

6. Mitchell (1968)

Canada in the twentieth century has been in the process of developing a national consciousness embracing the two main national groups as well as the diverse range of smaller ones and doing so not by melting all down into one common alloy, but by establishing unity with diversity. This developing sense of nationalism, neither British nor French, but essentially Canadian, is enhanced by resistance to being swamped by the great neighbour to the south.

[J. R. Mitchell, *The United States and Canada*, Basil Blackwell, 1968]

7. Forsey (1962)

The fact is that to talk of "developing something purely Canadian which will be neither British nor French" is literally nonsense: It makes "no sense". It is like the middle west-

ern American College which posted a notice: "The following are the traditions of this college. They will go into force at four o'clock tomorrow afternoon." Both the British and French traditions are bone of our bone and flesh of our flesh. . . . They have sustained each other. They have preserved each other. Together, they have preserved our national existence. Alone, neither can survive. They must preserve each other still: together they must still preserve our national existence.

[Eugene Forsey, Address to the University of New Brunswick, 1962]

Guidelines for Inquiry

1. With which of the commentators from 2 to 7 are you most in agreement? Why?
2. With which of the commentators from 2 to 7 are you least in agreement? Why?
3. (a) How many names among your profile choices are distinctively Canadian? Which category has the most Canadian names? Which has the least?
   (b) What does the profile reveal about you? About Canadians?
4. Do you think Canada can survive? How?

Part Two: One Economy?

As the 1970s arrived, Canadians found themselves faced with some very serious economic decisions. True, Canada's standard of living remained relatively high and its land, water, and mineral resources seemed immense.

But time seemed to be running out. As a young country Canada had welcomed foreign investment to get the wheels of industry started and to keep them turning. It had built its affluence on world trade. But now it discovered that much of its economy was American-owned and that approximately 70 per cent of its trade was with the United States.

Critics charge that Canada has produced an artificial prosperity, that the country has been indiscriminately selling its birthright, and that we no longer have a completely free hand in dealing with other nations. Is it as bad as the critics contend?

If it is that serious, what can Canadians do? Is it already too late to regulate American enterprises in Canada? Would the United States understand such a policy or would it retaliate? How can our policy-makers be fair to Americans and honour our past commitments while also being fair to Canadians and future generations? To what extent is our economic independence threatened?

A. THE ISSUES JOINED

1. Are You the Victim of Coca-Colonization?

This is an excerpt from Robert L. Perry's *Galt, U.S.A.,* which documents the extent of American influence and control in Galt, Ontario, in 1971.

An American salesman arriving in Galt today would hardly describe it as a foreign city. Galtonians eat American foods, chew American gum, drive American cars, watch American television programs, and respond to American commercial stimuli. What the salesman could sell in the States, he could sell in Galt. Galtonians are as eager a market for American-type goods as Americans themselves: in a word, CocaColonized. And they've been that way for a long time.

The advertising of the past in Galt newspapers offers a few clues about the timing of the CocaColonization process. In the 1890s and in the first decade of this century, advertising in the now-defunct weekly, *Galt Reformer,* was sparse and almost entirely Ontario-oriented.

After the United States emerged from World War I as an economic power, the flow of American-brand goods into Galt became significant, I suspect. The 1920 files of the daily *Reporter* show that Galtonians were familiar with American comic strips, Chiclets, Wrigley's gum, Post Toasties, Grape Nuts, Kodak cameras, Lifebuoy soap, Gillette razors and Hoover vacuum cleaners.

The migration of American brands into Galt had hit full stride by 1934. Vicks had become a household word; and Heinz, and Pepsodent, Noxzema, Pond's, Colgate, Listerine, Ford, Tums, Westinghouse, Palmolive, Kleenex, Bromo Seltzer, Campbell's, Libby's, Goodrich, Firestone, Goodyear, Kellogg's, Cities Service, Chevrolet, Pontiac, Oldsmobile, Buick, Jell-O, Life Savers.

[Robert L. Perry, *Galt, U.S.A.,* Maclean-Hunter Limited, 1971]

Guidelines for Inquiry

1. What does Perry mean by "CocaColonization"?

2. (a) Reconstruct a typical day in your life. What brand-name products do you rely upon to get you through the day? To what extent have you been CocaColonized?

(b) What alternatives are available to you to avoid this situation?

3. It has been suggested that "Canadian nationalism stops at the cash register". Does it? Should it?

2. American Investment in Canada: Facts and Figures

(a) What Is the Historical Trend?

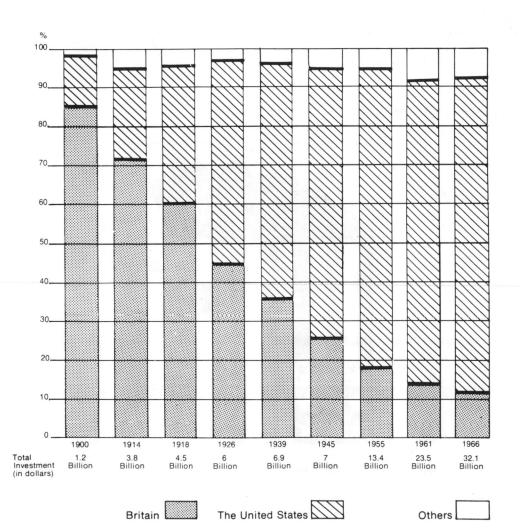

| Total Investment (in dollars) | 1.2 Billion | 3.8 Billion | 4.5 Billion | 6 Billion | 6.9 Billion | 7 Billion | 13.4 Billion | 23.5 Billion | 32.1 Billion |

Britain · The United States · Others

(b) What Are the Contemporary Patterns?

SOME FOREIGN-DOMINATED INDUSTRIES IN CANADA

foreign ownership ☐ domestic ownership

Oil and Gas Production

Petroleum Refining

Transport Equipment

Metal Smelting and Refining

Chemicals and Chemical Products

Machinery

Iron Mining

0 1 2 3 4 5

billions of dollars, U.S.

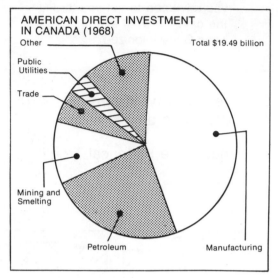

AMERICAN DIRECT INVESTMENT IN CANADA (1968)

Total $19.49 billion

Other

Public Utilities

Trade

Mining and Smelting

Petroleum

Manufacturing

[*The Economist,* September 19, 1970]

Jeff Wakefield

Debate the viewpoint expressed in the above cartoon.

3. Will It Pounce?

POWER RESEVOIR

CANADA

[Macpherson, *Toronto Daily Star*, March 3, 1970]

Guidelines for Inquiry

1. In what ways did foreign investment patterns in Canada change between 1900 and 1966? What are the implications?
2. In what sectors of the Canadian economy is most foreign investment concentrated? What important sectors are not included? Why?
3. If that cat in the cartoon has its way, what future developments in the Canadian economy might be in store for us?

B. DATA AND DEBATE

1. The Economics of Survival: Facts, Figures, and Questions

(a) The Vital Issues

This is an excerpt from "Facts and Figures on Canadian Independence", issued by the Committee for an Independent Canada. This committee is an independent Canadian citizens' organization, embracing people of all political persuasions who subscribe to its program.

Q: . . . What is the magnitude of foreign investment in Canada?

A: At the end of 1969, foreign investment in Canada (short- and long-term) is estimated by the Dominion Bureau of Statistics to be $46 billion, up from $40.2 billion a year earlier. Long-term investment (at book value) equals $41 billion, of which about 80% is American-owned.

Q: What has been the burden of dividends and interest payments to foreign owners paid out in recent years?

A: The increase of foreign investment has brought with it a corresponding increase in the outflow of dividends and interest payments. In the years 1966-69, for exam-

ple, the net outflow of dividends and interest was $3.6 billion. If you compare this with the net (new) capital imports during those years of $2.5 billion, it is apparent that there was a net *outflow* of funds from Canada of $1.1 billion during those years.

Q: Foreign-controlled Canadian firms are Canadian taxpayers too. Do they contribute in the same proportion to the overall Canadian tax bill as, say, Canadian-controlled firms?

A: Although foreign firms and subsidiaries are subject to the same corporate tax structure as domestic corporations, they can, and do, enjoy significant tax advantages in some cases. One major tax advantage is the remission of licensing and royalty fees to the foreign parent. These fees are not subject to Canadian taxes, since they are allowed as deductions in computing income subject to Canadian tax.

Q: Are the activities of foreign-controlled Canadian companies in any way governed by foreign laws?

A: Subsidiaries of U.S. corporations are an important case in point here. The actions of U.S. subsidiaries abroad are controlled by American laws and directives in three main areas: control of exports, control of mergers, and balance-of-payments policy. Legislation such as the Export Control Act of 1949, the Trading with the Enemy Act, the Sherman Act, the Clayton Act, and voluntary/mandatory guidelines relating to U.S. balance-of-payments problems, place U.S. subsidiaries in Canada under a measure of American government control. . . .

Q: In what ways do other countries regulate the activities of foreign-controlled firms?

A: Canada is one of the most liberal countries in the world as far as controls on foreign investment are concerned. Many countries, such as Brazil, Mexico, Japan and Sweden, have very strict controls on foreign

The Financial Post

What is the cartoonist trying to say about the relationship between the U.S. dollar and the Canadian dollar?

investment. These controls range from direct exclusion of foreign investment in certain sectors of the economy to various degrees of local participation in investment projects. Other controls include a required percentage of nationals on the board of directors, effective price and foreign exchange controls and a myriad of special tax rules on foreign investment.

Q: What are the present Canadian regulations in this regard?

A: Canadian regulations are presently limited to the following areas:

Broadcasting—a licence to operate a broadcasting station or network of stations can only be granted to a Canadian citizen or to a Canadian corporation of which the chairman and each of the directors are Canadian citizens and of which four-fifths of the shares are owned either by Canadian citizens or by Canadian-controlled corporations.

Financial Institutions—The Bank Act stipulates that at least 3/4 of the directors of a chartered bank must be Canadian citizens ordinarily resident in Canada. The proportion of shares of a bank which can be held by non-residents is limited to 25% and the proportion held by any one person (non-resident or resident) to 10%. With few exceptions these broad requirements apply to federally incorporated Canadian life insurance companies, loan companies, and trust companies.

Resources—Up until recently the major requirement in this area concerned oil, gas,

Air Canada Photo

Fly Air Canada on an American-built air liner. What are the technological implications for the Canadian economy?

and mining leases in the Yukon and N.W.T. Leases could only be granted to a Canadian citizen or to a Canadian Corporation of which the shares are either owned at least 50% by Canadians or listed on a Canadian stock exchange, or to a Canadian corporation which is wholly owned by such a corporation.

Taxation—The Income Tax Act gives a tax advantage to a corporation of which at least 25% of the issued shares are owned by Canadian residents; for such a company, the withholding tax on dividends paid to a non-resident is reduced from 15% to 10%.

Q: In addition to the high level of American ownership, is our economy linked to that of the U.S. in other ways?

A: The second major link is in the area of trade. In 1968, two-thirds of our exports went to the U.S. while 73% of our imports came from the U.S. Canada's dependence on the U.S. economy is greater than that of any other two industrialized countries. This dependence in turn poses serious problems for Canadian economic policy such as the control of inflation.

Foreign influence is also strong in the case of organized labour. If we exclude government employees, 71.3% of the unionized labour force in Canada are members of International Unions.

Q: What is the connection between foreign direct investment and the development of technology in Canada?

A: Foreign direct investment has had,

and continues to have, negative implications for the development of Canadian research and development capability. Because of the high degree of foreign ownership and control in Canadian primary and secondary industry, much of the [research and development] work is done in the head offices of these foreign concerns. As a result, the development of a distinctively Canadian R & D capability has been seriously retarded.

[Committee for an Independent Canada, "Facts and Figures on Canadian Independence"]

(b) Economic Nationalism: Sorting Truth from Half-Truth

W. B. S. Trimble sees things in a somewhat different light.

Fairness and intellectual honesty are part of the Canadian tradition . . . and I am beginning to think that the more extreme of our economic nationalists, with all their slogan slinging, are subverting our identity while claiming to enhance it.

It seems that a conventional wisdom has emerged in the nationalist movement and as so often happens, the conventional wisdom is wrong. You can test the extent to which you have fallen victim to it by answering the True/False quiz:

	TRUE	FALSE
1. Most major decisions about big corporations are made by the owners.	☐	☐
2. American residents who own businesses in Canada can easily influence Canadian political decisions.	☐	☐
3. When the people who make decisions about a Canadian business are Canadian citizens, their primary objective will be the health of the Canadian economy.	☐	☐
4. When the people who make decisions about an American business are U.S. citizens, their primary objective will be the health of the American economy.	☐	☐
5. When businesses located in Canada pay dividends to shareholders who live in the U.S., these dollars are lost to the Canadian economy.	☐	☐
6. In the interests of creating employment in Canada, we should encourage manufacturing industries.	☐	☐
7. Our material standard of living will go up if we keep out foreign competition.	☐	☐
8. We should be proud when the Canadian dollar is worth more than the American dollar.	☐	☐
9. If we stopped all U.S. investment in Canada, Canadian unemployment would get worse.	☐	☐
10. American-owned plants operating on Canadian territory have been subject to American restrictions against trading with communist countries.	☐	☐
	TRUE	FALSE

1. Most major decisions about big corporations are made by the owners.

This statement is false. In the early days of capitalism until well into the 20th Century, there was a close connection between ownership of a business and control. Those who invested the capital called the shots. . . .

Over the past 30 to 40 years, however, there has been a separation of ownership and control. Shareholders of big corporations, even major shareholders, no longer significantly influence the activities of the corporation. Control has shifted to committees of experts who are on the corporate payroll, but not on the board of directors. . . .

The shareholders of General Motors no longer make the decision to bring out a new model; hired experts do. The shareholders of AT and T do not decide to open a new plant; hired experts do. Selling prices, working conditions, industrial relations policy, marketing strategies, plant locations—all these are matters decided by committees of one kind or another, and then rubber-stamped by the owners' representatives on the board who often cannot know enough to interfere.

It no longer matters whether the owners of a big business are Canadian or American or Fiji Islanders. Shareholders still control in about the same way that the Governor-General governs Canada.

2. *American residents who own businesses in Canada can easily influence Canadian political decisions.*

This is false too. American residents do not vote in Canadian elections, and it is extremely difficult for pressure groups to significantly influence the Canadian government. To effectively bribe legislators in Ottawa, a corporation would have to bribe the whole political party in power, and there is no convincing evidence at all that even the most powerful U.S. corporations have ever successfully done so.

There is no way of knowing at present to what extent corporations—American or Canadian—make contributions to Canadian political parties. . . . The problem, however, remains just as serious, whether the donation is sent from Hamilton, Ontario or from Buffalo, New York. The expectations of the contributors in either case are . . . likely to be against the public interest.

In a very real sense, Canadians control the businesses that are owned by Americans, and located in Canada. Canadians, not Americans, legislate Canadian working conditions, holidays with pay, minimum wages, fair employment practices, industrial standards, labor codes and so on. The laws of the land are still in the hands of Canadians.

It is simply not true that we can maintain our political independence only by remaining independent economically. Norway, Sweden and Denmark have had closely integrated economies for many years without any surrender of political sovereignty.

3. *When the people who make decisions about a Canadian business are Canadian citizens, their primary objective will be the health of the Canadian economy.*

4. *When the people who make decisions about an American business are U.S. citizens, their primary objective will be the health of the American economy.*

These questions can be considered together. They are both false and for the same reason. The people who make corporate decisions are primarily interested in the growth of the particular corporation for which they work, regardless of what their passports may say. [The] motivations of people who make decisions about Canada's Massey-Ferguson Company are about the same as the motivations of those who make decisions about America's IBM. Neither Canadian nor American corporate experts care very much about the problems of a nation's economy.

A great deal of the Canadian antagonism toward Americans is really a variety of branch plant antagonism. . . . Most people who work in branch plants feel that people in head office do not understand them, and that policies coming from head office do not adequately take account of local conditions. If the head office is in Toronto, and the branch in Owen Sound, the branch plant antagonism is directed toward "those So-and-Sos on Bay Street who sit on their backsides all day in big offices and don't really know what is going on up here." When the head office is in the States, however, the hostility takes the form of anti-Americanism. Those on the receiving end draw the flak, not because they are American, but because they are from head office.

5. *When businesses located in Canada pay dividends to shareholders who live in the U.S., these dollars are lost to the Canadian economy.*

This statement too is false. American-owned enterprises in Canada do send about $1.5 billion per year to Americans, but the Americans do not burn or bury them. Eventually these dollars find their way back to Canada. If we reduce the number of dollars we send to Americans, they will have to reduce their purchases from us.

The dollars we send may be used by American tourists, or by those who want to buy Canadian goods, or by those who want to invest in Canada. The Canadian dollars may even go through several other countries on their way back. Ultimately, however, they come back here. Unless we send Canadian money out, other countries simply cannot buy from us. Those who really understand this simple truth, understand more than most U.S. congressmen, and more than the militant members of the Committee for an Independent Canada.

6. *In the interests of creating employment in Canada, we should encourage manufacturing industries.*

7. *Our material standard of living will go up if we keep out foreign competition.*

Both these statements are false. We would be only more ridiculous if we suggested we develop our own banana industry, or that we keep out the sun to create work for Canadian candlemakers.

We should concentrate our productive efforts on what we can do well, and then trade the results for the other goods and services which we want. There is no virtue in producing Canadian watches if we can get watches more easily by producing wheat and trading with the Swiss. There is no virtue in producing our own textiles if we can obtain textiles more easily by producing pa-per and trading with India. We do, of course, need to produce jobs but we can create jobs by encouraging industries which belong here—not banana-growing, candle-making or textiles.

The economic nationalists are afraid that Canadians may end up relying too heavily on primary industries like agriculture, mining, forest products and fisheries. It could just be, however, that Canadian primary products will become more and more valuable in terms of foreign manufactured goods as more and more countries of the world seem to opt for manufacturing. We may soon get a lot of pots and pans for a bushel of Canadian wheat.

The material standard of living in the world goes up if every country concentrates on what it can do best and then trades for its other requirements.

8. *We should be proud when the Canadian dollar is worth more than the American dollar.*

False again. We should be glad or sad, depending on where we sit.

Suppose our dollar is worth a whole lot more than the U.S. dollar. Let's say Canadians can buy a U.S. dollar for 90c. Any article marked $1.00 in the U.S. now costs a Canadian only 90c in Canadian money. In effect, all American goods are reduced in price for Canadians. The people who each year import about $12 billion worth of goods and services from the States should be pleased.

There is, however, another side to the coin. Everything in Canada bearing a price tag of 90c will now cost Americans $1.00 in their money. In effect our goods have gone up in price for Americans. Our exports to the U.S. will surely suffer as a result and a lot of jobs in Canada will disappear.

Be proud if you must when our dollar goes above the American. But you may end up proud and poor.

9. *If we stopped all U.S. investment in Canada, Canadian unemployment would get worse.*

This is true. As of February 1973, the federal finance minister estimated that one million Canadian jobs depended on foreign investment, most of which comes from the States.

And we must keep creating jobs at a very rapid rate. We have the fastest growing work force in the industrialized world with 240,000 new entrants each year and 668,000 unemployed already waiting in the wings.

To create each new job in Canada requires about $40,000. To create 668,000 jobs right now would require about $26.5 billion or $1,200 for each man, woman, and child in the country. We need all the help we can get.

It looks as if we are going to get less help rather than more. Latest figures show that American investors are getting fed up with their inhospitable Canadian hosts and are diverting their investment dollars to western Europe. There is trouble ahead for Canadian job seekers.

10. *American-owned plants operating on Canadian territory have been subject to American restrictions against trading with communist countries.*

This is true and we should be angered by it. This is the most legitimate cause for concern on the part of those who want an independent Canada. Canadian legislators, not American, should decide where goods made in Canada may be sold.

On several occasions, regulations made under the [American] Trading with the Enemy Act, which prohibited parent companies from trading with communist countries, have been extended to subsidiaries operating in Canada. Without too much difficulty, however, Canadian diplomats persuaded the U.S. government to reconsider, and in December 1969, Washington announced that foreign subsidiaries of U.S. firms would

no longer be included in the prohibition. If there should be further trouble in this respect, the Canadian government could easily establish an export trade agency to purchase goods from business for resale to any country approved by Canadian, not American, lawmakers.

Harry Johnson, famous Canadian economist, who holds academic appointments in both London and Chicago, has harsh words for the attitude of our more dogmatic economic nationalism. He refers to it as "the small town pettiness of outlook that is the shadow side of many Canadian virtues".

It is time we came out of the shadow.

[W. B. S. Trimble, "Economic Nationalism: Sorting Truth from Half-Truth", *Canadian Business,* June 1973]

Guidelines for Inquiry

1. How do the questions asked by the Committee for an Independent Canada differ from those asked by Mr. Trimble? Is this significant?
2. To what extent do the figures provided by the Committee for an Independent Canada dispute some of Mr. Trimble's opinions? To what extent do they support them?

2. The Canadian Economy and American Resource Needs

(a) We Need What You Have

Canada is precisely the country, of course, from which we seek the most. That is a natural result of geography. Only Canada, no other country, can be the geographical buffer between the United States and the U.S.S.R., the buffer between nuclear states. If we need water, we can't get it from Bolivia, only Canada. If we need a highway to connect the 48 states with Alaska, or to connect Buffalo directly with Detroit, we can't build it in Burma; we can only build it in Canada. Our electricity does not depend on all the plugs being in the right sockets in Finland, only in Canada. So the basic, long-range problem, or crisis, in U.S.–Canadian affairs, and the greatest obstacle to North American progress, is that the American people seek so much from a country whose independence they respect so little.

[Douglas Bailey, *Writings on Canadian-American Studies,* Harvard University Press, 1966]

(b) Let's Sell While We Can

Canada has no exclusive patents on raw materials or resources. These commodities are being produced and discovered in many areas of the world. The need for them can disappear overnight as new sources are discovered or the resources become obsolete. If we can't fabricate our resources into completely finished goods or consume these resources in our processing facilities, then it is time we started selling *now,* while the need exists. Perhaps those who do not share this viewpoint can advise the Canadian Government where we can sell our surplus uranium, potash, iron ore, oil, gas and, most important to our western farmers, surplus wheat.

[Stanley Randall, "Canada Can't Afford to Hoard Its Resources", *Toronto Daily Star,* February 22, 1971]

(c) To Sell Out Would Be Disastrous

When the heat went off in sub-zero North Dakota two weeks ago, the U.S. energy crisis became a harsh reality. The inability of U.S. sources of fuel to meet domestic demand was inescapable and public reaction was swift and predictable.

Within hours the problem became a continental problem (Americans are adept at exporting their difficulties). Canadian petroleum reserves—controlled largely by American-owned and other foreign-based corporations—were identified by U.S. public figures as the cushion for U.S. shortages and by the producing companies as a profit bonanza in a seller's market.

Prices increased immediately. The Alberta government which, in partnership with the producing companies, controls the primary petroleum reserves, heralded further increases. U.S. legislators began talking again about the urgent need for a "continental" energy agreement. President Nixon's executive reaction was to authorize an upward revision of oil import quotas for Canadian crude, an area in which his administration moved grudgingly and stingily only last year. But the word from North Dakota was that it was a new game.

The crisis, of course, is not a new one. Only the realization in the United States of its seriousness is new. And it is not just a U.S. crisis or even a continental crisis. It is a global condition that cannot improve much, according to experts, and is likely to deteriorate rapidly.

But it is not a Canadian crisis. . . . Proven Canadian petroleum reserves are sufficient to provide for this country's growth into the foreseeable future. In a toughening world market for all exports Canada's bountiful petroleum supply offers its industrialists a significant competitive edge.

If Canadians export their petroleum resources indiscriminately they also export the edge. If present pressures from outside the country and from within are successful, Canadian industry not only loses its advantage, it loses it to its most persistent and powerful competitor in the world market. . . .

The dimensions of the world energy crisis

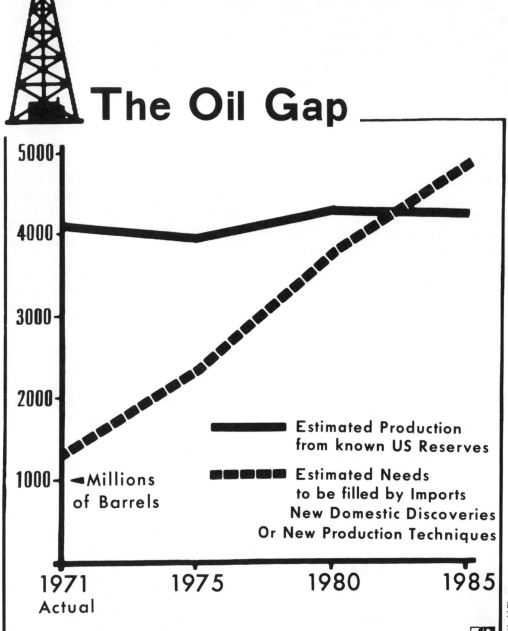

The Oil Gap

5000

4000

3000

2000

1000 — Millions
of Barrels

——— Estimated Production
from known US Reserves

■■■■■ Estimated Needs
to be filled by Imports
New Domestic Discoveries
Or New Production Techniques

1971   1975   1980   1985
Actual

Wide World Photo

This chart appeared in American newspapers in 1971. What does it show? What are the possible implications for Canadian-American relations?

have been roughed out over the past five years. Recently the Ontario advisory committee on energy stated them this way:

"The life index of world oil reserves is currently approximately 38 years, but this is likely to drop to about 22 years by 1980, assuming a continuation of recent trends. In the decade of the 1970s the world is expected to consume approximately 200 billion barrels of oil, roughly equivalent to total historic consumption to date and about 40 per cent of today's known oil reserves."

[Terrence W. Honey, "Energy: Whose Crisis?" *London Free Press,* February 3, 1973]

(d) The Economic Facts of Life?

The United States does not need Canadian natural resources to survive and is doing Canada a favor by buying them, Herman Kahn, a U.S. social and economic forecaster, said yesterday. . . .

He said the United States could just as easily deal with other resource-rich countries as with Canada. . . .

. . . He told reporters that Canada holds no monopoly on the natural resources needed by the United States. Australia has as many resources, Brazil has greater reserves than Canada and Australia combined, and Siberia has more than all three, he said. . . .

With modern transport systems, all countries on the Pacific or Atlantic Oceans are, in effect, next door to the United States, and Canada has no decisive advantage from its common border with the United States, he said.

If Canadians recognized this lack of U.S. dependence, relations between the two countries would improve, Kahn said. . . .

The United States could cut off all trade with the outside world "and we would be adjusted to it in about five years." There would be difficult problems, such as rationing water, extracting oil from coal instead of importing it, and operating industries without such metals as chromium, Kahn said. But they could be beaten. . . .

"There is an emotional thing in Canada about the Canadian identity and culture, but if there was ever a threat to the Western Hemisphere or another depression we would be back together again like this," he said, clamping his fists together.

Kahn said Canada now is strong enough to be economically independent, though many Canadians do not realize it.

"You are a big country now, but you still tend to feel small and fragile. If the U.S. gets a cold, you get pneumonia."

[*Toronto Daily Star,* August 23, 1972]

(e) Why Bury Our Heads?

There is one thing Canadians should always remember. In many parts of the world, including much of the southern United States, people will be uncomfortable if heating fuel is cut off; but in Canada, many people would die. We need our energy fuels just to stay alive in our rigorous climate, and fuel for our future is essential. We cannot return to the use of wood and coal, and nuclear power has not yet been developed as an adequate alternative to fossil fuels.

North America is today facing the problem met by all ancient peoples, that we are reaching the limit of our resources. Many nations and tribes in the past were unable to cope with the necessity to change, and perished; but the more successful of past civilizations [met the challenge], survived, and even flourished for centuries. . . .

Canadians can hope to do the same, but only if we recognize our problems in time, reduce our demands, conserve our resources, revise our philosophies and put far greater efforts into finding substitutes until alternatives, perhaps dependent upon energy from fusion, can be found. Nothing could be worse than to bury our heads in undeveloped tar sands.

[J. Tuzo Wilson, "Selling Today What We'll Need Tomorrow", *Maclean's,* March 1973]

Guidelines for Inquiry

1. What particular Canadian resources does the United States appear to be most interested in at the present time? Why?
2. On a page of paper, draw up a balance sheet with two columns: Reasons for Selling, Reasons for Not Selling. After completing the sheet, decide which alternatives seem most convincing. Are there other alternatives? Debate the issue.

3. Multi-National Corporations: Good Citizens or Subversive Agents?

(a) A Multi-National Giant in Canada: ITT

John Jones pushed away his ITT pie, brushed the crumbs off his ITT rayon shirt, switched off his ITT light fixture, went outside and climbed into his ITT rent-a-car.

He drove through downtown Toronto under several miles of ITT wire, passed the growing bulk of the new ITT hotel opposite City Hall, and went to his own company's new building, where he oversaw the installation of an ITT switchboard, gave orders to his secretary on an ITT intercom, watched the ITT window-cleaners at work and stopped off at the cafeteria for a cup of ITT coffee.

HOW LUCKY HE WAS

Then he drove to the ITT hotel on King St. for a few drinks, got back into his ITT rent-a-car and headed for home, thinking how lucky he was to live in a safe country, a land where ever-vigilant ITT employees were running the DEW line against any sneak attack from over the Arctic.

Alas, between his musing and his drinks, Jones became inattentive, swerved, and although he jammed on the brakes equipped with ITT brake shoes, it was too late.

His ITT rent-a-car plowed into a telephone pole. Soon after, an ITT insurance cheque was on its way to his weeping ITT widow. Poor fellow, he never made it into that ITT owned record, the International Who's Who.

This vignette may not be true, but it's possible. ITT is all around us, and the . . . resident who wants to spend a whole day free of the influence of this U.S. conglomerate will have his work cut out for him.

The company's holdings [in Canada] include Morton's Frozen Foods, a number of electrical companies, Avis Rent-a-car, one of [Toronto's] newest hotels (the 1,450-room Four Seasons-Sheraton), one of [its] oldest (The Sheraton-King Edward), Aimco Industries, which makes replacement brake shoes, and Abbey Life Insurance. . . .

IN 57 COUNTRIES

But ITT is not just an American company, it is a multi-national corporation, and a classic example of the breed.

It operates in 57 countries, from Surinam to Switzerland and from Thailand to Turkey, through 270 subsidiary and affiliated companies; has assets of $7.6 billion, annual sales of $7.3 billion; 392,000 employees; its own foreign policy and foreign intelligence services (a company director is the former head of the U.S. Central Intelligence Agency); and a controversial reputation. . . .

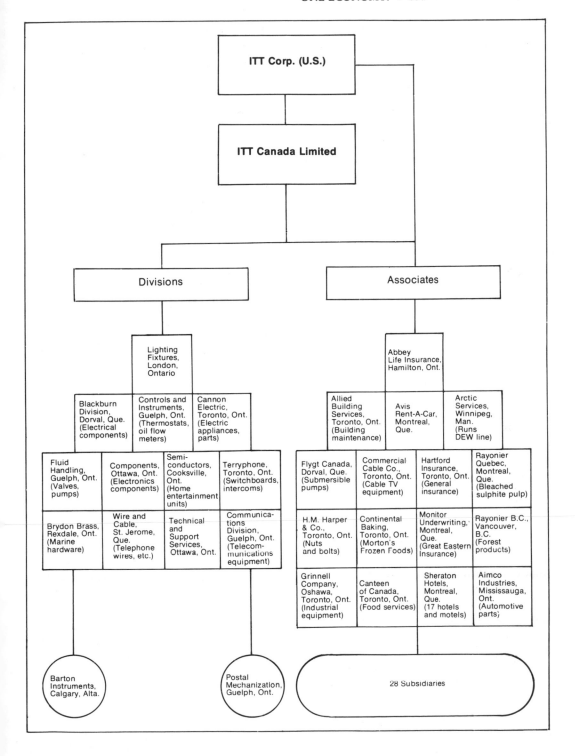

. . . ITT is like any other multi-national with arms and branches abroad, but control at home. Westinghouse, IBM, Du Pont are all run this way. However, ITT is a particular kind of multi-national; it is a conglomerate.

Wherever IBM goes, it operates as a producer and salesman of computers; it is a specialist in a particular line, and the same may be said of Westinghouse, Goodrich Rubber or Shell Oil.

SOME SPREAD OUT

But some multi-nationals spread out into any business that will bring growth and profits. These are the conglomerates—companies like Gulf Oil, whose activities range from pumping gas to making movies; Procter and Gamble, which sells toothpaste and runs pulp mills; and ITT, which turns its hand to anything that promises a profit, from window-washing to insurance selling.

In its scramble for growth, the U.S. ITT has purchased 16 companies with operations in Canada, and they in turn have 28 subsidiaries of their own. Only one of these firms—Aimco Industries, of Mississauga—was purchased in its own right: all the others fell to ITT as part of other deals.

These companies are direct subsidiaries of the U.S. concern, and while they appear on ITT Canada's roster as associates, neither their assets nor their sales are recorded on the Canadian company's books.

Rayonier Canada (B.C.) Ltd., ITT's largest Canadian holding, is a northern branch of Rayonier of New York, and came under the ITT umbrella with purchase of the parent firm. Abbey Life is part of Abbey International, Sheraton Canada is directly held by Sheraton U.S.

The Canadian heads of these companies make long monthly reports to New York, submit budgets, one-year and five-year plans to the appropriate executives there and make frequent pilgrimages to Park Ave. to hear the word from on high.

The degree of their independence may be judged from the statement of one of the Canadian presidents to The Star: "I can't tell you much; I could lose my job. I'm very nervous. I'm afraid."

The president of another ITT subsidiary was interviewed by The Star, and later said wonderingly: "I was given the answers to a bunch of questions by the ITT guy, but then you didn't ask the questions."

In short, the notion that ITT's divisions and subsidiaries in Canada are a sturdily independent bunch may be regarded, at best, as a polite fiction. . . .

. . . Harold S. Geneen, the U.S. President, described his company's decision-making process for the New York Society of Security Analysts. Geneen said: "I do not think even a routine question arises anywhere in the system that is not scheduled for review at the area and headquarters level within two weeks at most and usually in person by the top New York headquarters executives."

If ITT Canada is indeed a "good Canadian corporate citizen" it might be expected to make stock available to Canadians, disclose its operations adequately to the public here, make its own decisions, following Canadian priorities, and people its board of directors largely with Canadians.

WHOLLY OWNED

In fact it is a privately held corporation, wholly owned by ITT U.S., it discloses as little as possible to the Canadian public (even the names of its directors had to be obtained elsewhere) and, on the word of the U.S. president, delegates very little decision-making power across the border.

Of the 11 directors of ITT Canada, seven are in fact resident here, but the other four are the top officers of the New York firm, and it is difficult to imagine them losing any arguments.

ITT Canada follows McGill economist Kari Levitt's description of typical direct foreign investment: "The intrusion into the Canadian social and economic fabric of a tightly controlled private corporation whose operations are likely to diminish, not to enhance, the power and effectiveness of Canadian enterprise."

[*Toronto Daily Star,* May 6, 1972]

Guidelines for Inquiry

1. What is a multi-national corporation? What is a multi-national conglomerate corporation?
2. Why does the writer suggest that "the notion that ITT's divisions and subsidiaries in Canada are a sturdily independent bunch may be regarded, at best, as a polite fiction"?
3. Would you regard ITT in Canada as a good corporate citizen or a subversive agent? Why?

(b) Explanations: A Multi-National Corporate Executive

This is an excerpt from Robert L. Perry's *Galt, U.S.A.* The study documents the extent of American influence and control in Galt, Ontario. The following is an interview conducted by Perry.

I don't see anything wrong with foreign involvement. This is how you get international research, and that's really important. But this business of having people in Philadelphia making the final decision on whether you're going to do something in Toronto: I feel this is wrong.
[Ken Whittington, Director, Canadian Institute of Management]

The president of Allen-Bradley Canada Ltd. wears a red-and-gold, 15-year service pin in his lapel, and he works not in the usual posh office but from a no-frills open alcove sectioned off by glass partitions. His name is Keith H. Rapsey. If I asked a mildly radical-ized second-year sociology student to describe a Canadian businessman, he would probably describe Keith Rapsey or someone very much like him.

Rapsey is as acute and cool as a February icicle. He has an electrical engineer's affection for numbers and for things measurable in numbers, an indestructible faith in the wisdom of the free market, and after 40 years in industry a contempt for bureaucracy. He's articulate and stimulating, and his description of the operations and attitudes of a successful American subsidiary was brisk and to the point.

What did you join the company as? I asked him.

I encouraged Allen-Bradley Co. of Milwaukee to establish its Canadian operation. When this did take place in 1952, I started as general manager of the Canadian operation [Rapsey said].

You didn't take over an existing company?

No.

Was the parent company's capital involved in the investment?

Yes.

Has your growth over the last 10 years been financed by internal capital or that of the parent company?

Both, actually. Partly because in that period there has never been a nickel in dividends paid. Retention has been 100%, up to now, because the growth has demanded it.

The parent, I gather, is more interested in growth than immediate return.

Yes. Perhaps I should explain that it's not exactly the parent company, but the *related* company. Because we are not a subsidiary of Allen-Bradley Co. of Milwaukee.

The company in Milwaukee was originally a family concern. In order to retain this type of ownership, the shares quite some years ago were placed in trust so that death duties would not force the sale of the company. (They have the same problem in the

United States as we have here.)

Actually, it's these trusts that own the shares of the American company. They also own the shares of the Canadian company. So it's affiliated; technically it is not a subsidiary, although the effect is somewhat the same. But for that reason, the American company also finds it vital to grow from earnings. They are conditioned to this idea. They do not use the American capital market.

Do you have a position on the board of the American company? Are there interlocking directorships and executive responsibilities?

Yes. I'm a director of Allen-Bradley Co. as well as of Allen-Bradley Canada Ltd. I'm also a director of Allen-Bradley U.K. I also happen to be one of the five trustees who vote the stock of Allen-Bradley Co.

As a Canadian company, do you use, wherever it's economically possible Canadian input and supplies?

Yes. We have, as I think is common in all Canadian operations or practically all, a make-or-buy committee that meets every week, and we're always nibbling away. I don't think a month goes by without our finding it possible to transfer to a Canadian source, either making ourselves or buying in Canada, 25 or 30 items.

What types of items?

Parts and raw materials for the motor starters we build.

Do you do any design work here? Or do you depend largely on the affiliated company for that?

It all depends on what you call design. We do a certain amount, an increasing amount, of development work here, and actually we plan to do more. We've had recent discussions on stepping this up.

The fundamental component parts, the switches themselves, are probably likely to continue to be developed in the United States because the development time and facilities and so on are rather tremendous. The requirements are quite costly. But in the application and development of variations, as a matter of fact, we've already developed a couple of things which the American outfit has seen fit to copy.

Do you employ engineers for this purpose?

Yes. We have a number of engineers on staff. That, incidentally, is one of the limiting factors in more elaborate development work in Canada.

Generally speaking, there hasn't been too much of what you might call mechanical development, mechanism development, done in Canada. There aren't too many men around in Canada who have that experience. Recruitment, in many cases, has to be made from either the United States or Europe.

Is your staff largely Canadian?

We happen to have one American on staff. He was our chief engineer. We have recently moved him over to manufacturing manager.

One hears frequently the accusation that absentee-owned companies tend not to be good citizens in local community matters. Would you comment?

This is something that's a little difficult to prove by facts and figures, of course. My impression is a bit the opposite. The absentee owner feels in a somewhat sensitive position and tends to bend over backwards to make sure that he *is* a good citizen.

Can you give me a specific example of that?

An example of being a good citizen?

Of an absentee-owned company or operation bending over backwards.

No, I don't think I can. It's not one of those things you can produce statistics on really.

It is a difficult question.

By the way, that feeling is very strong in Ottawa. The feeling you mentioned.

About community matters?

About absentee-ownership. There was a meeting of the legislation committee of the Canadian Manufacturers' Association in Ottawa and we had arranged that Mr. Gray [Herbert Gray, minister of national revenue] would be present. Mr. Gray has been charged with the responsibility of pulling together all these various studies and articles and so forth on the subject of foreign ownership, with the idea of making a recommendation to the cabinet.

We met with him and some of his staff, and repeatedly it became obvious that they had the basic feeling that branch operations were not managed by the branch manager. That almost literally the branch manager had to get head office approval before he blew his nose. Now how do you disprove that? It isn't so; it's quite definitely not so.

In your case: does this company have a separate board?

We have a separate board.

Where does it sit?

We meet sometimes in Galt and sometimes in Milwaukee. This is partly a matter of convenience.

Are any local people on the board?

Yes. At the moment there are three Canadians on the board.

Including yourself?

That includes me, yes.

To what extent can the Canadian company's board make capital decisions, commit this company's capital to an expansion or some other project? Is it an [independent] board?

Well, what is [independent]? Obviously we're going to make decisions that are in the overall interest of the whole Allen-Bradley organization. And this requires consultation.

There's no such thing as complete [in-dependence] really. But there's quite a difference between running hat in hand and sitting down and consulting and deciding which is the best direction to move.

Do you have the authority to hire your own senior people?

Yes. That authority is absolute.

What is the actual procedure for linking your operations with those of Allen-Bradley Co. in the States? Do you have monthly meetings or telephone meetings?

At the board level, the coordination is very informal, really. The Allen-Bradley Co. Milwaukee board meets monthly. The Canadian board will meet only two or three times a year. But there's some interlocking of directorates, and we always know what's going on. If something comes up on the Canadian end, I would report it just as a matter of interest to the American board, although it doesn't directly affect them, but just to keep them posted.

What would your board and the American board think of a proposal to gradually put Allen-Bradley Canada Ltd. shares on the public market in Canada?

We would be strongly opposed to it, because Allen-Bradley shares are not on the market in the United States. Why should they be on the public market in Canada?

What do you think of this wave of economic nationalism you see around you? Do you think it's a passing thing?

I think the wave of nationalism is largely at Ottawa. It has been rather apparent that the provincial governments are becoming quite alarmed about this. So I'm convinced that it's largely at Ottawa. It is not a grassroots proposition. It is being pushed by a certain element largely based in Ottawa.

Trying to assess how this comes about, it's very difficult to pin down. I've tried repeatedly to get some of these people to explain. Foreign owners are supposed to be bad citizens. Why? Where? Give me examples. They don't have examples.

They occasionally make noises about the great drain upon the economy. There's no conceivable way that the figures would support a charge that foreign investment is a drain on the Canadian economy. It's quite the opposite.

The one thing that I do find recurring time and time and time again in all these reports such as Watkins's is the fact that a foreign branch doesn't want to trade with China or Cuba or something like that.

And more and more I am coming to the conclusion that the basic drive behind this antipathy to foreign investment is not any interest in the development of Canada or Canadian prosperity. It is out-and-out anti-Americanism. It is a desire to have Canada do business with every dictatorship and totalitarian country in the world *except* South Africa, which we're supposed not to do business with.

I find it very difficult to understand why it's desirable, in Canada's long-term interest, to do business with China at this time. I am forced to the conclusion that anti-Americanism is the underlying thing.

The other point that keeps coming up, and it came up again and again in our meeting with Mr. Gray: multi-national corporations. It stuck out that they [government officials] don't like multi-national corporations. And the reason they don't like them is that the multi-national corporation is rather more free to decide that it can locate a plant in Canada or locate it in Timbuctoo, depending on which of the two locations might be the more desirable business investment. This simply burns our friends who want to have business completely under the governmental thumb.

So it all boils down to the fact that I have to question either the intelligence or the integrity of these people who are making so much noise about foreign investment.

There is a feeling that multi-national companies bring more than economic influences, that they bring certain other influences. You've heard the same, obviously, in Ottawa. Do you want to say something about this, since Allen-Bradley is a multi-national corporation?

Again, this is an area that I don't believe anyone can produce statistics in. I'm quite convinced this is irrational, but how do you prove it? How do you prove that there is such a threat; how do I prove that there isn't such a threat?

What do you think accounts for the anti-Americanism in Canada?

I'd like to repeat that I think that anti-Americanism is almost entirely found in Ottawa. I don't think you'll find any strong waves of it elsewhere. And I think that it's based on a desire to have a strong central government, central planning, regimentation, and what to me is a denial of the ordinary democratic and free-market aspects of the economy which I think have brought us to where we are today. And they're in the process of being pushed down the drain.

Have you seen any anti-Americanism in Galt?

No. I haven't [Rapsey replied].

[Robert L. Perry, *Galt, U.S.A.*, Maclean-Hunter Limited, 1971]

(c) We Are Good Canadian Citizens!

The following was written in 1963 by Robert Yohe, President of B. F. Goodrich of Canada.

I have yet to find any American or any Canadian head of an American subsidiary who was any less a Canadian than the so-called pure Canadian in a comparable posi-

Joan Latchford

Here are students from Goderich, Ontario, and Chicago, Illinois, mingling in a supermarket. To what extent do such contacts prove or disprove the following view: "Canadian nationalists will always be frustrated in their extreme ambitions, for they ignore the most basic fact of Canadian-American relations: Canadians and Americans genuinely like each other."

tion with a wholly Canadian company. . . . Those that I do know are good citizens of Canada. In most respects they have to be, for their own individual success depends upon the success of the company with which they are associated and, in most cases, the success of the company depends upon how well it becomes integrated with the economy of the country in which it resides. . . .

The question is really one of obligation. I, myself, am still a citizen of the United States. Canada didn't send for me, didn't ask B. F. Goodrich to send me from Akron, Ohio, to Kitchener, Ontario. My company recognized this, and among a lot of other

admonitions which I shan't recount but which any businessman here could list for me, gave me the following direct [warnings]:

1. Be ever conscious of the problems of an American subsidiary in the Canadian economy.
2. Develop in every way possible, good community, provincial and federal relations.
3. Develop able Canadians to assume highest management positions in the company. . . .

Canada needs foreign investment but it has a right to expect this foreign investment, which has strictly a profit motive, to behave like a welcome visitor. What then are the obligations of such a visitor? . . .

1. Foreign-owned companies should have employment and other labour policies as good as or better than Canadian-owned companies. I believe that government officials will admit publicly that this is, for the most part, already standard practice.

2. Canadian managerial talent should be used to its fullest capacity and availability in the higher echelons of foreign-owned companies. Unfortunately, recent events would indicate that this obligation is not being met by some of our largest foreign-owned companies.

3. Canadian subsidiaries should export wherever and whenever possible. As for expecting them to compete with their parents, this is silly. The Canadian economy should not be subsidized by foreign investment and it never will grow up if it has to be so treated.

[Robert Yohe, "Do American Subsidiary Firms Doing Business in Canada Make Good Canadian Citizens?" *Fifth Seminar on Canadian-American Relations,* 1963]

(d) Multi-Nationals: Issues and Directions

Theoretically, . . . foreign-owned corporations are under the control of Canadian law, just as Canadian-owned corporations are. But, even the federal government has doubts as to whether they really are. The problem is that international (or multi-national) corporations have the ability to avoid, if not evade, government policy. They can shift their resources and alter their operations both geographically and through time. They can shift purchases and production among their subsidiaries. They can divert investments. They can transfer management and man-power. In other words, if

they aren't treated exactly the way they want to be, they can go elsewhere. And that can hurt the host country. The result, says Ron Basford, . . . Canadian Minister of Consumer and Corporate Affairs, is that "Because international corporations have alternatives, individual governments are in a negotiating rather than a controlling position." While me and thee are subject to the law, these privileged giant corporate concerns "negotiate" it.

But it goes much further than that. One of Basford's greatest concerns is that these corporations, because of their size and foreign nationality, can frequently ignore Canadian policy entirely. For example, to the extent that a multi-national corporation can generate funds independently from such sources as its parent company or from retained earnings, it may be able to limit the effectiveness of a country's monetary policy. Or it may escape tax laws in the absence of adequate monitoring facilities. Or it may frustrate laws against monopoly or restrictive trade practices by simply doing acts banned in Canada somewhere outside the boundaries of Canada where Canadian law doesn't apply. Thus, if two or three international firms carve up a world market between them and engage in price fixing, market allocation arrangements and other restrictive practices, there is little or nothing the government of Canada—or any other country acting alone —can do about it. . . .

The solution? The recently-established Canada Development Corporation? Ownership restrictions? Cooperation among governments to control gigantic corporate organizations? Establishment of so-called "world" corporations under the auspices and regulation of the United Nations? All have been suggested. Whatever the eventual choice, it might be well to bear in mind the following: In 1969, multi-national corporations accounted for 7.5 per cent of the free world's economy. But a recent study by the Economic Council of Canada predicts that, within 20 years, they may account for 50 per cent.

[Keith Bradbury, "The International Corporate Octopus", *UBC Alumni Chronicle,* Spring 1971]

Guidelines for Inquiry

1. Do either ITT or the Allen-Bradley Company appear to be guilty of the behaviour Bradbury outlines? Explain.
2. Which of Bradbury's proposed solutions seems most reasonable? Why?
3. It has been suggested that "multi-national corporations may be remarkable instruments for the enrichment of mankind." Suggest arguments to both support and refute this position.

4. What Should We Do?

What should we do about foreign investment in Canada? Encourage it? Discourage it? Outlaw it? In December 1971, the *Canadian Forum* devoted its entire issue to the Gray Report. Herbert Gray was the Minister of National Revenue in the Trudeau government and he had been delegated to write a report on foreign ownership in Canada. His report was "leaked" to the magazine, which reprinted it, and this action lead to a heated national debate about the report's proposals in regard to domestic control of our national economy.

(a) What Did the Gray Report Suggest?

The report discusses carefully three possible paths we can take to meet the challenge of foreign ownership. The first of these is for the government to say that all foreign corporations must be 51% owned in Canada. This would bring control back home, but

the report rejects this option because of the financial problems in buying back the industries, the confusion and opposition it would arouse among businessmen, and various other hazards.

We might, secondly, say that key sectors of our economy are sacred to Canada and must not be owned elsewhere. We've already done this in such areas as banking and investment, and the list could be enlarged. But the report rules this one out also as being too rigid. Canada will continue to need some foreign investment, and limiting controls to certain key sectors doesn't leave us enough room to manoeuvre.

What we should do, the report believes, is to set up some kind of screening agency which will examine foreign-owned business, past, present, and future, and decide what action, if any, is needed, in the light of what is best for Canada. The report suggests three ways to establish this screening body without strongly recommending any one of them: (a) it could be a tribunal independent of the government; (b) it might be an agency reporting to a Cabinet minister; (c) it might be a federal-provincial agency. Each of these forms has advantages and disavantages which you can discover with a little thought and which are discussed in detail in the report.

The screening agency should have the power to decide each case on its merits. In other words, while it might operate under general guidelines, it would have the great advantage of being flexible. It could scrutinize any or all of these forms of ownership: (i) takeovers; (ii) new investment; (iii) licenses and franchises; (iv) expansions of foreign-controlled firms now in Canada; (v) foreign-controlled firms in Canada that are not expanding; (vi) Canadian multi-national companies.

These should be judged by what they will do for Canada over the long term. The screening body might ask questions like this: (1) If it's a takeover, what is the object —an easy profit for the parent company or genuine development of Canadian manufacturing and employment? (By and large the report says we should have a bias against takeovers compared to building a new company from scratch.) (2) If we are hogtied for lack of a certain technology, instead of importing it and losing control, should we not try to negotiate a license for it and develop the industry at home? (3) If it's a major new foreign investment, what's it going to do for Canadians? Will it deplete our natural resources, which some think are over-developed now, without adding much to employment? (4) Or will it help our weak manufacturing sector and employ large numbers of our fast-growing labour force? (5) Should foreign-controlled firms now in Canada be left alone, or should they, over a period of time, be made to measure up to the standards set for new investment?

[Charles A. White, "What Did the Gray Report Suggest?" *Canada & the World,* January 1972]

(b) A Maritime Reaction to the Gray Report

The Maritime region of the Canadian Chamber of Commerce will issue a formal protest against any possible ban on foreign investment in the Maritimes, Joseph Zatzman, president of the Maritime chamber, said here yesterday.

"We wish to express the strong view that, due to our geographic location and our under-developed economy, we want to encourage investment capital in this area," Zatzman said.

Zatzman said that high unemployment and low productivity pointed up the need for more investment in the Maritimes.

[*Toronto Daily Star,* May 1, 1972]

(c) What Does Mexico Do?

Mexico has long had legislation providing that in most industries ownership should be at least 51 per cent Mexican.

During the last year the Mexican government has brought in several regulations to tighten its control over foreign-controlled companies. The three most important [regulations] are a measure to provide tax discrimination against foreign-controlled banks; a law on foreign technology which provides for state control of licensing agreements between Mexican and foreign firms, and provides a national technology registry to decide whether any given licensing contract is useful to the Mexican economy and whether a fair fee is being charged. The third and most important bill is designed to promote Mexican investment and regulate foreign investment. It [provides] . . . that foreigners cannot own more than 49 per cent of any industry . . . and creates a national commission to control foreign investment. In addition it prohibits any foreign participation in certain fields such as oil and petrochemicals, forestry, transportation and utilities. Most of these [sectors of the economy] are already state-owned.

One aim of the government is to separate foreign investment from technology and management. The problem—which exists on an even greater scale in Canada—is that in order to secure the added productivity made possible through advanced technology and progressive management, a country may give up control of its economy to outside forces.

Every developing country wants to step up productivity, to make use of the most advanced technology and management. But they do not want to become economic colonies of the advanced countries. Many of them have just emerged from one form of colonialism and have no desire to trade it for

Liederman — L.I. Press, N.Y. (Rothco)

ROTHCO

another—even if it comes under the name of development, or even of economic aid.

[John K. Elliott, "Curbs on U.S. Investment", *London Free Press,* March 31, 1973]

(d) A Long-Time Economic Nationalist Speaks Out

Former finance minister Walter Gordon said today that the government's policy statement on foreign ownership shows that it is "lacking in appreciation of the seriousness of the problem Canadians are faced with". . . .

Gordon said that "as a minimum" the Canadian government should have demanded that foreign-controlled companies in Canada meet the following requirements over the next five years:

—Appoint Canadians to top executive positions;

—Appoint Canadians as a majority on their boards of directors;

—Sell a majority of their shares to Canadians.

Gordon said he agreed with the Government's decision not to impose restrictions on new foreign investment in industries or developments that would produce new jobs.

"A high level of unemployment is a social disease that should not be tolerated by any government," he said.

"But if we continue to allow foreigners to exercise control, directly or indirectly, over so many of our economic institutions . . . we are asking for trouble in the future."

[*Toronto Daily Star,* May 3, 1972]

Guidelines for Inquiry

1. What proposals did the Gray Report suggest for regaining control of our domestic economy? To what extent are you in agreement with the idea of a screening agency?
2. How did the Maritime Chamber of Commerce react? Why?
3. In what ways is the Mexican economy similar to ours? Different from ours? Why did the Gray Report reject the Mexican 51 per cent regulation?
4. On the basis of further research outline the policy proposals put forward by the government in regard to Canadian control of our domestic economy. How do they compare with your original preferences?
5. How do the government's proposals compare with those of Gray? Of Gordon?

(e) What Should Be Done?

There are many policy alternatives to consider regarding foreign investment in Canada. Each of them will have important effects on our economy. For each of the statements listed below, indicate where you stand on a five-point scale between strong agreement and strong disagreement.

1. Encourage foreign investment in Canada with attractive subsidies.

Strongly Agree		No Opinion		Strongly Disagree

2. Establish a government review board to monitor and report on foreign investment in Canada.

3. Insist that chief executive positions in foreign-owned companies be occupied by Canadian citizens.

4. Insist that there be a majority of Canadian citizens on boards of directors.

5. Heavily subsidize Canadian scientific and technological research and development.

6. Prohibit foreign investment in selected sectors of the Canadian economy.

7. Outlaw the application of foreign laws to any industry operating within Canada.

8. Outlaw foreign takeovers of any existing Canadian-owned enterprises.

9. Deny foreign investors more than 49 per cent control of any industry in Canada.

10. Nationalize foreign-controlled enterprises in key sectors of the Canadian economy.

L___|___|___|___|___|___|

Part Three: One Culture?

Many Canadians feel that the greatest threat to the development of a distinctively Canadian way of life is cultural pressures from south of the border. It is difficult for Americans to understand this attitude. They have been generous in granting Canadians financial support under such programs as the Rockefeller Foundation grants, and in making it possible for Canadians to teach, study, and research in American universities, or to assimilate into their business world. But Canadians seem to respond rather ungraciously by worrying first about the "brain drain" south, and then about the "faculty flood" north.

Some Canadians feel that Canadian culture is threatened by the growing power of American marketing and mass media: American ideas and methods seem to be everywhere. Other Canadians are not so alarmed. They believe that culture cannot be artificially fostered, and maintain that people should have the opportunity to choose freely among products and programs.

Many, however, feel that there is something special and worth preserving in this land of ours, that there is indeed a real difference between Americans and Canadians. Theirs is a melting-pot society formed out of revolutionary beginnings, while ours is a mosaic of peoples nurtured by evolution. Other Canadians, though, feel that it is petty and meaningless to raise a distinctive flag and to search for a unique identity.

What will the result of present trends be? Will there eventually be only one culture north of the Rio Grande? And what is a Canadian?

A. THE ISSUES JOINED

Our popular culture might provide some evidence for answering the question: do we have a distinctive national personality? Do movies, television programs, sports events, and books provide clues as to who Canadians are? Analyse the following information and list general statements about our national personality that can be drawn from it. These statements will form the hypotheses which you can test in the later sections of this unit.

1. Saturday Night at the Movies

[Vancouver Sun, March 31, 1973]

2. Saturday Night on Television

SATURDAY

⑥ 22 Van Der Valk
Van der Valk investigates the murder of a young woman whose body is found in a canal.

⑧ ☐ Movie
★★★ *The Manchurian Candidate* (1962, drama) Frank Sinatra, Laurence Harvey.

⑨ ⑬ Movie
★★ *Limbo* (1973, drama) Kathleen Nolan, Kate Jackson. The desperate lives led by three women mirror the tragedy of thousands of American wives of prisoners-of-war or missing-in-action servicemen.

⑩ ☐ Movie
Saturday Afternoon At The Movies On Saturday Night: Elwy Yost presents the second of three programs recreating the mystique of Saturday matinees of the 1930s and 40s. The series includes comments by Don Daynard of CFRB, cinematographer Don Hutchison and Peter Harris of Star Week. Tonight, Chapters 2-8 of *The Mysterious Dr. Satan* (1940) with Eduardo Cianelli. To 11:45 p.m.

㉕ Les Grands Films
Le Rideau dechire avec Paul Newman, Julie Andrews.

㉙ ABA Basketball Playoffs
Divisional championship, teams to be announced.

8:30 ④ ⑩ Bob Newhart Show
Bob's decision to meet the rising costs of living by raising his rates sets off a revolt among members of his therapy group. (R)

⑤ ③ ⑧ ⑩ ⑫
The Whiteoaks Of Jalna
A 13-episode drama series based on the Jalna novels of Canadian author Mazo de la Roche, about the Whiteoak family on their country estate, Jalna, on the shores of Lake Ontario. Tonight's episode, *The Past:* In the carefree summer of 1914, the Whiteoaks attend a gymkhana. *The Present:* Renny attempts to rally the current generation to save the ancestral home. (R)

⑪ Lawrence Welk

㉙ Stampede Wrestling

9:00 ④ ⑩ The Carol Burnett Show
with guests Tim Conway and Steve Lawrence.

⑥ 22 Global Journal
Florida: Beavers In The Sand.

⑦ ⑬ Owen Marshall, Counsellor At Law
Owen's efforts to help an ex-convict regain custody of his son from his ruthless sister-in-law are complicated when the man abducts the boy. (R)

9:15 ⑰ Elizabeth R
Sweet England's Pride: Conclusion of a 6-part series.

9:30 ③ Movie
Partners In Crime (1973, made for TV) Lee Grant, Richard Jaeckel. A retired judge begins a private-eye business with a paroled convict as her right-hand man. To 11:00 p.m.

⑤ ⑩ ⑫ Shabby Tiger

⑥ 22 The Canadians

⑪ Wrestling

㉙ Grand Prix Wrestling

10:00 ④ ⑦ ⑩ News; Sports

⑥ 22 World Of Wicks

⑨ The Saturday Night Show With Norm Perry
with co-host Percy Saltzman. *Can People Be Brainwashed?; What To Do If You Want To Sue; How To Fight Inflation;* and *Crisis In China.*

⑬ Wrestling

---

⑬ ☐ Movie
★★ *What A Way To Go!* (1964, comedy) Shirley MacLaine, Paul Newman.

㉙ The 700 Club

10:30 ② ⑧ News; Sports

④ Movie
★★★ *La Dolce Vita* (1961, drama) Marcello Mastroianni, Anita Ekberg. A gossip columnist sees his life in shallow Rome society as worthless but can't change.

⑤ ⑩ ⑫
Singalong Jubilee
with guest Floyd King from Amherst, N.S.

⑥ 22 ☐ Movie
Red (1970, drama) Daniel Pilon. Genevieve Deloir.

⑦ Movie
★★½ *Kisses For My President* (1964, comedy) Fred MacMurray, Polly Bergen. The story of the first woman president of the United States and the problems her husband faces.

⑧ To Rome With Love

⑩ Movie
★½ *The Snow Creature* (1954, science fiction) Paul Langton, Leslie Denison.

⑪ Movie
★★½ *Murphy's War* (1971, drama) Peter O'Toole, Sian Phillips. The lone survivor of a German submarine attack sets out to get revenge with a battle-weary plane. To 12:40 a.m.

㉕ Telejournal

㉙ Point After
Sports Hot Seat with host Ron Hewat:

10:45 ㉕ Nouvelles Du Sport

11:00 ② Movie
★★ *Masque Of The Red Death* (1964, horror) Vincent Price, Hazel Court. A tyrannical prince of the 12th century takes a young girl to his castle to be taught the ways of the court.

⑤ ③ ⑧ ⑩ ⑪ ⑫
CBC National News

⑧ Rock Concert

⑨ ⑬ CTV National News

㉕ Cinema
Rien n'est trop ·beau avec Hope Lange, Joan Crawford.

㉙ Point After

11:15 ⑤ ③ ⑧ ⑩ ⑫
Provincial Affairs
A representative of the NDP Party.

11:20 ③ ⑧ ⑩ ⑫ ⑬
News; Sports

⑤ Toronto Tonight
A late night wrap-up of news, weather and sports with Jan Tennant.

⑨ Night Beat News

11:43 ⑤ Rock Concert
with guests Todd Rundgren, Graham Central Station, and Wishbone Ash.

11:45 ⑧ Movie
★★ *The Savage Innocents* (1959, drama) Anthony Quinn, Peter O'Toole.

⑩ Heritage Highways

11:50 ⑩ Movie
★½ *A Talent For Loving* (1968, drama) Richard Widmark, Caesar Romero.

⑫ Movie
★★½ *The Heroes Of Telemark* (1965, war drama) Kirk Douglas, Richard Harris. Resistance fighters attempt to destroy a heavy water plant which could lead to the manufacture of a Nazi atom bomb.

12:00 ③ Movie
★★★ *Becket* (1964, spectacle) Richard Burton, Peter O'Toole. Based on Jean Anouilh's story of the friendship between Becket and the king of England and Becket's subsequent appointment as Archbishop of Canterbury.

⑨ Movies
★★ *Counterpoint* (1968, drama) Charlton Heston, Maximilian Schell. While on a tour during World War II, an American symphony conductor and his orchestra are taken prisoners by the Germans. Also, ★★★ *Everybody Does It* (1949, b&w) Paul Douglas, Linda Darnell. A wife thinks she can sing so her long-suffering husband decides to try opera.

⑬ Movie
★★ *The Movie Maker* (1967, drama) Rod Steiger, Robert Culp. An aging movie producer, the last of the really big film moguls, wages an unsuccessful battle to maintain control of a film company.

12:40 ⑪ Movie
The Connection (1973, made for TV) Charles Durning, Ronnie Cox. A tough ex-newspaper reporter becomes the · go-between for jewel thieves and insurance companies. To 2:10 a.m.

1:00 ② The Story

1:03 ⑤ ☐ Movie
★★ *None But The Brave* (1965, drama) Frank Sinatra, Clint Walker.

2:55 ③ Movie
★★ *The Bandit Of Zhobe* (1959, adventure) Victor Mature, Anne Aubrey.

4:30 ③ ☐ Movie
★★ *The Legend Of Tom Dooley* (1959, adventure) Michael Landon, Jo Morrow.

3. The Sports Scoreboard

(a) The National Hockey League

STANDINGS

East Division	W	L	T	F	A	P	West Division						
Montreal	50	10	16	319	180	116	Chicago	42	26	8	278	217	92
Boston	51	20	5	322	223	107	Minn.	37	30	11	254	230	85
Rangers	47	22	7	293	198	101	Phila.	36	29	11	282	249	83
Buffalo	36	27	14	254	218	86	St. Louis	31	33	12	225	246	74
Detroit	36	29	11	258	238	83	Pittsburgh	31	36	9	250	254	71
Toronto	26	41	9	236	272	61	Los Ang.	30	36	11	226	242	71
Vancouver	22	46	9	230	333	53	Atlanta	25	38	14	187	235	64
Islanders	12	59	5	164	333	29	Calif.	16	46	16	213	323	48

(b) Coming Sports Events

TONIGHT
HOCKEY
National League
Vancouver at Los Angeles
NY Rangers at Montreal
5:00—Boston at Toronto, chs. 2, 6
NY Islanders at Philadelphia
Chicago at Detroit
Pittsburgh at St. Louis
B.C. Junior B
9:00—Kitimat vs. Norwes. North
Van Rec. Centre (Second game
best-of-three, semi-final).
TENNIS
1:00—Rothmans International, semi-
finals, PNE Agrodome
BOXING
8:00—12 bout amateur card. Queens
Park Arenex.

SUNDAY
HOCKEY
Montreal at Boston
Toronto at Chicago
Detroit at NY Rangers
NY Islanders at Atalnta
St. Louis at Buffalo
Philadelphia at Pittsburgh
Western Canada
7:00—New Westminster vs Edmonton,
fourth game, b e s t-o-f-s e v e n
quarter-finals, Q u e e n s Park
Arena
TENNIS
1:00—Rothmans International, finals,
PNE Agrodome
SOCCER
Pacific Coast League
1:00—SFU vs. Vancouver Sporting
Club, Empire Stadium.
3:00—Inter-Italia vs UBC, Empire
Stadium
Seggie Cup
10:30—Wesburn vs S. Burnaby, Wes-
burn
Provincial Cup
(First Round)
East Van. vs Club India (11:00),
Norquay Park; Hungarians vs
Safeway, Clinton Park; Fort
Langley vs NW Blues, Fort Lan-
gley; Richmond Labs vs Kolp-
ing, RC Palmer Park; Avalons
vs Norburn, Boulevard Park;
Firefighters vs Olympics, Nor-
quay Park; St. Alice vs NW
Luckies, Mahon Park; Greek
Olympic vs Villa Esso, W. Me-
morial Park.
(All Games at 2 p.m.)
FRASER VALLEY LEAGUE
PACKENHAM CUP
Second Round
Bradner Reds vs Sasquatch,

Bradner; Chehalis vs Langley
Borsato, Harrison; Surrey Cards
vs Aldergrove, Newton Park.
LEAGUE GAMES
Second Division
K i l g a r d vs Mission, Yale
School; Surrey United vs Port
Coquitlam, Holly Park; Pen-
guins vs Bradner Royals, B.C.
Pen (1:30); Silverdale vs Chilli-
wack Royals, Silverdale.
Exhibition Game
White Rock Labs vs Juggern-
auts, Crescent Park.
(all games start at 2 p.m.)

(c) Golf

GREENSBORO OPEN

Billy Casper,	67-64—131
Lou Graham,	68-64—132
Sam Snead,	66-67—133
Doug Sanders,	65-68—133
George Knudson,	68-66—134
Rod Funseth,	65-69—134
Ken Still,	66-68—134
Chi Chi Rodriguez,	68-66—134
Buddy Allin,	68-67—135
Butch Baird,	66-69—135
Bob Dickson,	68-68—136
Mike Hill,	68-68—136
Gay Brewer,	68-68—136
John Lister,	66-70—136
Martin Bohen,	69-67—136
Lee Elder,	64-72—136
Hubert Green,	67-69—136
Leonard Thompson,	68-69—137
Bert Yancey,	66-71—137
Arnold Palmer,	69-68—137
Lee Trevino,	71-66—137
Mac McLendon,	68-69—137
Jim Jamieson,	67-70—137
Bobby Nichols,	66-71—137
Jerry McGee,	69-68—137
Don Bies,	70-67—137
Mason Rudolph,	65-73—138
Ed Sneed,	66-72—138
Charles Coody,	69-69—138
Jim Wiechcr,	71-67—138
Johnny Miller	67-71—138
Art Wall,	67-71—138
Andy North,	68-71—139
Tom Jenkins	72-67—139
Labron Harris,	68-71—139

Tom Kite,	71-68—139
Paul Purtzer,	68-71—139
Bob Goalby,	69-70—139
Rick Rhoads,	68-71—139
Orville Moody,	69-70—139
Tom Weiskopf,	68-72—140
Mike Wynn,	73-67—140
Pat Fitzsimons,	69-71—140
Ron Cerrudo,	69-71—140
Phil Rodgers,	68-72—140
Rocky Thompson,	72-68—140
Jim Ferriell,	69-71—140
Larry Wood,	70-70—140
Jim Simons,	69-71—140
Mike Kallam,	74-66—140
Rod Curl,	72-68—140

ALAMO OPEN

Betsy Cullen,	34-35—69
Betty Burfeindt,	34-38—72
Joyce Kazmierski,	38-35—73
Sandra Palmer,	34-40—74
Sandra Post,	36-38—74
Noni Schneider,	36-38—74
Gerda Boykin,	37-37—74
Karolyn Kertzman,	40-34—74
Mickey Wright,	37-37—74
Susie McAllister,	36-38—74
Kathy Ahern,	38-37—75
Rene Powell,	38-37—75
Betsy Rawls,	38-37—75
Jayne Huntsberger,	38-37—75
Sue Roberts,	38-37—75
Shelley Hamlin,	36-39—75
Marie Astrolges,	37-38—75
Mardell Wilkins,	37-39—76
Mary Lou Crocker,	40-36—76
Kathy Martin,	38-38—76
Marlene Hagge,	40-36—76
Beth Stone,	39-37—76
Mary Bryan,	39-37—76
Sandra Haynie,	39-37—76

(d) Baseball

American League

New York	17	6	.739
Cleveland	14	7	.667
Oakland	12	8	.600
Detroit	12	11	.522
Boston	12	11	.522
Chicago	11	10	.514
Kansas City	11	11	.500
Baltimore	11	11	.500
Minnesota	10	13	.435
Milwaukee	7	10	.412
Texas	7	10	.412
California	6	11	.316

National League

Cincinnati	14	7	.667
Montreal	12	7	.632
San Francisco	11	6	.625
Los Angeles	12	10	.545
Chicago	10	9	.526
St. Louis	11	10	.514
Houston	10	10	.500
Philadelphia	9	10	.474
Pittsburgh	9	14	.391
New York	7	11	.389
San Diego	5	13	.278
Atlanta	4	15	.211

New York (A) 4, Texas 1
Baltimore 8, Kansas City 4
Minnesota 1, Houston 0
Cincinnati 3, Atlanta 1
Pittsburgh 11, Louis 1
Detroit 9, Philadelphia 5
San Diego 2, Cleveland 0
San Francisco 6, Milwaukee 0
Oakland 4, Chicago (N) 3
Boston 4, Chicago (A) 2
California 5, Los Angeles 4

[*Vancouver Sun*, March 31, 1973]

B. DATA AND DEBATE

1. The Media: About Magazines, T.V., and Textbooks

(a) A Case Study

A prime example of the lengths to which the American government was willing to go in protecting United States investment against Canadian laws involved the successful intervention by both the White House and the State Department to win an exemption for *Time* and *Reader's Digest* from the measure in Walter Gordon's 1965 budget that disallowed advertising in foreign-owned newspapers and periodicals as a tax deduction.

The vehemence with which the American State Department expressed its opposition was a shock to Ottawa officials, used to the give and take of most United States policies. One senior Canadian civil servant reported privately to the Prime Minister that he had never seen the State Department so unyielding. "There seems nothing, but nothing, that we could do which would upset Washington more," he wrote. "I have the impression that if we dared touch the Canadian operations of *Time* and *Digest,* the State Department would view it as far more serious than if, for instance, we sold tanks to Fidel Castro." . . .

The American pressure proved so great that the Pearson Government capitulated and Walter Gordon brought in a law that exempted the only two publishing operations it might have affected. It was Grattan O'Leary, speaking in the Senate on June 28, 1965, who had the final word. "If this House votes for this legislation," he told his fellow senators, "it will be voting for the proposition that Washington has a right to interfere in a matter of purely Canadian concern, and voting a probable death sentence on Canada's periodical press, with all that this can

entail for our future voyage through history."

[Peter Newman, *The Distemper of Our Times,* McClelland and Stewart Limited, 1968]

(b) The Teenage Perspective

A decade ago, the book that most often protruded from the hip pockets of Canadian teenagers' blue jeans was *The Catcher in the Rye,* J. D. Salinger's tale of a pre-hippie dropout in New York. Today's book-to-be-seen-with is *Soul on Ice,* in which Eldridge Cleaver expresses his black rage at honky injustice. Salinger's Holden Caulfield could conceivably have been a Canadian private-school boy—Cleaver is thoroughly American.

The top sellers in the Canadian teen-magazine market are, in order: *Miss Chatelaine* (Canadian), *Seventeen* (U.S.), *Mademoiselle* (U.S.) and, in tied position, *Ingenue* and *Teen* (both U.S.). *Miss Chatelaine*'s circulation is 130,000; combined circulation of the American top four, 154,000.

Close behind the teen periodicals are the movie-fan magazines that chart a kind of emotional electrocardiogram of Liz, Debbie, Mia, Jackie and, recently, the Teddy Kennedys.

All of which is by way of demonstration that the various print media read by young Canadians are predominantly—perhaps increasingly—American. The book breakdown is, however, debatable. Mel Hurtig, an Edmonton publisher and owner of western Canada's biggest book store, argues that teenagers are turning increasingly to Canadian authors as a result of new-found national pride, and better books. One in four books Hurtig sells is Canadian—hardly reason to wave the flag, but in 1956 the ratio was one in 10.

"Canadian books will never be dominant," Hurtig admits. "We buy as many from the U.S. each year as it exports to all other countries combined."

School officials report that almost all history texts are now written for and by Canadians. On the other hand, a trend to teachers individually selecting texts has fragmented the market, thus discouraging Canadian publishers who rely on bulk sales.

Except for the very young, whose parents seem to favour English fantasy (C. S. Lewis, A. A. Milne, Kenneth Grahame), Canadian youngsters look to the U.S. for most of their light reading, from westerns and science fiction to the sort of skin magazines that mothers find under boys' beds. But the biggest-selling U.S. periodicals (*Mad* magazine excepted) are aimed at the 18-year-old female mind—that is, at 15-year-old girls. They buy them for fashion news, dating etiquette, romantic fiction and the latest on their heroines and heartthrobs: Americans all.

[*Maclean's,* November 1969]

Guidelines for Inquiry

1. How do your preferences compare with those indicated in "The Teenage Perspective"?
2. Desmond Pacey has argued that "we are half-hearted in our support of Canadian magazines, films, painting, music, and literature, and then have the nerve to complain that we are swamped by American products." Why do you agree or disagree with this statement?

(c) The Massey Commission (1951)

It may be added that we should also have been forced to produce our own educational materials—books, maps, pictures and so forth. As it is, the dependence of English-

speaking Canada on the United States for these publications is excessive. In the elementary schools and high schools the actual texts may be produced in Canada, but teachers complain that far too much of the supplementary material is American with an emphasis and direction appropriate for American children but unsuitable for Canadian. As an illustration of the unsuitability of even the best American material, the statement was made in one of our briefs that out of thirty-four children in a Grade VIII class in a Canadian school, nineteen knew all about the significance of July 4 and only seven could explain that of July 1.

In our universities the situation is very much more serious. The comparative smallness of the Canadian university population, and the accessibility of American publishing houses with their huge markets has resulted in an almost universal dependence on the American product.

[*Report of the Royal Commission on National Development in the Arts, Letters and Sciences,* Queen's Printer, 1951]

(d) Textbooks in 1970

Just how bad is U.S. domination of the Canadian textbook industry? According to Tim Reid, Liberal education critic in the Ontario legislature, of new textbooks authorized in Canada, the percentage of wholly Canadian ones has dropped from 77 per cent in 1965 to 59 per cent in 1967 and is still dropping.

[Margaret Daly, "How the Textbook Sellout Threatens Our Schools", *Toronto Daily Star*, November 14, 1970]

Guidelines for Inquiry

1. Look carefully at each textbook that you are using this year, and determine

if it has been written and published in Canada. Compare your findings with those of Tim Reid.

2. To what extent do you believe your textbooks should be written and published by Canadians? Why?

3. Debate the following statement: "Knowledge, especially in the sciences, is universal, and we owe it to our students to provide them with the best available anywhere, even if it is written, printed, and sold in the United States of America. Americans don't know everything, but then neither do Canadians. If we let it, our distinctively Canadian brand of anti-Americanism will lead us down the garden path to ignorance. I don't see that I have to be stupid in order to be a Canadian."

(e) An Identity Crisis in Social Studies Class

". . . it's a painting he's done of Washington crossing the St. Lawrence . . . they're talking about it in school now . . ."

[*Toronto Daily Star*, April 26, 1971]

(f) Writers Do Not Need a Nationalist's Dog Licence

In 1972, the Canadian government announced a policy of subsidizing Canadian publishers and authors. This is an excerpt from an American news report about reaction in some parts of the literary community.

The surging Canadian nationalism that today affects so much intellectual activity in this country has inevitably drawn Canadian literature into the vortex of nationalist controversy.

To satisfy the nationalists' demand for "more Canadian content" in books and magazines, the government is offering subsidies to publishers and grants to authors. But not all publishers and very few authors are happy. Mordecai Richler, to name one of the more prominent Canadian writers, is incensed.

"Good Canadian writers stand in no need of a nationalist's dog licence," said the author of *St. Urbain's Horseman*, "and the rest are simply not worth sheltering."

On the nationalist side, the issue is one of surviving the onslaught of Yankee, and of earlier British, culture. Survival, says Margaret Atwood, critic, poet and rising young novelist, has preoccupied all Canadians for 400 years.

[For those who are not extreme nationalists], the crucial literary aim is not just to beat off the Americans, but rather to break out of the bleak, suffocating bounds of tradition and into the fresh air of international literary exchange, no matter how rough-and-tumble the going may be.

A new school of writers warns that if the nationalists have their way, Canadian literature may revert to the popular regionalism of the past: to Ernest Thompson Seton, who portrayed the Canadian West chiefly as the habitat of wild beasts; to Mazo de la Roche, who in her Jalna books made an Ontario country family more British than the British; and to that regional darling, *Anne of Green Gables,* the imaginary Prince Edward Island girl created by Lucy Maud Montgomery.

But what the Canada of today needs, say the newer writers, are not preservers, but innovators—a Faulkner, a Hemingway, a Fitzgerald.

[*London Free Press,* May 9, 1973]

Guideline for Inquiry

Mordecai Richler has often contended that "culture cannot be legislated or budgeted or protected with tariffs." To what extent do you agree with him?

(g) An Image of Ourselves on the Movie Screen?

Last year, of 548 films submitted to the Ontario Film Censorship Board, 166 were listed as American features—but many of the remainder were also American, made abroad. Canadian feature films among the 548 totalled six.

The ratio stands up anywhere you look in Canada. At random, consider the films playing on a recent Saturday in Victoria: *West Side Story* (U.S.), *African Safari* (U.S.), *The Gay Deceivers* (U.S.), *Oliver!* (British), *The Love Bug* (U.S.), *Goodbye, Columbus* (U.S.), *If* (British), *The Chairman* (U.S.). One theatre was screening an 18-minute Canadian short, *A Dime's Worth,* made in Toronto. (A film buff who saw this effort suggested that it should have been titled *A Plugged Nickel's Worth.*)

Youths under 21 now comprise 50 percent of the Canadian movie audience. Something of the effect on them of the U.S. film barrage is suggested by the Victoria lineup. With the exception of *African Safari,* an imaginatively-filmed travelogue marred by trite narration, and, possibly, the star-crossed lovers of *West Side Story,* the U.S.-produced films are subjective self-appraisals, insular comments on a uniquely American society. Propaganda-adventure (*The Chairman*), beat-the-draft comedy (*The Gay Deceivers*), ethnic drama (*Goodbye, Columbus*), car-culture fantasy (*The Love Bug*)—here is America talking to and of itself, absorbedly. Canadian young people strain their ears to listen.

Question: Why do we watch so many U.S. movies? Answers: "What else is there?" "They're just movies, that's all." "Steve McQueen is cute—who have we got?" "European movies are too arty." "Why not? They're better than U.S. TV shows." "You saw *Isobel* and you have to ask?" "They're slick, you know." "I don't watch them. I just like to go to the drive-in." "Because they're the best." "To kill time." "I like them." "They're where it's at." "Their actors are the best." "I don't know."

[*Maclean's*, 1969]

(h) An Image of Ourselves on the Television Screen?

The Canadian Radio and Television Commission ruled in 1970 that 60 per cent of programming by Canadian broadcasting stations should be distinctively Canadian. The cartoonist Ting comments on that regulation.

M. R. Tingley, courtesy of *London Free Press*

"PSST! YANKEE PITCHURES?"

"STAY WITH THE **LEAFS**, WE GOTTA GET OUR 60% CANADIAN"

M. R. Tingley, courtesy of London Free Press

[*Ting Cartoons*, London Free Press, 1970]

(i) What Price Nationalism?

After four years of agonizing over how to go about it, the Canadian Radio-Television Commission (CRTC) has launched its long expected holy war to rescue this country's television from the staggering competition of U.S. border stations.

The average Canadian viewer is both the prize and a pawn in the battle. If he'd just spend more of his time watching Canadian channels and less with the Americans, the problem wouldn't exist. But he doesn't. So it does.

Federal law says TV is here to help carry Canadian thinking across the country—to help us understand each other and feel more like a nation. But that doesn't work if the people are watching U.S. stations and absorbing their thinking instead.

So, since the average viewer has taken naturally to watching U.S. stations, he's now to be enticed into watching more Canadian stations. Or you might say goaded. Or you might say manipulated.

A lot of people are saying manipulated.

The tactics put a spotlight again on Pierre Juneau, the CRTC chairman, who is being hailed by some as a crusader for the Canadian dream and damned by others as a federal censor trying to jam Canadian culture down the viewer's throat.

Juneau explodes when he's accused of censoring the American flow. "That's sick!" he charges. "Anyone who would say that must be obsessed. We're just getting a whisper of our own material into the picture. We're just trying to breathe, for God's sake, in an atmosphere completely dominated by U.S. material."

The CRTC has a two-pronged attack started to help break the U.S. medium's grip. One attack is to stuff more Canadian stations on the dial to outnumber the American choices. The other is to discourage foreign viewing by making their stations harder to find or fuzzier to watch. They say this is coincidental.

Already three extra outlets have been licensed for Toronto, with CITY-TV (Channel 79) due on the air this month, and the CBC's French Channel 25 due next April, and the new Global Communications to reach Toronto with two transmitters in early 1974.

But as the Canadian competition is building up, the U.S. competition (which is the problem, after all) is supposed to be breaking down, if the theory works.

Buffalo's Channel 4 expects reception trouble in mid-town Toronto in nine days when CBLT, the CBC's flagship station, moves its booming signal from Channel 6 right beside it to Channel 5. For a lot of people, it will be "scratch Channel 4" as a major threat to Canadian stations.

Then Sept. 28, when CITY starts on Channel 79, local cable systems have been ordered to carry it on Channel 7. This will mean bumping WKBW-TV, Buffalo's most popular station, off its own Channel 7, to be relocated on Channel 12. Viewers searching for it should be confused enough to cost it at least some of its big Toronto following. Scratch a little of the Channel 7 problem.

Local cable companies have been showing WNED, Buffalo's brilliant non-commercial . . . station on Channel 12. . . . But when they move WKBW to 12, WNED has a problem. No space. Some cable firms will move it to Channel 3. At least one—the 58,000-home Metro system—will drop it.

Meanwhile WUTV, Buffalo's upstart UHF (ultra high frequency) Channel 29 outlet, remains banned from cable here. With four of Buffalo's five outlets due for some measure of grief (only Channel 2 escapes for now), Toronto ratings for them could be knocked down substantially, especially with new Canadian stations on the horizon to fill any gaps.

Obviously, cable TV is a key in the CRTC plan. But it hasn't been an obedient key all the way.

The commission favoured . . . cutting commercials out of the signals of U.S. stations that . . . would [be picked] up, then letting local Canadian stations sell ads to run in their place. The idea has been called outright piracy even by some CRTC staff members, but the commission saw this as a great money-maker for Canadian TV—one that would make the stations here so wealthy that they could afford lots of extra Canadian programming.

This dream has stopped dead after Vancouver's big Premier Cablevision system [had already] spent $50,000 for special equipment to do the job of [cutting commercials. But] . . . Premier became afraid U.S. stations would sue if [it] started selling their programs to sponsors. And Premier couldn't be sure it would win.

Last year Buffalo stations split $21,-365,000, but about $5,000,000 of that came from Canada. Meanwhile, Toronto advertisers spent about $31,000,000 on TV. But with $5,000,000 of that going to Buffalo, there was about $26,000,000 left to finance the industry here. If all the money on both sides had stayed in its own country, TV in the Toronto area would have been about twice as wealthy as Buffalo's—able to afford more stations and stronger competition.

At least, the Buffalo stations are legitimate in that they serve a city of their own that's big enough to support them. They could lose the entire Toronto bundle and still show a profit of up to 20% of their gross revenue (as it is, they pocket 40-45%).

But the CRTC grits its teeth at the example of KVOS-TV in Bellingham, Washington, and KCND in Pembina, North Dakota. Both are licensed for U.S. hamlets but both are wealthy on Canadian money. KVOS takes an estimated $4,000,000 a year out of Vancouver—roughly 1/3 of all the TV money available there. And KCND lives off Winnipeg, drawing about $780,000 of its $950,000 annual revenue from the Canadian city.

There's the angle, too, that Canadian stations have to produce far more of their own programs than the U.S. outlets, most of which can plug into a New York network line and relax all day—so the Canadians need more money.

And Canadian stations carry almost half U.S. programs in the evening, and U.S. stations carry all U.S. programs. So if viewing is evenly divided between the two, the audience here will see Canadian material only one-quarter of the time.

[Jack Miller, "TV Viewer's Just a Pawn in the Nationalism Battle", *Toronto Daily Star,* 1972]

Guidelines for Inquiry

1. Are you in agreement that radio and T.V. programming in this country should have 60 per cent Canadian content? Why?
2. Do the CRTC strategies mentioned by Miller amount to censorship? Why? How far are you willing to see the government go in providing distinctive Canadian television programming?

2. Good Sportsmanship: Canadian-American Style

(a) The Home Team Appears To Have Lost

Virtually every aspect of Canadian sport has been conditioned by American influences. Our sports heroes, with the exception of our hockey favourites, are mostly Americans— not surprisingly when our media constantly bombard us with as much American sporting news as Canadian, and when our sports commentators consider "American" to be the standard of excellence. Our best professional athletes seek their fortunes in the United States and our best amateurs seek

the semi-professional status and the specialized coaching and facilities that are available through U.S. athletic scholarships. Canadian sport impresarios—from track and field to tennis and golf—depend upon the "drawing power" of U.S. athletes to attract spectators to their events. Canadian physical educators rely upon their American counterparts to prepare their teaching manuals, conduct their coaching clinics, and so on. Even our fitness fads are imported. Lloyd Percival has preached the benefits of jogging for more than twenty years, but it was an American Air Force major, Dr. Kenneth Cooper, who fathered the present jogging boom. Canadians in search of a distinctive national culture get no help from sports.

To be sure, not every Canadian sport has been Americanized. . . . In track and field and swimming, for example, the lack of adequate year-round facilities and the scarcity of good coaching has forced many Canadian athletes to go south: as a result, half the members of our 1968 Olympic team in these sports attended university in the United States. In football, on the other hand, opportunities for professional employment in the Canadian Football League have encouraged many American athletes to come north.

[Bruce Kidd, "Canada's 'National' Sport", in *Close the 49th Parallel,* ed. Ian Lumsden, University of Toronto Press, 1970]

(b) The Winner and Still Champion—Big Money?

Jack Batten discusses the expansion and Americanization of the National Hockey League.

A few Canadians got rich . . . when they took the final step of many Canadian businessmen: sell out to the Americans. It's an old story. It's what we're all protesting. It's too familiar. But what makes the sell-out achingly painful in this case is that hockey —The Game—is a peculiarly Canadian product. When Canadian businessmen who used to make cars right here in Canadian factories sold out to the Americans, it was, you could rationalize, really giving back to them something that was theirs. But hockey is ours, and giving it away seemed a special crime.

The expansion of the NHL into seven U.S. cities . . . followed normal business practices. "To stay in business," Clarence Campbell said in 1969, "you place your operations in places that will keep you in business. The difficulty is that in Canada there are no places outside Toronto and Montreal that have the consumer spending to support an NHL organization." All of which, for Canadians who cared about hockey, was deplorable and ugly. But the worst was still to come. When the NHL decided [in 1970] to allow in another Canadian city, Vancouver, no businessmen came forward in our country to ante up the National League's admission fee of six million dollars. And the Vancouver Canucks are therefore owned by the Medical Investment Corporation of Minneapolis, a company originally set up as a tax shelter for five Minnesota doctors. Their team plays in a brand new arena built with money put up by the Canadian federal, B.C. provincial and Vancouver Municipal governments.

[Jack Batten, "Who Killed Hockey? Greedy Businessmen, That's Who", *Saturday Night*, January 1971]

Guidelines for Inquiry

1. Batten argues that "hockey is ours, and giving it away seemed a special crime." Explain why you agree or disagree with this statement.
2. "Hockey is no longer ours, just as baseball is no longer America's. Sport is international. In fact, we ought to be proud of Canada's contribution: imitation is the sincerest form of flattery." Debate this view.

Part Four:
One Diplomacy?

Can Canada function usefully as an independent state in the American orbit? Does our reliance on American arms for the defence of Canada reduce us to a satellite status? What are the implications for Canada's foreign policy of defence-production agreements with the United States? How should we exert influence in Washington?

The origins and history of the NORAD agreement will be used in this section as a case study, in order to analyse problems such as those mentioned above. The fundamental issue is, however: to what extent is Canada a rubber-stamp state?

A. THE ISSUES JOINED

1. Tell 'Em To Go Jump in the Ocean

A two-day visit to Canada made me realize that United States–Canadian relations are at low ebb. Everywhere I went, Canadians complained to me that the United States had been ignoring Canada and, although the country is now in the midst of a hot election campaign, no one south of the border really cared.

"We care about your elections," a friend said. "Why don't you care about ours? It seems nothing we do up here makes any impact on the United States."

I had to agree, but I told my friends it was their own fault.

"You haven't given us any trouble in a long while," I reminded them. "The difficulty is that relations between the two countries are so good they're starting to deteriorate. In order for us to pay any attention to

anybody, the United States must be provoked."

"How can we provoke you?"

"It isn't easy," I admitted. "It would help if you had a serious Communist problem. We're always ready to step in and help a country being threatened by Communists. If you had a real Red threat coming up in the elections, you would not only get our attention but military and economic aid as well."

"But we don't have a Communist threat," the friend protested.

"Then why don't you pull a de Gaulle on us?"

"How's that?"

"Why don't you threaten to pull out of the Western Hemisphere defense alliance? Tell the United States you want to set up your own DEW line and start working on your own atomic bomb."

"That would be expensive." . . .

"It's obvious that what Canada needs is a Nasser, a Sukarno, or a Chou En-lai—someone to tell us to go jump in the ocean."

"Diefenbaker has been hinting at it, but nobody seems to be paying any attention."

"Well, I can't help you then. We're willing to help you in any way we can, but only if you're willing to make life difficult for us. We have too many enemies we're trying to win over to spend much time on wooing our friends."

[Art Buchwald, "Phooey on Friends", *Washington Post,* October 24, 1965]

2. We Are Good Friends

This is an excerpt from an address given by Mitchell Sharp, then the Canadian Minister of External Affairs, to the Council on Foreign Affairs in New York in 1969.

Nothing is in itself more important to Canada than our relationship with the United States. It is probably the closest and most complex relationship existing between any two nations. It covers the whole spectrum of affairs from the maintenance of jointly-owned border monuments to the orderly development and effective defence of the North American continent. As Canada's foreign minister, I am also aware of your country's position as leader of the Western nations and as a [major] influence in the world as a whole. Canada is a sovereign nation and acts as such. It is also, we like to think, a . . . realistic nation. We pursue a foreign policy designed to promote our own national interest, but we know that in the development of every aspect of our foreign policy the foreign policy, objectives, initiatives and activities of the United States must be taken into account. . . .

The Communist world, and indeed other countries that [should] know better, like to refer to Canada as a satellite of the United States. This suits their purpose. When Prague dared to differ ideologically with Moscow, it encountered the mailed fist of Soviet armed might and Czechoslovakia's satellite status was affirmed before the whole world. When Ottawa and Washington differ, there is straight talk—and so there should be—but the principle of sovereignty is honored in the spirit as well as the letter of the law.

Canada's right to differ from the United States is important, perhaps more to us than to you. But I don't want to dwell on it any further. More important is that Canada and the United States share the same great national objectives and the same hopes for mankind. Where we will often differ is in the means by which each of our countries works toward the fulfilment of these objectives and these hopes.

[Mitchell Sharp, "Canada, a Middle Power in a Changing World", *External Affairs,* December 1969]

3. Anti-Americanism Causes Blindness

John Holmes is the Research Director of the Canadian Institute for International Affairs.

I reject the view that the United States is [an evil] force, an attitude found not only in Canada but in the rest of the world and in the United States itself. It seems to me as intellectually wrong-headed as McCarthyism, which [blamed] all the evils of the world [on] the conspiracies of Moscow. Belief that the United States is wrong in some or many of its policies . . . is different, of course, from the fixed attitude that United States policies and American influence should be opposed and rejected on principle. If one holds the view that the United States must be purged of its sins, then certain conclusions on policy follow which have their own logic. It is not a view held by many Canadians, although a somewhat larger number, with less logic, borrow arguments from those who do. . . . I don't believe it is likely to be a dominant opinion in Canada and . . . I cannot see any practical line of policy we could follow from this conviction. Ours is a long border on which to erect a Berlin Wall.

[John Holmes, "Canada and the United States: Political and Security Issues", *Behind the Headlines,* March 1970]

Guidelines for Inquiry

1. Compare the views of Buchwald, Sharp, and Holmes.
2. Develop your own statement of the role Canada should play in the world. State how Canada can achieve such a role while, at the same time, maintaining a firm and practical defence against potential aggressors.

B. DATA AND DEBATE: A CASE STUDY

1. The Origins of Continental Defence

(a) Roosevelt (1938)

The Dominion of Canada is part of the sisterhood of the British Empire. I give to you assurance that the people of the United States will not stand idly by if domination of Canadian soil is threatened by any other empire.

[Franklin Roosevelt, Address at Kingston on August 18, 1938]

(b) King (1938)

We, too, have our obligations as a good friendly neighbour, and one of them is to see that . . . our country is made as immune from attack or possible invasion as we can reasonably be expected to make it, and that, should the occasion ever arise, enemy forces should not be able to pursue their way, either by land, sea or air to the United States, across Canadian territory.

[Mackenzie King, Reply of August 21, 1938, to President Roosevelt's Remarks, 1938]

(c) *Ottawa Journal* (1940)

The Prime Minister and the President have discussed the mutual problems of defence in relation to the safety of Canada and the United States.

It has been agreed that a permanent joint board on defence shall be set up at once by the two countries.

This permanent joint board on defence shall commence immediate studies relating to sea, land and air problems including personnel and material.

It will consider in the broad sense the defence of the north half of the western hemisphere.

[Announcement of the Ogdensburg Agreement, 1940]

Guidelines for Inquiry

1. What special conditions in the late 1930s and early 1940s demanded increased Canadian-American defence co-operation?
2. How was such co-operation established?

2. NORAD: The American First Line of Defence

With their reluctance to tie themselves so closely to the United States matched only by their wisdom in accepting the necessary, the Canadians in the 1950s entered upon an extraordinary adventure in enlightened generosity. They allowed their country to become another's first line of defense through a network of radar, ballistic-missile early-warning systems, and a variety of air-surveillance plans. A nuclear-age trip-wire was strung across Canada from Alaska to Greenland. In 1957, this effort [resulted in] . . . the North American Air Defence Command—NORAD—at once the symbol of devastating destruction for any enemy, and the object of Canadian anti-U.S. sentiment. It is typical of U.S.–Canadian relations to realize that while NORAD to most Canadians is the most blatant example of the interdependence they cannot avoid, it is almost totally unknown in the United States. In a poll of 1000 high-school seniors in the American states bordering on Canada, only 70, or 7 per cent, could identify NORAD.

NORAD consists of 170,000 personnel in 400 bases. Ninety-four per cent of these men are Americans. Canada contributes ap-

This is the entrance to the Combat Operations Centre, Colorado Springs, Colorado, while it was still under construction. The Centre is three storeys deep, under 520 m of granite. It is said to be strong enough to withstand a direct hit by an H-Bomb. From here, all NORAD air forces would be controlled if a world war broke out.

proximately $115 million to its budget—and the United States $2 billion, or seventeen times as much.

Many Americans may ask the question: "Why do the Canadians complain about NORAD? We are supplying most of the money. We are supplying most of the men." It is important to understand that $115 million is 8 per cent of the total Canadian defense budget, while $2 billion is barely 4 per cent of the total U.S. defense budget. But it is even more important to understand that in a very real sense the Canadian contribution cannot be measured in money or in men, for the Canadian contribution is their future as a nation.

Through NORAD, Canada sacrifices the capacity to pursue a fully independent course. Through NORAD, Canada sacrifices the ability to influence . . . other nations by [presenting itself as independent] from the United States. Through NORAD, Canada commits itself as the one sure battleground in a nuclear-age exchange between the powers that face each other across her land. To Canadians it is of small consolation that geography and technology give them no alternative. . . .

. . . Canada has no more choice than the United States, for with or without BMEWS [Ballistic Missile Early Warning System], with or without NORAD, if there is a battle to stop a Soviet nuclear attack on the United States, it will be fought over Canadian territory. If the attack is by plane, it will be intercepted over Canada. If the attack is by missile, it will be intercepted over Canada. This is the harsh, unavoidable, unchangeable, and irrefutable fact of North American defense.

[Stanley Tupper and Douglas Bailey, *One Continent—Two Voices,* Clarke, Irwin and Company Ltd., 1967]

3. Rain Drops Are Fallin' On . . .

FRINGE BENEFITS

[*Ting Cartoons,* London Free Press, 1970]

M. R. Tingley, courtesy of *London Free Press*

4. Has Canada Become a Military Satellite?

It is a close, military alliance. And probably it is illegal, for while it was hotly debated in the Canadian Parliament, it never came before the United States Congress and did not receive the Senate's advice and consent.

NORAD established authoritative control of all air defence weapons which must be employed against an attacker, including the Distant Early Warning lines in the far north of Canada, subsequently backed up by the Mid-Canada Line and the Pinetree Line. They were spectacularly extravagant, of limited utility, and have long since been rendered obsolete by the BMEWS installations in Alaska, Greenland, and England. The DEW-line was never designed to deal with anything but bombers, and only bombers which obliged by flying overhead at an appropriate height; it got its best work-out on geese. It was a crash program, which can be defined as costing three times what it should and carried out just when it was becoming obsolete. It was in fact set up against a nonexistent threat from Russian bombers which were never built.

NORAD did little for defence but much to reduce Canada to the role of a military satellite of the United States. For that, in fact, is what a small nation becomes when it places its armed forces or portions of them under a foreign commander in peacetime, in a lonely, two-way, horse-and-rabbit alliance.

The Canadians battled for years to win the right to determine for themselves, at Ottawa rather than at Westminster, whether or not they would go to war. NORAD transferred that decision abruptly from Ottawa to Washington, or not improbably to the commander-in-chief, NORAD, Colorado Springs, Colorado.

[James M. Minifie, *Open at the Top: Reflections on U.S.-Canada Relations,* McClelland and Stewart Limited, 1964]

Guideline for Inquiry

James Minifie contends that "NORAD did little for defence but much to reduce Canada to the role of a military satellite of the United States." Explain why you agree or disagree with that statement.

5. The End of NORAD?

Canada will get rid of its two squadrons of nuclear-equipped Bomarc anti-aircraft missiles in defiance of U.S. requests, a defence white paper revealed today.

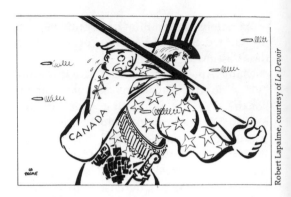

Quand l'U.S. s'en va t'en guerre.

Defence Minister Donald MacDonald, at a news conference called to coincide with the publication of the policy document, described the once-controversial missiles as "obsolete".

He said that U.S. Defence Secretary Melvin Laird and his advisers, when informed of Canada's decision to liquidate this part of its contribution to North American air defence, were "not enthusiastic".

["White Paper Defies U.S.", Victoria *Daily Times,* August 24, 1971]

Part Five: The Debate Goes On—But Will Canada?

1. Our Persistent Dilemma

At any rate, it is small wonder that Canadians are thoroughly ambivalent in their response to the United States, another trite adage in our bundle called the great cliché. They must be. Throughout their history they have been so constantly helped or hampered by America and the Americans. But they have always been utterly involved. One is tempted to conclude, in fact, that there could not be a Canada without the United States—and may not be a Canada with one.

[J. M. S. Careless, "Hooray For the Scars and Gripes", *The New Romans,* ed. Al Purdy, Hurtig Publishers, 1968]

2. The Land—and Survival

"Canada is not," as Professor W. L. Morton has noted, "a second-rate United States, still less a United States that failed. Canadian history is rather an important chapter in a distinct and even unique human endeavour: the civilization of a northern and arctic land. Because of its separate origin on the northern frontier, Canadian life to this day is marked by a northern quality and a strong seasonal rhythm. The line which marks off the frontier from the farmstead, the wilderness from the baseland, the hinterland from the metropolis, runs through every Canadian psyche."

This, it seems to me, is the right approach to the search for a Canadian identity: that we can find ourselves in the land. . . .

Our power structure is not rigid; it is open

Wide World Photo

Senator Mike Gravel of Alaska, flanked by two Canadian M.P.s, demonstrates outside the White House against a planned American underground nuclear test in Alaska. The test, it was feared, would set off an earthquake in Alaska and adjoining areas in Canada. To what extent can Canadians form alliances with certain American regions that have similar interests? To what extent might this be a more effective approach in Canadian-American relations than having our government confront Washington directly?

to anyone with ability and ambition. We are a country that is in the process of becoming; the aura of the frontier is still with us.

[Peter Newman, "The Testament of a Canadian", *The New Romans,* ed. Al Purdy, Hurtig Publishers, 1968]

3. What Is Your Will?

It is just impossible, by any policy whatever, to isolate Canada against the *outward* impact of American culture. No nation can be so isolated from currents gushing out of a technology that all nations imitate, an affluence that they all seek for themselves, an appetite that they all share.

In style of living, in use of gadgets, in hunger for goods and easy, predigested ideas, the whole world is being Americanized—not by any deliberate design but simply because no one really wants to stanch the technological flood. It moves under its own momentum, blindly, massively, irresistibly, everywhere. And nowhere so fast as across the Canadian border.

If we cannot resist the worldwide American gloss is our nationality therefore condemned to extinction? By no means, provided that we do not confuse gloss with reality. . . .

How . . . do we preserve the inner contents of Canada, the only thing that can be preserved or is worth preserving?

Certain measures already taken, or about to be taken, are obvious and generally approved.

We can retain for ourselves the ownership of vital Canadian assets like communications, transportation, banking and others.

We can make foreign investors obey our laws.

We can save more of our money, invest it in our own enterprises and run the risks that the more daring foreigners accept.

We can shape our tax laws to encourage native investment.

We can and should take the initiative in devising an international set of rules like GATT to police the rootless multi-national corporations that obey no single government, care nothing for any nation's convenience and will soon control much of the world's business while our Canadian eyes are fixed on lesser perils.

Yet all these measures, plus the old weapon of the tariff, even if they escape ruinous retaliation from our trading partners, cannot succeed, lacking broad national agreement within Canada. They will worsen our situation if they further divide our unequal geographic regions and set us quarrelling among ourselves. . . .

. . . The decisive question is clear and simple: How much are we prepared to pay in work, money, goods, and above all, in wisdom for the privilege of being Canadian?

[Bruce Hutchison, "Bruce Hutchison Writes an Open Letter to Pierre Elliott Trudeau", *Maclean's,* July 1971]

Guideline for Inquiry

How much are *you* "prepared to pay in work, money, goods and above all, in wisdom for the privilege of being Canadian"?

unit 4: Canada in the World: Selected Issues

by Robert Clark and Cary Goulson

Duncan Macpherson. Reprinted with permission—the *Toronto Star*

INTRODUCTION

All countries have foreign policies. A foreign policy can be described as the way in which one country relates to the other countries of the world. Of course, not all countries have the same foreign policy. There are over 150 separate nations in the world, and each one must mould its foreign relations to suit its own particular needs and characteristics. Thus no two foreign policies are exactly alike.

The cartoon at the beginning of this unit gives some insight into Canada's foreign policy. What can you tell about our role in the world from looking at the cartoon?

The importance of an effective foreign policy is undeniable. Questions of war and peace, the development of world trade, the spread of nuclear weapons, and the improvement of human living standards are all questions that Canada must consider when formulating its foreign policy. To give you a better understanding of the factors at work in creating Canada's foreign policy, this introductory section will look at three important areas: (1) the major factors affecting our foreign policy; (2) our foreign policy in the past; and (3) the direction in which our foreign policy appears to be heading. By the end of this section, you should have a clear idea of the general outline of Canada's foreign relations, and you should be ready to look at some of the specific foreign policy issues facing Canada today.

Part One: Canadian Foreign Policy: An Overview

1. Factors Shaping Canada's Foreign Policy

There are many domestic and external factors that influence Canada's foreign policy. Some of the most important of these are discussed below.

Geography Canada occupies the northern half of the North American continent and borders on only one other country, the United States. Because Canada and the United States occupy a common land mass, many of our main geographical features, such as the prairies and mountain ranges, continue in north-south directions across the border. But although we may share some common geography, in other aspects most Canadians want Canada to remain distinct from the United States. To help us do this, Canada has looked across the three oceans that border us on the east, west, and north. Traditionally, the Atlantic has been our communications link with the rest of the world. Now the Pacific is increasing in importance as we develop better communications with the Orient. And the Arctic, with its untapped energy potential, has drawn our focus northward in recent years and has had a significant impact on our relations with the Soviet Union.

Population Canada has a population of 23 000 000. Approximately 43 per cent of these people are of British origin, 29 per cent of French origin, and 26 per cent of other origins (mainly European); 2 per cent are native Indians and Inuit. The variety of ethnic origins, and the fact that

Canadians tend to maintain their ethnic identities, often leads to differing views about Canada's international relationships.

Language The strength of the French language and culture in Canada naturally has affected our relations with the French-speaking nations of the world. Officially, Canada is a bilingual country, and an important part of our foreign policy is to develop our image abroad as a land of two languages and cultures.

Political System The parliamentary system of government, where the Prime Minister and the Cabinet must account for their policies in the House of Commons, gives the opposition the opportunity to probe foreign policy decisions. Thus the government must pay close attention to all foreign policy matters.

The provincial governments are also factors in determining our foreign policy. Because the provinces exercise a great deal of power in a federal system, the national government must be sure that their interests are taken into consideration.

Economics Canada, although a rich country, is underdeveloped in that we still do not have the capital or the labour to exploit our resources to the fullest advantage. In addition, the prosperity of our nation is very dependent on the growth of world trade. These factors make it difficult to be as independent in our diplomatic relations as we might like to be, for they indicate that we must give some priority to commercial matters when formulating our foreign policy.

Nationalism Canada's desire to build a North American nation distinctively different from the United States also gives direction to our foreign policy. For example, in recent years we have tried to develop closer links with Western Europe, to establish détente with the Soviet Union and China, and to maintain our image as a middle power with some freedom to act independently in international affairs.

Power Realities One of the most obvious limitations on the development of our foreign policy is the fact that Canada is not a powerful nation and does not have the influence that countries like the United States and the Soviet Union have. There is very little we can do to alter American foreign policy decisions, and at times we may have to bow to outside pressures and revise our own way of thinking.

World Opinion The pressure of widely accepted international positions on some issues occasionally pushes Canada to take stands it might prefer to avoid. For example, we may be pressured into cutting off trade relations with a country because of its racial policies, even though trading with that nation may be very advantageous to us.

Idealism While foreign policy, like domestic policy, is largely motivated by self-interest, there are some commonly accepted positions on such issues as foreign aid and disarmament that have a definite bearing on our foreign policy decisions.

2. Canadian Foreign Policy in Perspective

(a) Early Foreign Relations

At the time of Confederation in 1867, the Canadian government had no control over its foreign policy. We were given the right to control our domestic policy (what happens inside our country), but as soon as we stepped outside the door of our national house the British government took over and made our decisions for us. At the time, our leaders regarded this British link as desirable. The Civil War in the United States had finally ended, and with their internal problems put to rest, the Americans were dreaming of an expanded American nation; some individuals and groups favoured the conquest of Canada as the first step towards fulfilling this dream. Canadians viewed the British connection as a form of protection from their threatening neighbour.

Fortunately for Canada, any differences between the British and the Americans were settled through negotiations. The most significant of the agreements was the Treaty of Washington in 1871. Sir John A. Macdonald, the Canadian Prime Minister, was part of the British delegation at the talks. The Prime Minister was there, of course, to represent Canadian interests, but he found that the British often disregarded

Public Archives Canada #C17243

UNCLE SAM: "National Policy! British Connection! Protective Tariff! Canada Pacific Railway! Colonization! And this is your 'friendship', Sir John! Pshaw!"

In this cartoon, Uncle Sam, personifying the United States, is listing the aspects of Sir John A. Macdonald's National Policy, which was designed to create a strong economic base for a Canada stretching "from sea to sea". Why would Uncle Sam be angry about these developments?

the Canadian viewpoint; unfortunately, he was powerless to do anything about it. However, the Treaty of Washington did much to create a degree of harmony in British-American relations, and such accord was crucial for Canadian security. In fact, in 1871 all British troops except the Halifax naval garrison were withdrawn from Canada; hence, it was vitally important that Canada do its best to ensure that friendly relations continued to prevail between Britain and the United States.

Although our foreign policy was in the hands of the British, we were given jurisdiction over trade and immigration. In 1880 we sent a High Commissioner to London, and in 1882 an Agent-General to Paris, to act as our representatives and to handle business dealings with the British and French governments.

As Canada's interests developed both inside and outside the Empire, Britain, in 1887, began consulting with authorities from the Dominions at periodic meetings known as Colonial Conferences. (The name was later changed to Imperial Conferences.) At the first conference, Canada won the right to refuse to be bound by British commercial treaties if they were regarded as harmful to the Canadian economy.

During the 1880s and 1890s there was much debate in Canada between those who wanted to maintain a common foreign policy and a strong imperial tie with Britain and those who wanted greater independence and freedom from British decisions, unless, of course, they were in our own best interests. Sir John A. Macdonald and Sir Wilfrid Laurier were both followers of the latter position. At the Imperial Conference of 1897, the British Colonial Secretary, Joseph Chamberlain, tried to sell the idea of common trade regulations and unified military planning to Laurier and the other Dominion leaders. Laurier, however, backed away from such a suggestion, stating that Canada would take voluntary initiatives in these fields.

Laurier's position was strongly tested with the outbreak of the Boer War in 1899. Canadians with strong imperial sentiments pressed the government to rush to Britain's aid, while the nationalist elements and the French-speaking Quebeckers wanted no part of a British colonial war which did not threaten Canadian security. Laurier tried to reach

Public Archives Canada #C1659

Members of the Colonial Conference, 1902. What initiatives did Laurier (front row, third from the left) take toward developing an independent Canadian foreign policy?

a compromise by authorizing the recruitment of volunteer contingents while claiming that this action was not to be regarded as a precedent for future Canadian participation in British military activities. He asserted, "I claim for Canada this, in the future she shall be at liberty to act or not to act".

(b) Moving Toward an Independent Foreign Policy

Laurier continued to press Canada's national interests when the occasion demanded. In 1903, in the vote to settle the Alaska Boundary dispute, the single British delegate sided with the three American delegates to vote in favour of the U.S. claim by a margin of four to two. Laurier was incensed by this action, and he became determined that the Canadian government should take more control of its own affairs. The following year, he replaced the English Commander-in-

CANADA : DON'T BE SCARED : I'M HERE

Public Archives Canada #C14556

How does this cartoon symbolize a Canadian viewpoint of Canada's role in the First World War?

Chief of the Canadian armed forces and virtually ended direct British military involvement in this country.

Laurier was also responsible for the creation of an independent Department of External Affairs in 1909. This new portfolio was to be held by the Prime Minister. (Provision for a separate minister was not made until 1946.) The first office of the Department of External Affairs was located over a barbershop in Ottawa; for the next twenty years it was staffed by an undersecretary, three assistants, and a few clerks and secretaries. It was a very modest beginning. However, it did allow all of the papers and correspondence related to Canada's dealings with other countries to be consolidated in one specialized department and it was responsible for the monitoring of foreign mail.

The First World War served as the major impetus to the development of an independent Canadian foreign policy. When war broke out in 1914, Robert Borden, an ardent imperialist, was Prime Minister. Our diplomatic bonds with England were so strong that when that country declared war in 1914, Canada was automatically and legally committed to war as well. However, our enthusiastic and unquestioning allegiance to Britain was quickly transformed by wartime conditions into a yearning for much greater Canadian independence. Borden protested to Britain that, by virtue of our contribution of 500 000 fighting troops to the Allied war effort, Canada deserved more consideration in policy-making. His protests must have been heard, for starting in 1917, he and other Dominion premiers were invited to participate in the discussions of the Imperial War Cabinet. In addition, Canada received a seat at the Paris Peace Conference, signed the

During the First World War, Canada contributed over 500 000 fighting troops to the Allied war effort. How did this involvement change Canadians' perception of themselves and the world?

Treaty as a member of the Imperial delegation, and, most significantly, in 1919, gained independent membership in the League of Nations.

(c) Achieving an Independent Foreign Policy

For most of the inter-war period, Mackenzie King was Canada's Prime Minister. His priority during these years was to heal the racial divisions within the country, which had been aggravated by the First World War. He carefully avoided overseas commitments and established the principle that only the Canadian Parliament would decide Canada's role in international affairs. Up to this time, a British representative signed all Canadian treaties, even if these had been negotiated by Canada itself. This practice was broken in 1923 when the Halibut Treaty with the United States was negotiated and signed by a Canadian.

The evolution to independence reached a high point at the Imperial Conference of 1926, where it was announced that the United Kingdom and the Dominions were "autonomous communities within the British Empire, equal in status, in no way subordinate to one another in any aspect of their domestic or external affairs, though united by a common allegiance to the Crown." Five years later, this statement was given the force of law by the Statute of Westminster in 1931. Henceforth, Canada was free to develop an independent foreign policy and diplomatic service.

Our new status meant that Britain had to appoint a High Commissioner to Canada, which it did in 1926. Britain also had to deal with our Department of External Affairs rather than with the Governor General, who now represented only the Crown. It also meant that Canada was free to establish its own diplomatic relations. Thus, in 1927 Canada posted its first diplomat to the United States, and by 1939 we had exchanged diplomatic offices with France, Japan, Belgium, and the Netherlands.

However, Mackenzie King was not eager to pursue foreign relations at this time. In the 1920s and 1930s he adopted a policy of isolationism. Confronted by the aggressive actions of Mussolini and Hitler, King—and indeed most Canadians—applauded policies of appeasement. When, for example, in 1935 the Canadian delegate at the League of Nations took an independent stand and voted in favour of economic restrictions against Italy to discourage its aggression in Ethiopia, King forced the delegate to change his position and to oppose any actions against Italy. In effect, King's decision contributed to the collapse of collective security through membership in the League of Nations. In the end, the League took no action. Most countries, including Canada, were just too preoccupied with their own internal problems resulting from the Great Depression to have much concern for external events.

(d) New Power in International Relations

As the threat of a second world war increased, however, Canadians began to lose their preoccupation with their domestic problems. When Britain declared war, Canada followed suit only one week later. Significantly, our declaration was an independent act of the Canadian Parliament, thus indicating our change in status since 1914.

The war did much to enhance Canada's position on the world scene. Our provision of over 1 000 000 fighting troops, together with Allied training programs and precious war materials, made Canada one of the leading nations during the war. And unlike our attitude after the First World War, we emerged from this war eager to play an active role in world affairs. Evidence of this was the appointment in 1946 of Louis St. Laurent as the first full-time Secretary of State for External Affairs; Lester B. Pearson became his Undersecretary. Two years later, when Mackenzie King retired, St. Laurent became Prime Minister and Pearson took over the External Affairs portfolio.

While the war-damaged countries of Europe and Asia were working to rebuild, Canada became a significant country on the international scene. We conceived of our new role as that of a middle power and one of the aspects of this role was to act as a liaison between Britain and the United States and between developed and developing nations.

Canada also played a prominent role in the creation of the United Nations in 1945, particularly in attempting to ensure that its charter did not make it a helpless instrument of the great powers. The Canadian government sought the peaceful resolutions of many early post-war international disputes through the United Nations. The UN, however, did not turn out to be the successful peacekeeper the Canadians had hoped for. The wartime alliance between the Soviet Union and the Western Allies was shattered and the Soviets seemed determined to expand their area of influence and control, particularly in Europe. The resulting Cold War between the two superpowers, the United States and the Soviet Union, with the latter paralysing the UN with its vetoes, blunted the effectiveness of the international organization to maintain the security of its members.

Now wary of the effectiveness of the existing UN security arrangements, the Canadian government sought an alternative form of security. This new alliance came in the form of the North Atlantic Treaty Organization (NATO), established in 1949. Lester Pearson, one of the architects, hoped that, despite the lack of interest on the part of the Americans, this pact would become more than a military alliance to stem Soviet aggression in Europe. He had visions of a transatlantic community with nations co-operating in many fields of endeavour. At the time of its founding, however, the overriding concern of most member countries was to pose a military counterweight to the U.S.S.R. in Europe. Accordingly, in 1951 Canadian forces

As Canada's minister of external affairs, Lester Pearson headed the Canadian delegation at the UN General Assembly in Paris in 1948. Here he talks to a delegate from the Soviet Union. It was hoped that the United Nations would be a forum where verbal clashes would replace military clashes. To what extent has this hope materialized?

Canadian Press

were dispatched to Europe as part of the NATO agreement. Regional collective security had now become part of Canadian policy.

When North Korea invaded South Korea in 1950, Canada sent troops to join the United Nations' forces defending South Korea. In fact, Canadian diplomatic and military resources were for a time unstintingly devoted to UN peacekeeping activities. This was most noticeable during the Suez Crisis of 1956, when Pearson, through skilful negotiations, convinced the powers involved to agree to assign UN forces to defuse the fighting in that area. He received the Nobel Peace Prize for his efforts, and for the next decade Canada played a leading role in UN peacekeeping operations in many countries of the world.

(e) In the Shadow of the American Superpower

The threat from the Soviet Union meant that Canada had to provide for its own defence in North America as well, and in 1958 we entered the North American Air Defence Command Agreement (NORAD) with the United States. Canada had traditionally relied upon Great Britain as a counterweight to American influence, but the war had seriously weakened Britain, and the United States emerged as the dominant power in the Western world. The question that many Canadians began to debate in the post-war period was to what extent Canada was, or would, or should become a military, economic, and diplomatic satellite of the United States. However, the Canadian government had decided against developing nuclear weaponry, and, given the nature of the strategic balance of power in the world, the shelter of the American nuclear umbrella seemed imperative.

By this time, the former British Empire had been transformed into the Commonwealth of Nations, a free association of sovereign states as originally envisioned by the 1926 Imperial Conference. The Commonwealth was essentially an informal organization, but as former British colonies in Asia and Africa joined and the multiracial character of the association developed, Canada proceeded to advance its own role as a bridge between developed and developing nations. In the 1950s, Canada channelled much of its development aid through this organization.

From 1957 to 1963, the Canadian government, under Prime Minister John Diefenbaker, attempted to re-establish our British connection in the face of increasing American influence. Times had changed, however, and Britain was trying to establish its own special relationship with the United States. Still, the Canadian government proceeded on its course. It rejected American suggestions that NORAD missiles in Canada be equipped with nuclear warheads provided by the United States; in so doing it decreased American confidence in Canada as a reliable military partner. Lester Pearson, who succeeded Diefenbaker as Prime Minister in 1963, accepted the warheads, but he was criticized by a significant group in Canada who argued that we would now become totally subservient to the United States in our foreign policy. Instead, they suggested, Canada should assume a neutral role in international affairs. Most Canadians, however, believed that this was an unrealistic option which would destroy our relations with traditionally friendly countries like the United States.

As Prime Minister, Pearson presided over a foreign policy which was beset by quite different challenges than he had confronted in the Department of External Affairs in the early post–Second World War period. The UN now had more than 100 members, many comparable in size and influence to Canada. As a result, our prestige in that forum waned. The war-damaged countries had now recovered and Western European nations in particular were regaining their previous economic and political strength. Internally, Canadians were faced with the growth of Québec nationalism, and Pearson's Liberal government was compelled to be preoccupied with domestic policies as it attempted to resolve this and other crises at home. Canadian foreign policy seemed somewhat adrift as the government and the people began to recognize their diminished significance in world affairs since the 1940s and 1950s. For the most part, we pursued a "quiet diplomacy" with the United States, with discreet consultations that seemed appropriate to our friendly relationship. On the other hand, we wanted to retain an independent position in world affairs. In one such display of independence in 1965, Pearson publicly suggested a change in American policy in Vietnam. He was sternly rebuked by President Lyndon Johnson, and Canada's relative weakness in the Canadian–American relationship was quickly underlined. The episode clearly illustrated that a major review of Canadian foreign policy was in order.

Canadian Forces Photo

The Distant Early Warning (DEW) Line stretches across the Canadian Arctic for 8000 km. Its purpose is to alert NORAD should any Soviet bombers attempt a raid on North America from a polar approach. To what extent do you think Soviet bombers pose a serious threat to Canada today?

(f) Evaluating our Foreign Policy Goals

Shortly after becoming Prime Minister in 1968, Pierre Trudeau initiated a complete reassessment of Canadian foreign relations, stating that, "It must be a policy which is pragmatic, realistic, and which contributes effectively both to Canada's political survival and independence and to a more secure, progressive, free and just world society." With the complexities of the world situation, the task would not be an easy one.

In the meantime, the Trudeau government undertook some radically different initiatives in foreign policy. In 1970, Canada officially recognized the People's Republic of China. Large sales to China of Canadian wheat were followed by the exchange of diplomatic representatives between the two countries. In another significant gesture, diplomatic recognition was accorded to the Vatican, in keeping with the desires of many Catholic Canadians. The Canadian government also pressed ahead to develop stronger relations with the Francophonie, an association of French-speaking countries similar to the English-speaking Commonwealth of Nations. This move was a continuation of a policy which was initiated in the 1960s

The figure on the left is Mitchell Sharp, who was Secretary of State for External Affairs from 1968 to 1974. What is the cartoonist saying? Do you agree or disagree? Why?

and which reflects the bicultural character of Canada.

On another front, the size of our military contingent to NATO was reduced and the nature of our contribution changed. This caused dismay among our allies, who feared we were retreating into an isolationist shell. The Canadian government, however, believed that some changes were in order. European countries had recovered from their low ebb after the Second World War, and thus their security was no longer entirely dependent on NATO forces. Canada believed that some of the money and resources now could be channelled into other areas without jeopardizing the security of NATO members. Some of these resources were needed for the defence of our own territory, particularly in the North. And there was an increasing need for new initiatives and actions against the problems of the Third World countries. In addition to all this, Canadian nationalists had long maintained that we were simply an instrument of American policy in NATO. Still, the government pledged to refurbish smaller Canadian forces in more specialized roles in NATO, which quieted those allies who had thought that we might abandon the alliance altogether.

In 1970, the Trudeau government extended Canadian territorial waters from 5 km to 19 km and claimed control over pollution in the Arctic to 1600 km from Canadian land. This served notice—particularly to the Soviet Union and the United States—that our sovereign interests over the North and its potential resources were to be heeded.

Beginning in 1970, the Canadian government issued a series of papers entitled *Foreign Policy for Canadians*, which outlined our goals in this field.

Trudeau argued for a more modest and realistic foreign policy which served our domestic needs. He had four foreign policy goals: to avoid too great a dependence on the United States by strengthening our relationships with other countries; to increase our economic growth; to aid national unity by encouraging bicultural policies abroad; and to contribute to world peace in whatever way our limited circumstances permitted.

In relations with the United States, our foreign-policy makers considered three options. One was to leave the relationship unchanged. The second was to deliberately pursue greater integration between the two countries. The third was to take a more independent position by developing closer economic and political ties with other countries. The government chose this "Third Option", a somewhat difficult path given the fact that the United States is by far our largest trading partner, our principal defensive ally, and a dominant influence in the cultural and industrial life of our country. However, this was not really a new policy. We had traditionally sought counterweights to American influence, beginning with Great Britain. After the demise of British power, we had hoped that NATO might be a useful medium for balancing our relations with the Americans. But the United States proved to be the dominant power in that organization. In still other attempts to establish a more independent position, the Canadian government recognized China, sought détente with the Soviet Union, and moved to explore closer relations with the nine-member European Economic Community and with the countries of the Pacific Rim and Latin America.

(g) Foreign Policy Issues for Canadians Today

The issues that face our country in the sphere of foreign relations are very complex. How do we maintain a very close friendship with the United States, yet avoid becoming a satellite in its powerful orbit? How do we maintain our military strength in NATO and NORAD while seeking détente with the Soviet Union? How do we establish closer economic relationships with the Western European members of the EEC as that organization becomes more powerful? How do we create a broader trading base with Japan and China? What emphasis should we place on our participation in the United Nations when our peacekeeping role has proven frustrating and our political influence has been lessened? How can we continue to produce nuclear reactors for export and yet attempt to reduce the use of nuclear resources for military purposes? How do we best assume our moral responsibility as the gap between rich and poor nations seems to widen? How much importance should we attach to such organizations as the Commonwealth and the Francophonie given their loose and informal structures?

3. Canadian Foreign Policy: Trudeau's Views

This excerpt from a biography of former Prime Minister Pierre Trudeau outlines his priorities for Canada in conducting our foreign policy between 1968 and 1979.

Although it is an area that has contributed handsomely to his prestige, Trudeau came late to an interest in foreign policy, and his involvement in it remains quite selective. Says Ivan Head, his foreign-policy advisor: "He's a man who had probably done more foreign travel than any person who has ever come into high public office in Canada, and yet who was willing despite that background to be quite indifferent to foreign affairs. That was not what interested him, not what he regarded as important. It was something he was quite willing to delegate to others from the very beginning and have nothing to do with. As he's become aware of not only the usefulness but the personal interest to him—the attractiveness to him as a person—of personal diplomacy, often in the form of summits, that has changed."

Trudeau regards foreign policy, for the most part, as the pursuit of Canada's domestic interests abroad, and he is sceptical about assigning the country any larger international role. "We shouldn't be trying to run the world," he has said. "We should be trying to make our own country a good place.[1] . . . We're perhaps more the largest of the small powers than the smallest of the large powers.[2] . . . Personally, I tend to discount the weight of our influence in the world. If we have influence, so much the better. But I don't think this should be our purpose, sort of, to tell the world what is morally right and what is morally wrong and go around voting properly on the right issues and being all things to all men."[3] His foreign-policy goals are accordingly modest: to assist Canada's economic growth, to further the cause of national unity at home by ensuring that Canada maintains a fully bicultural presence abroad, to avoid excessive dependence on the United States by strengthening Canada's ties with other countries, and to make whatever limited contributions to world peace our circumstances permit.

Relations with the United States are one of the few foreign-policy areas to which Trudeau accords "first category" attention.

Here, as in most other fields, his preoccupation is with maintaining a fine balance. On one hand, he considers a certain amount of domination by the United States inescapable, if only because few Canadians would be prepared to pay the economic price that would be required to end it: "I think the problem of economic domination is somewhat inevitable, not only of the United States over Canada but perhaps over countries of Europe as well. . . . These are facts of life and they don't worry me.[4] . . . If the whole country became nationalistic in an economic sense, it would soon find itself trying to eat its pride, you know, but you don't go far on a proud stomach."[5] But, on the other hand, Trudeau believes it is his government's role to ensure that this domination does not extend so far as to cause serious damage to Canada's economic, political, or cultural well-being or sense of identity. This, to him, is less a matter of erecting across-the-board barriers to U.S. influence than of determining on a case-by-case basis whether a threat exists, and what protective action is required. In such subjective judgments, of course, his perception is quite different from that of economic nationalists who are convinced that the present level of U.S. ownership in this country is, in itself, a threat to Canada.

Trudeau's pursuit of what he considers a proper balance in the Canada–United States relationship takes two forms. First, it involves an attempt to wean Canada away from over-dependence on its southern neighbour by developing closer economic and political ties with other countries. This strategy constitutes the "Third Option" outlined on behalf of the government in 1972 by Mitchell Sharp, who was then external affairs minister; the other two options identified and rejected by the Trudeau government were to leave the Canada–United States relationship unchanged, or

to move deliberately toward closer integration between the two countries. As Trudeau explains it: "The object of our policy, simply stated, is that we are trying to create counterweights. . . . It's a very simple strategy of creating other channels of interest than the automatic easy, north-south, Canada–U.S. ones in which we are always the smaller and minor partner."[6] This strategy of diversification underlies much of Trudeau's foreign policy, including the recognition of China, the rapprochement with the Soviet Union, and the pursuit of closer and more active relations with the countries of the Pacific Rim, Latin America, and the European Economic Community.

The other element of Trudeau's approach, which has sometimes been misinterpreted as anti-Americanism by the United States and even by some Canadians, involves selective government intervention to assert or protect Canada's independence. As Trudeau puts it: "We can't expect, without becoming much poorer, to control all of our economy. What we can do is make an effort to control those economic or financial institutions which are of greater importance in the free development of this society. . . . The same thing in cultural fields."[7] These selective interventions have included blocking the sale of Canadian uranium mines to U.S. interests, introducing legislation to prevent the World Football League from expanding into Canada, encouraging the Canadian Radio and Television Commission to impose stringent Canadian-content requirements on broadcasters, and driving the Canadian editions of *Time* and several other U.S. publications out of the country by ending their tax concessions. Apart from such specific interventions, Trudeau also established the Foreign Investment Review Agency, a screening body whose limited mandate is designed not to block or discourage foreign investment but to ensure that it takes place in forms which carry some benefit for Canada. In a more general sense, Trudeau has also periodically asserted Canada's independence by pursuing policies—such as trading with, and even visiting, Cuba—that defied pressures from the United States, by vigorously resisting the extra-territorial application of U.S. laws to American corporations operating in Canada, and by such actions as making American draft-resisters and deserters welcome in this country during the Vietnam War.

A second area of foreign policy to which Trudeau accords "first category" attention is the matter of nuclear non-proliferation. The intensity of his feelings about nuclear weapons and the prospect of their use has changed little since he wrote in 1961: "Massacres is too weak a term. Twisted, charred, liquefied, vanished into thin air. . . . Of all humanity nothing will remain but traces of shadows stamped on the concrete debris, on the stones in the fields, on the cliffs of the ocean, as if they were so many stains on a bad photographic plate."[8] He has not been prepared to take Canada out of the business of making nuclear reactors—which, although designed for peaceful purposes, can be used to produce nuclear bombs—but he has insisted that those reactors be sold under safeguard agreements which greatly reduce the danger of misuse, and he has consistently pressed the issues of non-proliferation and disarmament in his talks with foreign leaders.

The third foreign-policy area in which Trudeau takes a strong personal interest is the changing relationship between developed and developing countries, a subject on which he said in 1968: "We must recognize that, in the long run, the overwhelming threat to Canada will not come from foreign investments or foreign ideologies or even—with good fortune—foreign nuclear weapons. It will come, instead, from the two-thirds of the people of the world who are steadily falling farther and farther behind in their search for a decent standard of living."[9] He believes that Canada, because it is both an industrialized nation and a country whose economy is heavily dependent on the production of raw materials, can well understand the problems of both developed and developing countries and therefore can sometimes serve as a bridge between the two. Though domestic economic and political considerations have deterred him from matching his sympathy for the concerns of developing countries with concrete generosity, he has succeeded in establishing close personal rapport with such leaders of the Third World as Julius Nyerere of Tanzania, Lee Kuan Yew of Singapore, and Michael Manley of Jamaica. . . .

1. CTV interview with Charles Templeton, Dec. 18, 1968, PMO transcript.
2. *Toronto Star*, April 27, 1968.
3. CTV interview with Charles Templeton, Dec. 18, 1968, PMO transcript.
4. Interview with J. Walz, *New York Times*, Nov. 22, 1968, PMO transcript.
5. Interview with Gerald Clark, *Montreal Star*, Dec. 1, 1969, PMO transcript.
6. Interview with three European journalists, February 21, 1975, PMO transcript.
7. Interview with Dick Duncan, *Time* magazine, Feb. 20, 1970, PMO transcript.
8. P. E. Trudeau, *Cité Libre*, December 1961.
9. Speech at University of Alberta, Edmonton, May 13, 1968, PMO transcript.

[George Radwanski, *Trudeau*, Macmillan of Canada, 1978]

4. Is the Third Option Dead?

The following article reviews the status of the Third Option, the policy adopted by the Trudeau government in the early 1970s to govern our relations with the United States. It raises the old issue of continentalism (closer ties between Canada and the United States in the

North American continent) versus the Third Option, which was intended to lessen our dependence on the United States. For further evidence to assess the arguments on both sides, you should refer to the previous chapter in this book entitled "The Americans and Us".

"The Third Option would lessen the vulnerability of the Canadian economy to external factors, in particular the impact of the U.S., and . . . develop a more confident sense of national identity."

External Affairs Minister Mitchell Sharp
October, 1972

Officially, no one talks any more about the Third Option policy of trying . . . to prevent our north-south ties from binding us too closely. . . .

What then about the Second Option? (The First Option, which even Ottawa didn't take seriously, was to do nothing). It meant, said Sharp, "closer integration with the U.S."

No, no, no, said Sharp, in 1972. Cuddling up to the U.S. would "threaten the Canadian identity."

Today, without admitting and without perhaps even realizing it, we are curled up at the foot of the U.S. bed. We can't cry rape. We can't even claim to have been seduced. We have been drawn together, it seems, by the most powerful body chemistry of all— economic geography.

Two examples of the change in attitude:

In 1975, the Economic Council of Canada report "Looking Outward" suggested, timidly and circuitously, Canada–U.S. free trade as a last choice alternative to all other forms of free trade. In reply came a storm of editorial and political protest that almost flattened the council.

Two months ago, the Senate Committee on Foreign Affairs concluded its study of Canada–U.S. relations and recommended

that Canadians "seriously examine" North American free trade. Scarcely an editorial voice has squeaked. "The silence has amazed me," said committee chairman Senator George van Roggen.

Again, late in August, "after two years of pondering about it and wondering whether I should do it," Carl Beigie, director of the C. D. Howe Research Institute, broke a long silence and called for a "Canada–U.S. economic deal" based upon free trade. Beigie's, to him, agonized conversion earned him the same response as the report of the Senate committee—none at all.

Continentalism, once the most potent issue in Canadian politics except for that of national unity, has become, it seems, conventional wisdom. Not even a policy any longer, so much as a resigned acceptance of the inevitable.

Economics isn't the only force pushing us together. The U.S. no longer repels Canadians as it did when it was at war in Vietnam and when its own cities were battlegrounds. More than three million Canadians a year now depend upon the U.S. as a winter resting place, whether for a few days or permanently. If our magazines have never before been so Canadian, our television, which is the only cultural force that really matters, has never been so Americanized, and, which matters even more, without public protests any more.

Yet economics is still the force that counts. In a chilly world, Canadians are finding themselves shivering alone—the only industrial country, almost, without free access to a market of 100 million or more.

Bleakly, the Senate committee listed the alternatives to Canada–U.S. free trade; "de-industrialization," as U.S. branch plants hurry back home; "diminished competitiveness" as Canada struggles to implement an industrial strategy without a market within which to implement it; and, as the end result, "a declining standard of living."

The price of economic expansion, continentalist critics always have argued, would be political contraction. The Senate committee disagreed: "An economically strong Canada is in a much better situation to maintain political and cultural independence than an economically weak Canada."

There's the rub. The Second Option is familiar. It amounts, though its advocates haven't realized it, to the Parti Québécois' formula for "political sovereignty/economic association," with the U.S. in place of Canada, and Canada in place of Quebec. If Canada could negotiate a free trade-for-sovereignty deal with the U.S., so could Quebec with Canada, more easily so in fact because the partners would be more equal in size.

To push the analysis a step further, if Canada did indeed initiate free trade discussions with the U.S., Quebec would be far better able to protect its own interests as an independent country than as a member of a federation that was due, soon, to cease to exist as a distinct common market. So would, by extension, Canada's western and eastern provinces.

Canada's "confident sense of national identity" would be threatened less by slow political and cultural assimilation within a North American common market, as Sharp feared in 1972, than by national disintegration the instant the trade talks began.

The Senate committee, wisely, did not advocate free trade as such but only that it be examined seriously, "without prejudice." Its economic appeal remains as strong as ever, perhaps stronger than ever. Its political appeal has never been weaker, which may only be a measure of how unconfident our national identity now is.

[Richard Gwyn, "Like It or Not, We're in Bed with U.S.", (October 1978). Reprinted with permission—the *Toronto Star*.]

5. Canadian Diplomacy: A Case Study

This case study deals with an incident in international affairs in which Canada played an important role. It illustrates some of the primary motives behind Canadian foreign policy and, to some extent, the way in which our foreign policy is conducted.

A country can be a world leader in many ways. Quite often, a country is called a world leader because it has much industry and wealth. Also, world leadership is often defined in terms of the military power of a country.

Although Canada has a fair amount of industry and a small but modern army, we are not thought of as a world leader in these terms. However, Canada has established a foreign policy which has allowed us to become a world leader in diplomacy and international affairs.

One of the best examples of this leadership was Canada's role in helping to solve the Suez Crisis of 1956 which threatened to break out into a major war.

After the Second World War, Britain was given the task of supervising Palestine, where thousands of Jews left homeless by the war had decided to settle. Tension developed between the incoming Jews and the Arabs who were living in Palestine. Britain found herself unable to handle the situation and turned her responsibility over to the United Nations.

The United Nations examined the problem, and after much debate in its General Assembly offered a recommendation. It proposed that Palestine be partitioned—(divided) into two states, one Arab and one Jewish. The recommendation was not completely popular. The Arab countries opposed the partition and threatened to resist it with force. They followed through on this threat and war broke out between the Arabs and Jews in December 1947.

CANADA OPPOSED FORCE

Although Canada supported the recommendation of the United Nations she, along with Britain and others, did not want to use force to bring about the partition. Matters were out of her hands, however, and in May 1948, the Jewish Government announced the creation of the state of Israel. The U.S.A. and U.S.S.R. formally recognized the new country immediately but Britain and Canada did not.

The Canadian government and its United Nations representative, Lester B. Pearson, were very active during these troubled times. They attempted to find a solution acceptable to both Arabs and Jews. They also spent long hours trying to keep relations friendly between the U.S.A. and Britain, who were disagreeing with each other on many points. This was a role which Canada was to play often in the future.

The war between the Arabs and Israelis was finally ended by the signing of a ceasefire agreement in January 1949. The United Nations had brought the two sides together and managed to stop the fighting for the time being.

The situation between the Arab states and Israel remained fairly peaceful for the next few years. In 1952 the Egyptian government of King Farouk was overthrown by the army and Colonel Gamal Abdel Nasser came into power. Nasser was determined to modernize Egypt and he sought economic aid from other countries to do so. One of Nasser's key projects was the desire to build a huge dam on the Nile River. He secured the promise of large loans from Britain and the U.S.A. to pay for its construction. But, in 1955 the U.S.A. withdrew its support and Britain did the same.

Determined to build the dam, Nasser decided to nationalize and take control of the Suez Canal. He intended to use the money which the Canal would make to pay for construction of the dam. Because the Canal was formally owned by various governments, principally Britain and France, a great protest developed.

CANAL THREATENED

Britain, who saw her route to India being threatened, led the protest. France and the United States, who also used the Canal a great deal, joined the outcry. Representatives of these three countries met and out of the conference two attitudes developed. Britain and France agreed to move in troops and take over the Canal.

The two countries felt that this would ensure the operation of this important international waterway. The United States opposed such a move and recommended that the Canal come under international control. The Egyptians rejected this plan and Britain and France began to move ships and troops into the Mediterranean Sea.

Canada, through the Minister for External Affairs, Mr. Pearson, was very actively involved in trying to resolve the problem. The Canadian government supported the American recommendation and urged Britain not to use force to settle the matter. Above all Canada wanted to prevent a major split between Britain and the U.S.A. This desire was and continued to be the cornerstone of Canadian foreign policy.

After Egypt had rejected the American plan to international control, American Secretary of State Dulles suggested forming a Suez Canal Users' Association. The Association would run the Canal and pay Egypt for its use. Nasser and the Egyptians rejected this idea.

Finally the matter was brought to the United Nations by Britain and France. Before any major discussion could take place the

Israelis attacked Egypt. This brought the whole dispute into a new light. Britain and France demanded that the Arabs and Israelis cease fighting. They warned that if they would not that British and French forces would move in to guarantee the safety of the Canal.

The new outbreak of war in the Middle East became the main interest of the United Nations. The General Assembly met in an emergency session to try to resolve the matter. All of the member nations wanted to stop the fighting but no one could find a method which would satisfy all of the parties involved.

CANADIAN PLAN

The Canadian delegation seemed to have an idea that might work. It suggested the creation of a United Nations peacekeeping force to move into the area and keep the two fighting countries apart. This move would prevent Britain and France from becoming directly involved and maintain good relations with other countries. At first, the reaction to this Canadian idea was not positive, but after a few days, when no solution was able to be found, the reaction changed.

Mr. Pearson presented the idea in a resolution to the General Assembly and it was passed without opposition.

The next major question was what countries would supply troops to this United Nations Force. Before this could be decided, it was announced that the first British and French troops had landed in Egypt. The U.S.S.R., which had been selling large amounts of arms to Egypt, threatened to step in and use force to stop the British and French "aggression." The U.S.A. then warned the U.S.S.R. not to become involved.

The crisis had now developed to the point of a possible large-scale war.

The United Nations acted quickly. A cease-fire between Israel and Egypt was arranged. The Emergency Force was quickly put together, sent to the area, and British and French troops sent home. There were still some difficulties. Nasser objected to the Canadian troops being sent because of Canada's traditional ties with Britain. However, after some discussion, a smaller Canadian force did take part in the peacekeeping.

These were exciting times for Canada and for the world. Canada, and her representative at the United Nations Lester B. Pearson, had come to the fore as a leader in international affairs. For his efforts in helping to solve the Suez Crisis, Mr. Pearson was awarded the Nobel Peace Prize. He is the only Canadian to have ever won that honour.

The Middle East problem had not been

Lester Pearson accepts the Nobel Peace Prize from Gunnar Jahn of the Nobel Committee on December 10, 1957. How did the winning of this prize symbolize our attitude towards the UN during this time?

Canadian Press

completely cleared up. A solution to stop the fighting had been found. However, there was no "political solution," and there were no permanent borders between Israel and the Arab states. As a result war again broke out in the Middle East in 1967.

[George Black, "The Suez Crisis, 1956— Canadian Diplomacy at Work", *Canada and the World*, September 1974.]

Guidelines for Inquiry

1. Using the list of factors that shape Canadian foreign policy, analyse the historical development of this policy and explain where and how these factors have had an influence.
2. (a) To what three foreign policy issues does Trudeau give highest priority? Do you agree with his ranking? Why?
   (b) Assess Richard Gwyn's comments about the Third Option in our foreign policy.
3. Using the case study of the Suez Crisis:
   (a) Identify the influences which shaped our foreign policy at that time.
   (b) Describe how we put that policy into practice.
4. As a study base for this unit, prepare a preliminary statement outlining what you think our current priorities in foreign policy should be. As much as possible, relate your ideas to the factors shaping our foreign policy and to the historical evolution of that policy. Be prepared to revise this statement after you have examined the specific foreign policy issues in the rest of this unit.

Part Two: Canada and Europe

Canada's relations with the countries of Europe, and in particular with Great Britain, have always been strong, but since the Second World War they have been overshadowed by the importance of our ties to the United States. However, the ancestral roots of over 90 per cent of Canadians are in Europe, and recently Canada has sought to draw closer to that continent as part of its Third Option foreign policy.

Our principal post-war connections with Western Europe have been within the North Atlantic Treaty Organization. Although our initial enthusiasm and support for this organization had declined by the mid-1960s, we have continued to play an active, though somewhat reduced, role in its councils. In recent years, our diplomats have advocated a policy of détente, or a lessening of tensions with the Soviet Union, while at the same time maintaining a commitment to NATO.

The reconstruction of Europe after the war led to the formation of the European Economic Community. The purpose of the EEC was to establish closer economic ties among Western European countries. Canadians feared that British entry into this organization would harm our trade with that country, and one object of our foreign policy has been to establish a special connection with the EEC to promote trade with that powerful economic bloc and thus reduce our dependence upon the United States.

One difficult aspect of our European foreign policy was the strained relations which developed between France and Canada when General Charles de Gaulle assumed power. De Gaulle cultivated a special relationship with the province of Quebec, a relationship that was dramatized by his public cry of "Vive le Québec libre!" in Montreal in 1967. Québécois nationalists responded warmly to the new attention being shown to them by the French government, and Canadian government officials began a concerted effort to assert the leadership of the federal government in our foreign relations. Subsequent leaders of France have ceased to openly advocate the independence of Québec and have acknowledged the central role of Ottawa in foreign policy.

1. Canada and NATO

(a) Historical Background

In a major defence policy statement in 1971, the Canadian government reaffirmed its membership in NATO and noted that "Canadian security continues to be linked to West Europe and Europe is still the most sensitive point in the East-West balance of power." The North Atlantic Treaty Organization was formed as a mutual defence pact in April 1949 to counter the threat of Soviet expansion in Europe. When the war ended, Russia maintained substantial forces in Eastern Europe and installed Communist governments in these countries. It threatened both Turkey and Greece and attempted to squeeze the Allies out of their administrative role in Berlin by blockading that city. A massive airlift overcame the latter move, but in 1948 the Soviet Union supported the illegal takeover of power by the Communists in Czechoslovakia.

The Western European countries had been shattered by the war, and in their weakened state they grew increasingly nervous about the spread of Soviet influence. Their solution to the problem was NATO. The original members included Britain, France, Belgium, Italy, Denmark, the Netherlands, Luxembourg, Norway, Portugal, Iceland, the United States, and Canada. The members agreed that they would enjoy collective security against any threat. The treaty stated that, "an armed attack against one . . . shall be considered an attack against them all." Their fears were further intensified when, in September 1949, the Soviet Union exploded its first atomic bomb.

(b) Structure of the Organization

The membership of NATO was expanded first in 1952 when Greece and Turkey, although removed from the North Atlantic, sought protection in the alliance from a common enemy, and again in 1955 when West Germany was admitted. Today there are 15 members of this organization operating under the North Atlantic Council in Brussels, and each member is represented by a special NATO ambassador. The chairing of the Council and the supervising of the day-to-day work of NATO are the responsibilities of a Secretary-General.

The military headquarters of NATO is also in Brussels. It is composed of the Chief-of-Staff of each member nation, with the exception of France, which is represented by a military mission. Four regional commanders report to the central NATO Military Committee: the Supreme Allied Commander, Europe (SACEUR), the Supreme Allied Commander, Atlantic (SACLANT), the Commander-in-Chief, Channel, and the Canada–United States Regional Planning Group. To date, the Commanders-in-Chief of SACEUR and SACLANT have been Americans, recognizing the contribution and power of that country in the alliance.

(c) Canada's Role

In the first eight years of participation, Canada spent more than 50 per cent of its defence budget in support of NATO. We sent an armoured brigade of 6500 troops and 12 fighter squadrons to Europe and made our Atlantic fleet available to SACLANT. After 1957, however, our enthusiasm diminished somewhat. Our economy was going through a troubled period. In 1958, we joined NORAD, thus turning our attention to North American continental security. In the early 1960s, there was a vigorous debate about the wisdom of equipping our NATO forces with nuclear weapons. Prime Minister Pearson agreed to do this, but his critics contended that he was simply adding to military tensions rather than contributing to peace and that Canada was merely a servant to American wishes. In 1967, as a result of Canadian pressure, NATO agreed to seek détente with the U.S.S.R. through diplomatic negotiations while at the same time maintaining its military strength. Positive steps in this area began in the early 1970s.

When Pierre Trudeau came to office in 1968, he committed himself to a reappraisal of our role in NATO. Supporters of the organization noted that it had halted

Ben Wicks, the London *Times*

"PARADE . . . ATTEN-SHUN!"

This cartoon appeared at the time that Trudeau announced the reduction of the Canadian troop commitment to NATO. What was this British newspaper's view of that decision?

aggression in Western Europe, provided military protection while European countries recovered from the war, helped integrate West Germany into the Atlantic community, and provided helpful Canadian diplomatic access to European countries with important economic and political results. On the other hand, many critics argued that our contribution was so small that we should pull out completely and devote our resources to more effective international purposes.

The Trudeau government decided to bring half of our forces in Europe home and to transform the role of the remaining forces from a tactical nuclear assignment to a specialized mobile and support role. In 1975 it was announced that Canada would increase its defence budget considerably in order to buy new equipment for our armed forces, including the most advanced battle tanks. Canada proceeded to purchase ultra-modern jet fighter aircraft to replace aging equipment. These actions indicated that we were willing to make up for the reduced quantity of our commitment with much higher quality. NATO was still to remain a cornerstone of our foreign policy.

(d) NATO's Internal Problems

In attempting to co-ordinate the defensive efforts of fifteen members, NATO has been plagued by many problems. Under President de Gaulle, France withdrew its military support from NATO command and compelled the headquarters of the organization to be moved from Paris to Brussels. De Gaulle resented American dominance in the organization and sought to develop France's own independent nuclear force. However, France did not withdraw completely from NATO and more recent French leaders have tended towards increased co-operation.

In 1968 fighting over Cyprus broke out briefly between Greece and Turkey and both countries threatened to withdraw from NATO. Only intensive diplomatic efforts and the arrival of a UN peacekeeping force in Cyprus quietened the situation.

Britain and Iceland also have had their differences, although not as serious as those between Turkey and Greece. However, relations are strained over the issue of Icelandic offshore fishing rights.

Economic issues have at times threatened the stability of the alliance. The Western European countries formed the European Economic Community, a customs union, in 1958, and after finally accepting Britain's entry in 1973, the group came to account for approximately 25 per cent of the world's trade. Whereas once the United States was the undisputed economic power in the Atlantic community, by 1970 it was experiencing severe trade deficits—that is, more money was going out of the country than was coming in. Inflation in the United States resulted in higher wages and prices in relation to European and Japanese goods. Although inflation was not solely an American problem, it and other financial difficulties created problems for the members of the alliance as they attempted to stabilize their relationships.

Another source of friction was the Arab oil embargo of 1973–74. At first, each of the European countries tried to secure its own oil supply under the best possible terms. Only after considerable pressure from the United States did the NATO countries resolve to present a united front to the Organization of Petroleum Exporting Countries (OPEC).

The most recent problem to confront NATO was the increasing strength of the Communist parties in Italy, France, and

Portugal in the mid-1970s. Although the party leaders claimed independence from Moscow, members of the alliance remained suspicious. Would the Communists guard military secrets and remain loyal to NATO's aims if they ever took power in these countries?

(e) NATO and the External Threat

The counter-alliance to the NATO forces in Europe and on the Atlantic and the Mediterranean is the Warsaw Pact, a union of nations under Soviet influence, formed in 1955. The membership consists of the Soviet Union, Czechoslovakia, East Germany, Poland, Rumania, and Hungary. Generally, the alliance is more unified than NATO because of the firm, direct control exerted by the Soviet Union. For example, when rebellions

took place in Hungary in 1956 and in Czechoslovakia in 1968, they were quickly suppressed by Soviet tanks.

The military forces of the Warsaw Pact countries outnumber those of NATO in virtually every category, and they are continuing to expand. By 1978, it appeared that the Warsaw Pact could win a war in Europe with conventional, non-nuclear weapons. American nuclear weapons seemed to be the main deterrent discouraging any acts of aggression on the part of the Warsaw Pact members. Some of the NATO allies in Europe, however, wonder if the United States would resort to the use of nuclear weapons to avoid takeover of European territory. Would the United States risk the destruction of major American cities to stop the advance of Soviet tanks into

Canadian Forces Photo

Delegates from the Warsaw Pact nations have been invited to observe NATO exercises like the one we see in the picture above. Why do you think NATO would extend such an invitation?

Western Germany? This is a troubling dilemma for NATO as the Moscow-backed alliance continues to build its armed forces at a steady rate.

(f) Pursuit of Détente

In the early 1970s both NATO and the Warsaw Pact made official noises in favour of détente, or a lessening of military tensions between the two sides. Formal talks took place over a period of seven months between late 1972 and June 1973. These and subsequent discussions have focussed upon two essential themes: reduction of arms, or Mutual Balanced Force Reduction (MBFR), and the free flow of people and ideas. The NATO countries have advocated the reduction of armed forces to a position where the forces on both sides are equal or balanced. However, the Warsaw Pact nations will agree only to limit military forces to their existing sizes, thereby leaving themselves in a superior position. Thus far, the two sides have been dead-locked over this fundamental issue.

Canada has taken a leading role in pushing for broader economic, scientific, technological, and humanitarian contacts between NATO countries and Warsaw Pact countries, with the hope that such contacts would reduce the fears and tensions that could result in war. Our negotiators have pressed the Warsaw Pact countries to open their borders for freer movement of people, particularly to reunite families; the Soviet bloc countries have done so to a certain degree.

Another area in which some agreement has been reached is in commercial relationships between the two blocs. For example, Muscovites are now drinking Pepsi-Cola and Torontonians are buying Russian Lada cars. But tensions still exist and it is not likely that they will be dramatically reduced in the near future.

Canada will continue to evaluate its role in NATO. For the present, however, our participation appears to be vital for our own security and for our political and economic relations with Europe, which are necessary if we are to achieve a balance in our relations with the United States.

(g) Statistical Confrontation

In February this year [1978], Britain's Labor government produced a report saying the Russians are spending between 11 and 13 per cent of their resources on the military. In comparison the U.S. spends 5.5 per cent of its gross national product on defence, NATO European members spend 3.5 per cent and Canada spends 1.8 per cent.

Says the British report: "Soviet forces have, in many areas, been strengthened in size and quality on a scale which goes well beyond the need of any purely defensive posture." It outlines the balance of forces, Warsaw Pact versus NATO in the Eastern Atlantic and in Central Europe. In surface ships the Communists have 1.2 vessels for every single NATO warship; in submarines the ratio is 1.4; there are 1.2 Communist troops to every NATO soldier; and 2.7 main battle tanks against each NATO tank.

Of the Soviet Union's 168 army divisions, 27 are in Eastern Europe along with 31 East German, Polish and Czechoslovak divisions. They could attack northern Germany from a "standing start" with less than 48 hours' preparation. NATO has about 25 divisions in West Germany, the most powerful being the 11 West German and five American divisions in the south. France, which has not participated in NATO formally since 1966, has two divisions in West Germany and another eight in France.

The bulk of Russian forces in East Germany are stationed on the North German

Plain, a 100-mile [1600 km] belt of rolling countryside stretching south from the North Sea. The terrain would allow rapid movement by a westbound tank force while providing ample cover to interfere with the anti-tank missiles on which NATO relies. NATO's vital air support could be severely hampered by the low cloud cover and heavy morning fogs that are common there in late fall and winter. . . .

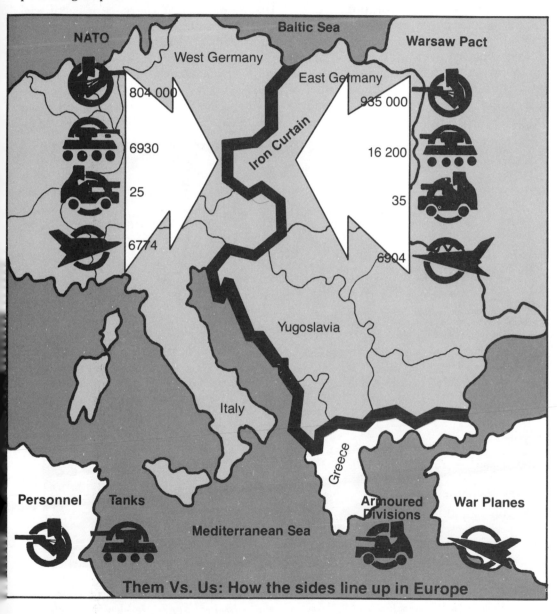

Them Vs. Us: How the sides line up in Europe

[William Lowther, "The Gathering Storm", *Maclean's*, May 29, 1978. © 1979 by *Maclean's* Magazine. Reprinted by permission.]

2. Canada, Quebec, and France

In 1967, President de Gaulle of France chanted "Vive le Québec libre!" while speaking to a crowd in Montreal. The Canadian government was infuriated with de Gaulle's behaviour, which it regarded as unwarranted interference by a foreign country in our domestic affairs. The following article provides an overview of this incident, which introduced a Cold War in Canadian–French diplomacy that has only recently started to thaw out.

The July 1967 visit of French President Charles de Gaulle to Canada is now regarded as an historic moment in the rise of Québécois national sentiment as well as in Franco–Canadian relations. On 1 November 1977, a day before the start of his official visit to France, Premier René Lévesque unofficially visited de Gaulle's tomb at Colombey-les-Deux-Eglises. There, on a hill overlooking the village, beside a giant cross of Lorraine, de Gaulle's wartime symbol, Lévesque wrote in the guest book: "Ten years later, accompanied I am sure by

Canadian Press

President de Gaulle is pictured here flanked by the mayor of Montreal, Jean Drapeau, on his right, and Premier Jean-Jacques Bertrand of Quebec on his left, just after his arrival in Montreal in July 1967. How did de Gaulle's behaviour during this visit affect both our domestic politics and our external relations with France?

the immense majority of Quebeckers, my homage to the memory of a great French-man and a great friend of Quebec. René Lévesque." "He was," Lévesque told waiting reporters, "probably the first political figure from outside who understood what was going on." The president would have been pleased, for such recognition was his hope and belief. In his valedictory, as he left Quebec for the last time in 1967, de Gaulle had said: ". . . quand je vous aurai quittés, . . . vous gardiez l'idée que la présence pour quelques jours de Général de Gaulle dans ce Québec en pleine évolution, ce Québec se révèle, ce Québec qui se décide, ce Québec qui devient maître de lui, mon voyage aura pu contribuer à votre élan."[1]

De Gaulle's contribution to the spirit of Quebecois nationalism and separatism is unquestioned, but were his actions of 1967 part of a deliberate pattern which he expected to impose upon history? Were his words premeditated or the intense emotion he felt after his journey from Quebec City to Montreal? There can be no definitive an-swer to these questions. President de Gaulle died before he completed his memoirs of the period, and his private papers remain inaccessible to researchers. Many Cana-dians, including Prime Minister Lester Pearson, believed that de Gaulle's action was premeditated. Others, including Paul Martin, the Secretary of State for External Affairs, disagree, and de Gaulle's colleagues seem to support Martin's belief.

In a forum on the subject of de Gaulle's action, held in Paris in February 1977, most who knew de Gaulle argued that "Vive le Québec libre!" was a sudden response to the separatists in the large crowd at the Montreal Hôtel de Ville who were chanting the same slogan. Having uttered the slogan, de Gaulle characteristically refused to retreat; and after the summer of 1967, de Gaulle's support for the "liberation" of Quebec was unequivocally expressed.[2]

De Gaulle's support for separatism had developed slowly although his sympathy for Quebec's "Quiet Revolution" was pro-found. In 1964 when Pearson and Martin visited Paris, de Gaulle publicly assured his guests that nothing should undermine the "heureuses relations" of France with "votre État fédéral." The French officials also showed great willingness to seek closer relations with Canada at this time. They promised to keep the Canadian embassy informed of any initiatives by Quebec which might affect Franco-Canadian relations. There are several explanations for the warmth of the reception the Canadian visitors received. The French expected the Canadians to buy their Caravelle passenger jet, and they in turn hoped to purchase Canadian uranium. Moreover, de Gaulle was mainly interested in Europe and in the breaking down of American "hegemony" over Western Europe. In the eyes of de Gaulle and other French observers of the Canadian scene, the separation of Quebec from Canada would lead to the annexation of English Canada to the United States. Such an increase in American power and territory was certainly not desired.

Within a year and a half, the situation had changed. The Canadians did not buy the Caravelle, and they refused to sell uranium to the French. De Gaulle's vision of an independent Europe based upon Franco-German alliance also vanished as Germany's chancellor was unwilling to share the vision. The French thus began to court the Third World and to challenge the Americans more directly. Canada's refusal to criticize the American action in Vietnam seems to have convinced de Gaulle that the Canadian federal government was controlled by American puppets. What, then, would be lost by Quebec independence?

Identifying Quebec's desire for an independent relationship with France as a step towards a "free" Quebec, the French encouraged the Quebec government to take more initiatives in foreign relations. The Canadian government was outraged, and it reiterated its claim that only the federal government could make treaties and was entitled to diplomatic representation abroad. Quebec could not speak for French Canada internationally; that was the federal government's prerogative. As the debate became more acrimonious, de Gaulle's centennial year visit was planned. Federal officials feared the impact of de Gaulle's visit, but they knew that cancellation of the visit would cause great controversy. De Gaulle came and their worst fears were realized. The English–Canadian press denounced de Gaulle's actions, but Claude Ryan, editor of *Le Devoir*, reflected the view of most French Canadians when he called the English Canadian reaction hysterical and unnecessary.[3] Canada had divided once again, and the results of this division are still unknown. The French return to North America had proven as difficult as their departure two centuries before.

1 The *Globe and Mail*, 2 November 1977; and Charles de Gaulle, *Discours et Messages: vers le terme Janvier 1966-Avril 1969* (Paris, 1970), 197.

2 A full report of the Forum discussion is found in *Le Monde*, 16 February, 1977.

3 See Gérard Bergeron, *Du duplessisme à Trudeau et Bourassa 1959-1971* (Montreal, 1971), 437-83.

[John R. English, "Charles de Gaulle in Canada", *Past and Present*, University of Waterloo.]

LE CANADIEN
COAST GUARD

How does this cartoonist view the role of de Gaulle in regard to Canadian unity? Do you agree or disagree? Why?

3. Canada and the European Economic Community

This reading provides a general description of Western Europe's most important economic organization and Canada's relations with it.

On December 10, 1976, Canadian officials had their first meeting with representatives of the European Economic Community under a new framework agreement that could mean long-term changes in Canada's international trade. What was the nature of the agreement? What does Canada hope to gain from it? And what is the European Economic Community?

Take the last question first. The European Economic Community (EEC) is a collection of countries in Western Europe that have reached an understanding on how their economies should interact. They have formalized this understanding by setting up an administration with power over the individual member countries. When the EEC was first organized under the Treaty of Rome (1958), its members were France, West Germany, Italy, Luxembourg, Belgium and the Netherlands. Since then, Britain, Ireland and Denmark have joined the Community, making it "The Europe of Nine".

The EEC is Europe's best-known organization, but there are other Community bodies. The European Coal and Steel Community (ECSC) co-ordinates the member countries' activities in these industries. The European Atomic Energy Community (Euratom) directs projects in atomic energy development. Strictly speaking, then, there are three communities, but the EEC is dominant and its operations are representative of the other two communities.

THE BEGINNING

The intent of those who established the EEC was the economic, monetary and political integration of the countries of Europe. The proposed first step in this process was to break down barriers to trade, and to encourage the flow of productive resources from country to country. A little history can help explain why this was an objective in the early post–World War II period.

To put it mildly, Europe was badly damaged by the war. All routine economic, social and cultural patterns had been virtually destroyed, and Europe was in chaos. National leaders saw these conditions as very dangerous to the peaceful growth of democratic government, which was their goal.

It was believed that political stability would be achieved, at least partially, through rapid reconstruction (through the Marshal Plan) and high rates of economic growth. Political unrest was seen as a by-product of unemployment and of a pessimistic view of future economic conditions.

Theory, as well as experience, indicated that international trade could provide a boost to economic growth. In addition, economic integration between European countries could lead to some degree of political unity. A sense of common purpose would strengthen resistance to 'the external threat', posed by the U.S.S.R. and its communist government. The early drive for European economic integration had many forms, born of the unique conditions of the post-war period. The EEC today reflects those early circumstances. But more importantly, it reflects response to changes in the individual countries of Europe, as well as in Europe's relations with the rest of the world.

REMOVAL OF TARIFFS

The cornerstone of the EEC is the agreement among its members to form a common market. As a common market, the Europe of Nine is joined in a customs union, which means that no tariffs are charged on goods traded between EEC countries. In addition, these countries charge the same tariff on all goods purchased from countries that are not members of the EEC. In matters of trade, the EEC behaves as one country, despite national boundaries and differing priorities among national governments.

The different strengths and weaknesses of the EEC countries form the foundation for its co-operation. The free flow of traded goods encourages competition among producers in all member countries. Competition is expected to result in the success of companies best suited to making a given product. In the absence of barriers to trade, success usually depends on the resources of the country in which the producer is located. With specialization and trade, the resources of each country can be used more effectively.

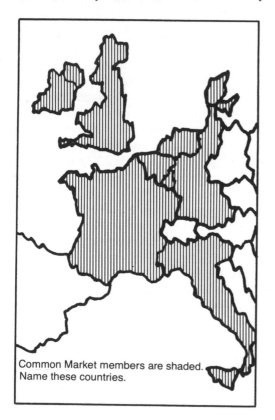

Common Market members are shaded. Name these countries.

Tariffs are not the only barriers to trade, however, and the EEC countries have taken steps to remove some non-tariff barriers. Efforts are being made to 'harmonize' member countries' legislation covering business rules and regulations, so that producers in all countries operate under the same conditions. Harmonization programs cover quality standards (e.g., metrication), combines legislation, labour migration and qualifications for professional (e.g., doctors) status across countries. Perhaps the most eye-catching attempt at harmonization is in taxation.

TAXATION POLICY

As can be seen clearly in Canada, tax policy is one of the strongest tools a government has for achieving its objectives. Taxation can be used to encourage some activities, such as business investment and to discourage other activities, such as alcohol and tobacco consumption. By their willingness to harmonize certain forms of taxation, the individual countries of the EEC have given up some freedom in the use of this tool to achieve national objectives.

Progress toward European tax reform is understandably slow. However, the EEC has stated its long-run intention to standardize rates and regulations for indirect taxes at least. The first step has been taken with the value-added tax (VAT)*. Under the EEC's VAT agreement, taxes charged against producers at each level of production may vary from country to country. However, within each country, VAT is charged on imports and domestic products at the same rate, and exports are not taxed. Eventually it is

*Value-added tax, which is not charged in Canada, is a tax payable at each stage of production. For example, on a loaf of bread, the farmer is charged VAT on the sale of wheat. the miller on the sale of flour and the baker on the sale of bread. Each process is charged according to the value of its contribution at that stage of production.

hoped that standard VAT rates will apply throughout the EEC.

The EEC also has a Common Agricultural Policy (CAP), which has major social, as well as economic, meaning. When CAP is working according to plan, tariffs and subsidies are used to standardize food prices among EEC countries, whether they import their food or produce it domestically. The CAP has helped European farmers resist competition from North American competitors, but, in some years, has resulted in much higher food prices for Europeans. However, since 1972, European food prices have been lower than world prices.

The running of CAP has been complicated by recent wide fluctuations in the value of EEC members' currencies. The price of imported food to the consumer depends not only on the asking price of the selling country but also on the exchange rate of the consumer's currency. With frequent large changes in the exchange rates of the EEC countries' currencies, the administration of CAP's tariffs and subsidies has been difficult.

ONE CURRENCY?

Broad fluctuations in exchange rates have also dampened hopes for a single currency in Europe. The founders of the EEC saw this as a brave step toward full European integration. Management of a single currency by one agency would mean the co-ordination of each country's monetary policies. Recently, however, domestic conditions, most notably rates of inflation, have varied widely from country to country. Programs undertaken to deal with individual domestic conditions have had varying effects on exchange rates. The dream of a single European currency is not taken very seriously at the moment.

In fact, one view is that the countries of Europe have given to the EEC as much of their individual power as they can be expected to give. This view sees future strength coming from an enlargement of Community membership (to include, perhaps, Greece, Turkey and Portugal), and from individual agreements negotiated as events dictate. Emphasis is put on the achievements of the Community to date. To expect further formal integration, in the form of monetary and political union, is to expect too much.

Whether or not this view of the future is correct, the EEC has made immense progress for Europe since 1958. The Europe of Nine is now the largest trading bloc in the world. As such, its friendship as an economic power has become very important to Canada.

CANADA AND THE EEC

Canada has done most of its trading with the United States, despite our historic trade ties with the Commonwealth. Canadians have become concerned about this close connection with the United States in other economic matters. The Canadian government saw three possible ways of changing our relationship with the U.S., as it stood at the beginning of this decade. One was to accept a much closer U.S. connection. This was seen as unacceptable. A second option might be to completely disconnect ourselves from the United States. This too was unacceptable—our economies are too closely tied, and geography alone encourages a close relationship. Canada's third option was to devote more effort to developing closer ties with other parts of the world, in order to balance our U.S. dependence. The choice of this third option led to the framework agreement mentioned at the start of this article.

Under this agreement, the Canadian government and the EEC are working together to identify opportunities for commercial and economic co-operation. To begin with, areas of mutual interest include non-ferrous metals, forest products, construction, telecommunications, and the nuclear/ uranium industries. The work of the Canada/EEC Joint Co-operation Committee will also include exchanges of information on fisheries, environmental protection, and joint ventures in third [world] countries.

Both parties have made it clear that the success of the agreement depends on the response of private business. The Joint Co-operation Committee will provide contacts and information on possible areas of partnership. But it will be up to the private sector to take advantage of the information provided.

This new agreement will not have much immediate impact on Canadian trade, or other international relationships. However, the success of the EEC over the past two decades offers many lessons in economic co-operation. The EEC has taken its place as an economic power, one that offers great potential to Canadian producers.

[Libby Joyce, "Strength from Co-operation", *Canada and the World*, March 1977]

Guidelines for Inquiry

1. At a recent NATO conference Canada agreed to increase its military spending in NATO over the next ten years.
   (a) Do you agree or disagree with this decision? Why?
   (b) How do you think increasing our NATO commitment will affect our policy of détente? Why?
2. (a) Why did de Gaulle decide to favour independence for Québec?
   (b) Through further research, find out how the position of the French government has changed since the death of de Gaulle. What reasons can you discover for these changes?
3. Discuss the advantages and disadvantages of developing closer ties with Europe.

Part Three: Canada and the Third World

What is the Third World? Generally speaking, Third World countries are former colonies, mostly non-white, and, in many cases, troubled by extreme poverty. (The First World is made up of the industrial democracies, mainly in the West; the Second World comprises the Communist states led by the U.S.S.R. and China.) The Third World countries have called for a "New Economic Order" to bring about a fairer distribution of the world's wealth in the face of an economic trend where the rich are becoming richer and the poor are becoming poorer.

Canada's involvement in the Third World has been principally with Commonwealth and Francophone countries in Asia, Africa, and the Caribbean. The Commonwealth is an informal association of 36 countries including the United Kingdom and former colonies which have achieved independent statehood. The only formal link between members is that they recognize the British sovereign as the "head" of the Commonwealth. A small Secretariat co-ordinates the periodic conferences and co-operative activities that characterize relations among member states. One of the questions frequently raised about the Commonwealth, however, is whether it is so informal that it is fundamentally useless in increasing our influence in international relations.

Just as the Commonwealth serves as a bond between the English–speaking countries of the world, the Francophonie serves as a bond between the French-speaking countries. The Francophonie, founded by General de Gaulle in 1962, embraces French-speaking countries (most of which are former colonies of France) with a common interest in sustaining the French language and culture.

As a bilingual nation, Canada wanted to obtain membership in the Francophonie as well as in the Commonwealth. De Gaulle, however, felt that only the province of Québec was legitimately entitled to membership, and that Canada as a nation should not be included. However, as a result of delicate negotiations and great perseverance, Canada was admitted into the Francophonie as a single member. The federal government was given the right to appoint the chairperson of the delegation, and Québec the authority to appoint the vice-chairperson; a provision was made for other provinces with significant French-speaking populations to be represented in the Canadian group.

Canada's main involvement in the Third World has focused on international economic development. As one of the wealthier nations in the world, Canada is in an economic position to give aid to countries that are in less fortunate positions. However, foreign aid can present a dilemma for the industrialized world. Conflict often exists between giving aid on a completely selfless basis—that is, where the donor country receives no beneficial returns for its assistance—and giving aid with strings attached, so that the donor nation ultimately will benefit from its own generosity. In addition, many questions must be considered when deciding what type of foreign aid we should give. What are our own employment and capital needs? Should we give outright cash grants or loans with long-term, low-interest rates? Or should we supply goods rather than money? To what extent should we require recipient countries to buy Canadian materials and skills with our aid? To what extent can we attempt to influence the domestic and foreign policies of these states? Or should we attempt to influence them at all?

1. Commonwealth Participant

(a) What is the Commonwealth?

WHAT IT IS: The Commonwealth of Nations is a free association of 36 self-governing nations. Queen Elizabeth II is the symbol of this free association and, as such, the head of the Commonwealth. The chief aims of the Commonwealth can be stated in two words: consultation and co-operation.

"The Commonwealth. Too ill-assorted by half to be called a proper family. Thirty-six disparate nations, old world, new world, third world, pedigrees all different . . . a *foster* family. The alumni of an empire. Resolved to keep in touch, not just for old times sake, but for the sake of something else that's not so easily expressed."

So spoke the narrator on a 1976 CBC program, The Family Prince. As he talked, Maori war canoes, Fijian dancers and Eskimo dog-sleds flashed across the television screen. Then, as a tight formation of planes zoomed by, he asked, "Why?" The answer came in the words of former Indian prime minister, Pandit Nehru:

"In the world today where there are so many disruptive forces at work . . . I think it is not a safe thing to encourage the breaking up of any association which may do good in the world."

To find out how the modern Commonwealth of Nations has developed, we must search our own history. The jumping-off point is Lord Durham's Report of 1840. Following the rebellions of 1837 in Upper and Lower Canada, Durham advised responsible government. All local affairs, including the taxing power, should be handed over to an elected assembly. The executive council (cabinet) should govern only as long as it had the support of a majority in the assembly. Nine years later responsible government passed its final test when the Governor General, Lord Elgin, signed the controversial Rebellion Losses Bill over violent Tory opposition.

The idea of self-government for the colonies began here and spread to other parts of the British Empire. In 1867, Canada became the first self-governing dominion. Australia achieved dominion status in 1901, New Zealand in 1907, and South Africa in 1909.

The first small step toward the idea of a Commonwealth came in 1897 with the Colonial Conference in London which was limited to those colonies that possessed responsible government. The Colonial Conference of 1907 decided that future meetings would be called 'imperial conferences' to reflect the rising status of the colonies.

The dominions made important sacrifices and contributions in World War I. When it ended, they were growing up and ready for more freedom. At the peace conference at the end of World War I in Versailles they insisted on separate representation. In the 1920s they expanded control of their external affairs by appointing their own diplomats in foreign countries.

By 1926 the Imperial Conference of that year was ready for a landmark decision. A communique from the conference defined Britain and the dominions as "autonomous Communities within the British Empire, *equal in status*, in no way subordinate one to another in any aspect of their domestic and external affairs, though united by a common allegiance to the Crown, and freely associated as members of the British

Commonwealth of Nations."

Responsible government, given its first nudge by Lord Durham, had at last grown to full independence and a free association under the crown. The Statute of Westminster, passed in 1931, put the legal seal on the decisions of 1926 and made the dominion parliaments the equals of the British Parliament.

Another result of the Imperial Conference of 1926 was a change in the status of the governors general. They now represented the British monarch only, instead of the British Government. In order to have direct inter-government contacts, therefore, Britain began to appoint high commissioners to the dominions. (The dominions, since before World War I, had already been sending their own high commissioners to London.) The commissioners did the same kind of job as ambassadors. From this two-way relationship with Britain the dominions went on to exchange high commissioners with each other. Most of them now do this, and the practice is another sign of the special relations which exist among Commonwealth countries.

World War II started the collapse of colonialism everywhere. As this went on, the Commonwealth showed it could roll with the punches. On August 15, 1947, two new nations, India and Pakistan, were carved out of the Indian subcontinent. A year later, Ceylon (since 1972, Sri Lanka) traded colonial status for independence.

India decided to become a republic* but still wanted to stay within the Commonwealth. A republic declaring allegiance to a monarch is an unlikely political animal, so the Commonwealth prime ministers came up with a new idea. From now on (this was in 1949), the British monarch would be a

*Republic. A government whose chief of state is not a monarch. Today, the chief of state in a republic is usually called a president.

symbol of the free association of its independent member nations and, as such, head of the Commonwealth, but not necessarily head of an individual member state. Thus members could adopt whatever constitution they liked.

Some, like Canada and New Zealand, kept the British monarch as their head of state. A few, like Malaysia and Swaziland, set up their own national monarchies, while many others chose to be republics. The word 'British' was dropped from the title and the association became simply the Commonwealth of Nations.

The Commonwealth carries some scars but has proved its hide is tough. During the 1960s, anti-colonialism swept Africa. New nations popped up at a dizzy pace and Commonwealth membership grew rapidly. All but three of the British African territories (Sudan, British Cameroons, Southern Togoland) decided to remain part of the family. The Commonwealth already had a multiracial face with the addition of India and Pakistan. Now, with African nations joining in numbers, it included every skin colour.

The new arrivals were unhappy with the apartheid (racial segregation) of South Africa. So many of them objected to the policy at the Commonwealth prime ministers' meeting in London in 1961 that South Africa decided to withdraw from the association.

Rhodesia has been another painful experience for the Commonwealth. When Ian Smith declared illegal independence in 1965, the Commonwealth began looking for ways to establish black majority rule in Rhodesia. A Commonwealth Sanctions Committee was established in 1966 to work along with the United Nations sanctions against Rhodesia (sanctions are trade boycotts against a nation). Financial help was given to Zambia, when its economy was damaged because it applied sanctions;

even Mozambique (not a Commonwealth member) received some aid for the same reason.

The Commonwealth has suffered a few losses apart from South Africa and Rhodesia. Burma chose to be an independent republic outside the association in 1948. Ireland left in 1949 because of strained relations with Britain. The most recent dropout is Pakistan, which left in 1972 because a number of Commonwealth countries recognized Bangladesh (formerly East Pakistan).

How does the Commonwealth work? What does it actually do? It isn't an organi-

Member Countries	Area (km²)	Population	Date of Membership	Capital	Constitutional (Monarchy or Republic)
Australia	7 682 300	13 548 000	1901 01 01*	Canberra	M (Br.)
Bahamas	13 864	218 000	1973 07 10	Nassau	M (Br.)
Bangladesh	144 020	76 820 000	1972 04 18	Dacca	R
Barbados	430	258 000	1966 11 30	Bridgetown	M (Br.)
Botswana	575 000	630 000	1966 09 30	Gaborone	R
Britain	230 609	55 930 000		London	M (Br.)
Canada	9 220 975	22 992 000	1867 07 01*	Ottawa	M (Br.)
Cyprus	9 251	639 000	1961 03 13	Nicosia	R
Fiji	18 272	588 000	1970 10 10	Suva	M (Br.)
Gambia	10 689	493 000	1965 02 18	Banjul	R
Ghana	238 305	9 600 000	1957 03 06	Accra	R
Grenada	344	107 000	1974 02 07	St. George's	M (Br.)
Guyana	210 000	800 000	1966 05 27	Georgetown	R
India	3 166 828	605 000 000	1947 08 15	New Delhi	R
Jamaica	4 243	2 080 000	1962 08 06	Kingston	M (Br.)
Kenya	582 600	13 800 000	1963 12 12	Nairobi	R
Lesotho	30 340	1 180 000	1966 10 04	Maseru	M (Nat'l)
Malawi	119 214	5 310 000	1964 07 06	Lilongwe	R
Malaysia	332 317	12 630 000	1957 08 31	Kuala Lumpur	M (Nat'l)
Malta	121 900	305 000	1964 09 21	Valletta	R
Mauritius	1 865	880 000	1968 03 12	Port Louis	M (Br.)
New Zealand	268 675	3 150 000	1907 09 12*	Wellington	M (Br.)
Nigeria	923 773	73 000 000	1960 10 01	Lagos	R
Papua New Guinea	475 300	2 489 000	1976 09 16	Port Moresby	M (Br.)
Seychelles	404	59 000	1976 06 28	Victoria	R
Sierra Leone	27 925	3 000 000	1961 04 27	Freetown	R
Singapore	602	2 280 000	1965 10 15	Singapore	R
Sri Lanka	65 709	14 270 000	1948 02 04	Colombo	R
Swaziland	17 400	527 000	1968 09 06	Mbabane	M (Nat'l)
Tanzania	952 003	15 000 000	1961 12 09	Dar-es-Salaam	R
Tonga	700	90 000	1970 06 04	Nuku'alofa	M (Nat'l)
Trinidad and Tobago	5 128	1 070 000	1962 08 31	Port-of-Spain	R
Uganda	236 860	11 200 000	1962 10 09	Kampala	R
Western Samoa	2 842	151 000	1970 08 28	Apia	R
Zambia	752 620	5 140 000	1964 10 24	Lusaka	R
Nauru (special member)	20	8 000	1968 01 31	Nauru	R

*Date on which dominion status was acquired.

zation, like the United Nations. It has no constitution, no flag, no voting, no headquarters. It is nothing more than an association, the kind you have in a grown-up family. Prince Charles, who will likely be the next head of the Commonwealth, puts it this way:

"The most important thing, I think, is that the whole idea of monarchy, certainly as far as the Commonwealth is concerned, is a family . . . that the strongest aspect of it is that you project the feeling that it's a family and that somehow everybody belongs."

Families have reunions and the reunion has become a Commonwealth custom. Nearly all the colonial and imperial conferences were held in London and were attended by prime ministers. From 1944 on, the gatherings were called Prime Ministers' Meetings and were held more frequently. By 1969, it was decided that this title too was out of date. In many cases presidents and kings, not prime ministers, were the political leaders of member countries. The 1971 conference in Singapore was called a Heads of Government Meeting, and this title has been used since.

At one time the meetings were held at irregular intervals but it is now the custom to hold a Heads of Government Meeting every two years. To stress the equality of the association, the get-togethers are no longer always in London. In 1973, the meeting was in Ottawa, and in 1975, in Kingston, Jamaica. The coming meeting from June 8 to June 16 [1977] once more goes back to London to honour the silver anniversary of Queen Elizabeth's coronation.

Though Commonwealth relationships are casual and informal, the association has had a Secretariat since 1965. The Secretariat's purpose is to act as a communications centre so that member governments can

talk to each other between meetings. It is an example of "the spirit of cooperation which animates the Commonwealth," and is staffed by officers from 20 Commonwealth countries. The money to run it comes from all member governments. It is a clearing house for the exchange of opinions in a friendly way. It also serves as organizer for the many Commonwealth institutions which work together to help member countries.

The Secretariat's first Secretary-General was a Canadian diplomat, Arnold Smith. Mr. Smith held the post for ten years; when he retired in 1975, he was succeeded by Shridath S. Ramphal, formerly Foreign Minister and Justice Minister of Guyana.

Because the Heads of Government Meetings are private, there is no need for playing politics. The talk can be frank and to the point, since it is off the record. However, there was worry for a while that the explosion in membership (from eight in 1948 to 36 in 1977) would destroy this intimacy. Leaders, it was feared, would not know each other as well, the goals of rich and poor countries would clash, and regional groupings might form.

Government heads set out to restore the old easy, flexible style at the Ottawa meeting in 1973. The friendly, informal mood established there has since been called the Spirit of Ottawa. This meeting was historic in another sense too. For the first time, the Queen, as the symbol and head of the Commonwealth, attended a Heads of Government Meeting outside Britain.

Commonwealth work goes on behind the scenes all the time. Senior government officials follow up the proposals made at Heads of Government Meetings. For example, in 1976 senior officials discussed how to establish a Commonwealth group of specialists on industrial cooperation. They believed that this should be done in a practical way and that such a group would also help other countries outside the Commonwealth.

The Heads of Government Meetings often refer ideas to specialist Commonwealth groups which must then carry the ball. At the Kingston meeting in 1975 they invited experts from member countries to suggest practical steps for closing the gap between rich and poor countries. The experts, chaired by Alistair McIntyre, Secretary-General of the Caribbean Community, presented an interim report entitled, "Towards a New International Economic Order" to the meeting of Commonwealth finance ministers in Georgetown, Guyana, in August, 1975.

A plan for industrial cooperation . . . a new international economic order. There's no hint here that the Commonwealth is interested only in its own narrow affairs. As a cooperating family it sees the urgent need for cooperation in the larger international family and offers what help it can.

The Commonwealth Youth Program got its start after a meeting in 1973 in Lusaka, Zambia. Once again, the emphasis is practical. Seminars and research in key problems such as unemployment, education, health, and urban adjustment are going on all the time, and three regional centres are training youth workers. A CYP awards scheme provides travel funds and cash for outstanding social and community projects organized by youth. One of the early winners was a youth group from Victoria, British Columbia. Canada contributes 30 per cent of CYP's budget.

Interested in writing? Try the Royal Commonwealth Society's annual essay competition for schools. Or, what about being a delegate to the Society's annual Student Commonwealth Conference sponsored by its Ottawa branch? You could represent Barbados, Ghana, Lesotho, or

even Canada in a model Heads of Government Meeting, discussing the latest Commonwealth and international issues.

And youth has its day too in the Commonwealth Games and the Associated Paraplegic Games. The eleventh Commonwealth Games will be held in Edmonton, Alberta, from August 3 to 12, 1978, and will involve more than 50 teams. Equality and sportsmanship are the two principles on which the Games are built.

The Commonwealth isn't all meetings of heads of government or high-level talks between cabinet ministers. Far from it. There is an unofficial Commonwealth which may be just as important as the official one. It owes its present health to a Prime Ministers' Meeting in 1965 which created the Commonwealth Foundation.

The Foundation's purpose is to link up professionals in all kinds of fields so that they can exchange ideas and everyone can benefit. Now there are over 200 nongovernmental bodies in constant touch with each other. Of the 50 Commonwealth conferences held in 1975, 23 were sponsored by non-government associations. Some, but not all of these, were financed by the Commonwealth Foundation. Though all members contribute to the Foundation's budget, Canada takes the heaviest load, assuming 32 per cent of the Foundation's costs.

The Commonwealth is, above all, practical. Its work goes on quietly, without fuss and horn blowing. The Colombo Plan, started way back in 1950, was the godfather of many another Commonwealth venture in self-help. Under the Plan, all members did what they could to help with the political and economic problems of South Asia. Non-Commonwealth countries in the area were invited to participate as well.

The Commonwealth Program for Technical Co-operation (CPTC) is another good example of down-to-earth cooperation. Everyone gives a hand, developing as well as developed countries. Canada, in 1975-76, gave $4 million to the CPTC, about 35 per cent of its total budget. The money goes to such things as technical assistance, export development, training, and education.

A lot more than money is involved, however. Developing countries do their bit by assigning their own experts in special fields to help other Third World countries; half of all specialists in the CPTC come from poorer member countries. The Program gives good value for its modest budget. In the year ending in June, 1975, it had completed, begun, or approved about 700 projects around the globe.

Although the Commonwealth has no charter, the Heads of Government Meeting at Singapore in 1971 did state the ideals of the association in a Commonwealth Declaration. In a preamble, the Declaration describes the rich variety of the membership. Association with the Commonwealth, says the Declaration, does not prevent members from being non-aligned, or from belonging to other alliances. It is a free association, based entirely on consultation, discussion, and cooperation. The Declaration then goes on to state a belief in principles which are shared by all. Briefly, they are these:

• International peace, and support for the United Nations as the best means of achieving it.

• Liberty of the individual and equal rights for all regardless of race, colour, creed, or political belief.

• A recognition that racial prejudice is a dangerous sickness and a pledge that each member will "vigorously combat this evil" at home.

• A belief that wide disparities in wealth are wrong. The Commonwealth aims at "their progressive removal" and seeks to raise standards of life in the developing countries "in a true spirit of partnership".

• International cooperation is essential for peace, tolerance, justice, and an improved quality of life. . . .

The Commonwealth is not a relic of the past, tied to a dead empire. It is, for the statesmen who have created it, an instrument to help shape the future, dedicated to the betterment of human beings everywhere. We should think of it as a living, changing organism, a force for good. Last year, Queen Elizabeth said she would like a special gift for her silver jubilee. The gift, she told her people in a Christmas broadcast, is reconciliation. "Remember," she said, "that good spreads outward, and every little does help. Mighty things from small beginnings grow . . ." it is in that spirit of reconciliation that the Commonwealth does its work.

[Charles A. White, "Commonwealth—A World-Wide Foster Family", *Canada & the World*, May 1977]

Duncan Macpherson. Reprinted with permission—the *Toronto Star*

This is a cartoonist's view of the 1971 Commonwealth Heads of Government Meeting. What attitude toward the organization does Trudeau appear to have had at that time?

(b) Case Study: 1977 Commonwealth Heads of Government Meeting

. . . For Trudeau, the London summit was a substantial success on three major fronts:

• He had insisted that Idi Amin's ruthless and bloody dictatorship in Uganda be condemned and it was.

• Hopes were raised substantially that the Commonwealth Games will take place in Edmonton next summer, though the African nations who have threatened a boycott will have the last word.

• And Trudeau received, in private talks, a

personal assurance from India's new Prime Minister, Morarji Desai, that he is committed to peaceful development of nuclear technology and that India does not plan further test explosions.

Trudeau did not dominate the conference, attended by 33 countries representing a quarter of the earth's people. On such issues as Uganda and southern Africa, says one Canadian official, "we wanted to avoid the impression of the white man pointing the finger from outside." For instance, while some Africans were arguing that Amin should not be criticized in absentia (Nigeria) and that censure might provoke him to further atrocities (Kenya), it was the persistence of leading Third World figures Michael Manley of Jamaica and Kenneth Kaunda of Zambia that carried the debate. Without naming Amin, the conference communiqué issued June 15 denounced the "sustained disregard for the sanctity of life" and the "massive violation of basic human rights in Uganda."

Trudeau did lead off the debates on the world economy and on human rights and he was particularly pleased that the attack on Amin lent credence to the parallel push for human rights in white-dominated Rhodesia, Namibia and South Africa. However, some saw traces of a double standard at a subsequent press conference when Trudeau was asked about an appeal by Kaunda to end "exploitation and plunder of Namibian wealth." Queried specifically about Falconbridge Nickel's operations in Namibia, he said his government had withdrawn Crown corporations from South Africa but "as far as the private sector is concerned, we are not interfering in any existing trade investment."

A revealing peek at the mysterious workings of the Commonwealth was provided during the negotiations over the Edmonton Games. For domestic consumption, partic-

ularly in Western Canada, Trudeau desperately needed a solution to the black Africans' boycott threat, which is based on New Zealand's continuing sporting ties with racist South Africa. But, New Zealand's flinty Prime Minister, Robert Muldoon, who came to power largely on pledges not to interfere with independent sports associations, was making his first Commonwealth appearance. Muldoon initially remarked that Trudeau should spend "less time with his African friends" and recognize that New Zealand's sports policy was not much different from Canada's—that is, federal funding is refused to teams that play against South Africans and Rhodesians.

But the night before the leaders flew off to Scotland, Trudeau turned up at a lively party hosted by the New Zealanders. In seclusion at the fabulous Gleneagles Hotel in Scotland—where the entire 700-acre estate was reserved exclusively for the Commonwealth party—the Canadian and New Zealand prime ministers found themselves working together on an informal committee headed by the charismatic Michael Manley. And by the end of a six-hour train ride back to London, the heads of government had initiated an accord drafted by the Commonwealth Secretary-General, Guyana's Shridath (Sonny) Ramphal. They agreed to take "every practical step" to discourage competitions with racist regimes—a phrase sufficiently vague to allow Muldoon to save face.

The spirit of Gleneagles, one of easy informality, also infused the 90-minute talk that Trudeau held with Desai, the remarkable 81-year-old ascetic who now rules the world's largest democracy. There was a substantive divergence in their approaches to global resources, with Trudeau submitting that industrialized nations can better share their riches when the economy is growing, Desai arguing that the pursuit of happiness through industrialization has become "a continuous, almost intolerable burden" on the world.

That exchange reflected the profound split between the haves and the have-nots. In 18 countries with more than 800 million people, average annual incomes are less than $500. Canada, in vivid contrast, is the wealthiest Commonwealth member, with a per capita income above $6,000. But Trudeau's enlightened message in London that Canadians are living beyond their means in a world of shortages has been greeted largely with indifference at home, where the debate over Quebec and the price of coffee are of greater concern. That indifference is intolerable in the poor countries where, as Desai put it, "it is not only a question of recovery, it is a question of survival."

There was similar intensity of feeling, again not reflected in Canada, on the key subject of black majority rule in southern Africa. Zambia's Kaunda cut to the heart of it all when he warned that unless there is a prompt transfer of power in Zimbabwe (Rhodesia) and Namibia, there will be an "explosion" that will make the "French Revolution look like a picnic."

The conference, as a result, recognized the inevitability of escalation in the arms struggle by liberation groups in southern Africa. But the consensus favored a negotiated settlement to remove the Ian Smith regime in Rhodesia, at the same time incorporating the radical phrases of the frontline black African states condemning South Africa for its aid to Smith. . . .

[Robert Lewis, "Canada: Local Boy Makes Good", *Maclean's*, June 27, 1977. © 1979 by *Maclean's* Magazine. Reprinted by permission.]

Guidelines for Inquiry

1. How did membership patterns of the Commonwealth change after the Second World War?
2. What is the nature and significance of Heads of Government Meetings?
3. Identify at least three different Commonwealth programs and describe the functions of each.
4. To what extent did the 1977 Heads of Government Meeting bear out Trudeau's comment that "we employ our energies in attacking problems, not in attacking one another"?
5. The Commonwealth has been attacked as an "old imperial hang-over, essentially powerless, and an unnecessary reminder of our British past that particularly annoys French-speaking Quebeckers." Do you agree with this? Why or why not?

2. Participant in the Francophonie

A comparison of Canada's involvement in the Commonwealth and in its French-language counterpart, the Francophonie, is a study in contrasts. In the first instance, she played a positive role in a long and gradual process; in the second, she was precipitated into an improvised activity in order to defend her national interests. The Commonwealth was moulded to suit her needs and concepts; the leaders of the Francophonie were opposed to them until she forced her way in, and almost literally sold her views to a majority of members. Such differences in beginnings notwithstanding, both associations offer useful links with large numbers of other peoples. They are also complementary, one serving as a channel to English-speaking countries, the other to French-speaking countries. Together they meet the requirement of the

Trudeau Administration that foreign policy must reflect domestic realities.

In one sense, the Francophonie was created as France's answer to the Commonwealth; in another, it was an integral part of General de Gaulle's *politique de grandeur*. As developed by President Senghor of Senegal, the concept is essentially cultural—a community of people whose attachment to the French language and culture transcends geographic, racial, and religious barriers. France, and Paris in particular, is its fountainhead. . . .

Prior to the 1960s, French Canadian contacts with other branches of the French cultural tree were limited largely to missionary activities in Africa and Haiti. However, the "quiet revolution" in Quebec in the early 1960s—in effect, the opening of Quebec society to modern influences—coincided with the emergence of a number of French-speaking nations in Africa. Less than three months after the election of the reform-minded Lesage Government in June 1960, Premier Patrice Lumumba was received with great enthusiasm and circumstance in Quebec, and ambitious plans were laid for Canadian assistance to the new Republic of the Congo. Individual Canadians and non-governmental organizations attempted to develop contacts with the former French colonies as well. But French control was still significant there, particularly in the field of education, and French officials in key positions made it clear that any Canadian interference in their areas of responsibility would be unwelcome. The Africans themselves were largely unaware of the "French fact" in Canada, and thought of it, if at all, as a quaint left-over of another age; what assistance French Canada could provide that they could not better receive from France, was far from clear to them. And within Canada, few structures had been developed

for dealing with new nations outside the Commonwealth. . . .

As the Province of Quebec developed its direct contacts with France in the early 1960s, French Canadians became aware of the potential advantages of being associated with the larger French-language community. This possibility was particularly appealing to Quebec separatists like Jean-Marc Leger, a journalist with strong Gaullist leanings, who wrote in *Le Devoir* in July 1963 that it was "humiliating, nefarious, and in the long run intolerable" for Quebec to pass through Ottawa in dealing with the French-speaking world. Thus, the claim to deal directly with France, which was already causing controversy between Ottawa and Quebec, was extended to encompass the entire international French-speaking community. This competitive situation served as a spur to the federal government, and in 1967-68 it sent a high-level mission to Africa that identified a series of projects which Canada might support. The cost of this aid was estimated to reach 100 million dollars per year by 1973, thus making the division of Canada's development aid between English-speaking and French-speaking countries roughly proportionate to the size of the two linguistic groups within her borders. In still another way, domestic realities had become a determinant of Canadian foreign policy.

The problem of developing the necessary instruments and procedures for dealing with French-speaking countries proved delicate and complex. In the first place, Canada had no tradition of contact with them, and no similar institutions, such as existed among members of the Commonwealth. Secondly, the French and Quebec authorities were working in collusion to negate the federal government's efforts in this regard. The natural vehicle of cooperation was the development agency that was then being discussed by the French and the French-speaking Africans, but it soon became evident that the original plan called for only Quebec to be admitted to it. In late 1967 the Canadian Government learned that Quebec was to be invited to have a delegation attend a meeting of the Conference of African and Malagasy Ministers of National Education, to be held in Libreville, Gabon, in early 1968; this was to be followed by a general meeting of the Francophonie later in the year to decide upon creating the agency. Citing the numerous precedents of Canadian delegations, composed in part of provincial representatives, taking part in international conferences on education and allied topics, the Pearson Administration sought an invitation to attend. In discussions with the Quebec authorities, Pearson even offered to name the Quebec Minister of Education as head of a Canadian delegation. However, no agreement was reached, and even a quick trip to Africa by Pierre Trudeau, as Prime Minister Pearson's personal emissary, failed to produce a mutually acceptable formula. In the end, only a Quebec delegation appeared in Libreville. In his last days as Prime Minister, Lester Pearson made a special effort to reach an understanding with Premier Johnson of Quebec on the composition of future delegations, even offering to restrict the role of any federal representatives to "aspects of those conferences which relate to the federal responsibility for international relations."[1] But when the next session of the continuing Conference of Education Ministers was held in Paris in April 1968, once again only Quebec was represented.

After Pierre Trudeau took office as Prime Minister, the Canadian Government took a noticeably harder line on this issue. However, even before he succeeded Pearson, the Department of External Affairs had expressed its displeasure with the Gabonese authorities by not appointing a new ambassador to that country when the incumbent's term expired; it also let it be clearly understood that diplomatic relations would remain, if not broken off, at least in a state of hiatus until the Gabonese recanted their position on Canadian participation in international meetings. Ottawa succeeded in obtaining an invitation from the former Belgian colony, the Congo Republic, to attend the next meeting in the series, in Kinshasa, presumably because French influence was less significant there. To the bemusement of the Africans, a Canadian delegation and no less than three provincial delegations appeared, each with its own flag to be flown in front of the *Palais des Nations,* and its separate identity within the conference. The Quebec delegation even included the popular *chanteuse,* Pauline Julien, a fervent separatist who became involved in a lively exchange with the leader of the Canadian delegation, Secretary of State Gerard Pelletier. The presence of the Ontario and New Brunswick delegations proved beneficial to Ottawa in the test of strength that ensued. Since the other national delegations were not willing to have Canada accorded several seats in the new agency, they urged the Canadians to settle their differences.

The actual founding of the agency, called the *Agence de coopération culturelle et technique,* took place at Niamey, the capital of Niger, in March, 1970. The French delegates lobbied hard to win support for separate Quebec membership, or at least associate membership, but most of the other delegations were unwilling to become involved in the power struggle, and eventually Pelletier, who again led the Canadian delegation, was able to win approval for a novel compromise formula. There would be only a single Canadian membership, it was agreed, but a spokesman from the Government of Quebec would automatically be vice-chairman of any future Canadian delegations, and representatives of the other Canadian provinces with French-speaking populations would be included as well. The Canadian Government would meet 33 per cent of the costs of the initial budget of the organization, France 45 per cent, and the other members the remainder. Jean-Marc Leger, the Canadian who until a short time earlier had advocated direct relations between Quebec and the Francophonie, was appointed the first Secretary-General, with headquarters in Paris. . . .

During a trip to Africa in March 1971, Mitchell Sharp was able to state that Canadian aid to francophone countries in that continent had reached the same level as aid to Commonwealth African countries. And the new French-speaking president of the Canadian International Development Agency, Paul Gerin-Lajoie, announced that he intended to give a still "greater impulse" to aid to French-speaking countries.[2] Whether or not this orientation of precious aid funds is the best possible contribution that Canada can make to the developing countries as a whole, it does meet two of Trudeau's requirements: it is an extension abroad of domestic policies, and it does reflect the bilingual and bicultural character of the country.

1 Letter to Premier Daniel Johnson. March 8, 1968. Quoted in *Federalism and International Conferences on Education.* p. 34. White Paper published by Secretary of State for External Affairs. 1968.
2 House of Commons. Standing Committee on External Affairs and National Defence. February 4, 1971. p. 11:6.

[Dale C. Thomson and R. Swanson, *Canadian Foreign Policy: Options and Perspectives,* McGraw-Hill Ryerson Limited, 1971, pp. 83-87]

Guidelines for Inquiry

1. In what ways did "the problem of developing the necessary instruments and procedures for dealing with French-speaking countries" prove "delicate and complex"?
2. Compare the nature and significance of Canadian membership in the Commonwealth with our membership in the Francophonie.

3. Canada and Development Aid Programs

(a) The Challenge

I believe that the great overriding issue in the world today is the gap between the rich and the poor nations, between the "have" nations and the "have not" nations. Here is a fundamental source of tension for the remainder of this century. Here is an issue which has profound economic and moral and political implications which we are not fully appreciating in our present policies or in our future plans.

In my judgment this great issue of our generation must be fully confronted in the next few decades. At the present time neither the processes of our government nor of our political leadership nor of public opinion have sufficiently comprehended the urgency and the magnitude of this problem. We are going to be guilty of a grievous failure in foresight if we do not recognize this issue with all its implications and if we do not seize fully the opportunity which exists for Canada as a middle power to play a leading role in the great adventure of world economic development.

We belong to a small group of privileged nations, comprising less than 20 per cent of the world's population, yet controlling among them more than 70 per cent of the world's wealth. Two out of every three people in today's world live in the less developed areas. Individual income in these countries is less than $130 a year. Life expectancy is under 30 years. 80 per cent of the people are illiterate. One out of every two persons does not have enough food. Some 8000 people die daily from one disease alone and countless other thousands fall victim to those great enemies of mankind, hunger, pestilence and disease. No schooling whatsoever is available for over 200 million children between the ages of 5 and 14. These facts are well known. However, they have not been sufficiently appreciated by many Canadians.

One of the most traumatic experiences for any member of one of the "have" nations, is to see at first hand the needs of a developing country. Any person who has had that experience can never be the same again. He must carry with him part of the burden of being involved inevitably in the greatest economic, philosophical, political and moral issue in the history of mankind. Just as in the late 19th and 20th centuries many of the nations of Western Europe and North America have developed individual national consciences from which have flowed the policies of the welfare state, so now in the remainder of the 20th century we must develop an international social conscience.

[J. Duncan Edmonds, "The Implications for Canada and U.S.A. of Interdependence", Sixth Seminar on Canadian-American Relations at University of Windsor, 1964. (pp. 217-18)]

(b) A View from a Canadian Dinner Table

Duncan Macpherson. Reprinted with permission—the *Toronto Star*

(c) Do We Help the People or Military Dictators?

EMERGING NATION TO SUPPORT

Trevor Hutchings, the *Financial Post*

(d) Foreign Aid: Do We Know What We're Doing?

For 3½ hours, my Bengali friend Rahat Uddin Ahmed and I bounced along Bangladesh's No. 1 Highway in a Land Rover. The early evening sky was black when he finally stopped in the jungle, 60 miles [96 km] out of Dacca. "Follow me," said Rahat as he hopped out.

We had gone scarcely 300 yards [270 m] along a winding trail before I found myself in a cluster of mud huts: the village of North Rampur. About 30 men stood waiting for us. They greeted Rahat warmly and led us into a small thatched hut where we sat on wooden benches under a single light bulb.

As I listened to their story, I was struck by their obvious respect and affection for Rahat. They had been landless peasants, broke, disorganized and despondent before he came to the village and persuaded them that they must work together and help themselves. Under his guidance, they pooled their labor and they were soon vaccinating cattle, raising chickens and stocking two fish tanks. In a year, their credit union had accumulated $1800, which was lent to three members to buy a little land. Then the group bought ten cows, later selling them for a profit. Now, they said, they were negotiating to lease one acre [0.4 ha] of land for each member of the co-operative to work, one third of the proceeds going to the landlord and two thirds to them.

Self-Financing. What I was hearing about was a new kind of Canadian aid in action. Since 1974, Rahat, a 32-year-old economics graduate, and some 300 other young Bengali men have been trained to go into the villages to teach the inhabitants new skills and organize them into self-help groups. And more are being trained, in classes of 20 at a time. Known as Proshika (a Bengali acronym for Leadership Training Center), this program was started by Raymond Cournoyer, Asian field representative for the Canadian University Service Overseas (CUSO). It is based on the simple but oft-ignored premise that the best kind of aid is aid that shows people how to do things better for themselves.

The Canadian government commitment, in funds supplied by the Canadian International Development Agency (CIDA), began with a modest $75 000, and will total $533 500. Eventually, Proshika will finance itself. During a recent six-week tour of Asia, I did not see a better use of Canadian aid.

At Cikembar in Java, close to the Indian Ocean, I visited a development center where Indonesian men and women are trained to become village "motivators." The selection program is rigorous. To prove resourcefulness, each volunteer must live for a month in a strange village studying the needs of the community with no support from the center. The director, Wimfred ("Ed") Laliseng, a 48-year-old, Dutch-educated Indonesian, explained why. "Everything depends on our motivators persuading the villagers that they are partners and friends. They have to be able to share the awful housing and sanitation conditions. They need patience, a clear idea of what a village needs, and, besides their own technical skill, some respect for the people's own way of doing things. They must not make them dependent."

This Indonesian program has so far resulted in the installation of water, health facilities and credit unions in 47 villages at a total cost of $763 000. Of that, CIDA has contributed $200 000, the United Church of Canada $63 689 and the Alberta government $63 543, with the balance coming from international church groups. Its example, and that of Proshika in Bangladesh, showed me that our aid dollars can be spent to very good effect indeed.

Poor Image. Yet foreign aid is in bad odor here at home. Many Canadians look upon our present foreign-aid budget of $1.1 billion as money pitched into a bottomless hole. When the government cut foreign-aid spending from 0.56 down to 0.46 per cent of the Gross National Product last year—thus letting it slip even farther below the UN target of 0.7 per cent—not a protest was heard.

One reason, of course, is that some spectacular blunders have given foreign aid a poor image. In 1974, CIDA bought a fishing vessel for $175 000 to be used in a training program in Colombia. It cost CIDA $628 000 to refurbish the vessel and convert it into a school and research ship. Various tests then demonstrated that the vessel was unstable when fully loaded, and Colombia turned down the gift. It was subsequently determined, however, that the tests themselves had been faulty. Even though a parliamentary committee learned that CIDA was not to blame, since another government agency had handled the testing, a public impression of incompetence resulted.

In another case, construction of a

poultry-processing plant in Dominica had to be abandoned because a local group had built a plant in the time between CIDA's approval and the arrival of the equipment from Canada. In Indonesia, I saw the footings of a CIDA bridge that had collapsed; a Canadian supervisor was not empowered to overrule what he knew was the bad judgment of a local engineer using weak material.

On balance, such horror stories distort public appraisal of CIDA, which manages some 1000 projects in 70 countries at any one time. More serious has been the 1976 report of the Auditor General of Canada, who criticized the unsatisfactory state of financial control in CIDA. Moreover, the imperial style of Paul Gérin-Lajoie, president of CIDA from 1970-77, who was welcomed by Third World presidents with more acclaim than foreign ministers usually receive, was a lightning rod for critics at home. MPS were irritated, too, by such excesses as an expenditure of $20 544 for the preparation and printing of one of his speeches.

CIDA's new president, career diplomat Michel Dupuy, has set out to improve the agency's credibility and management. Gone are the lavish luncheons and first-class flights. In his first four months, Dupuy informed parliamentary committees that he had already implemented more than half of the Auditor General's recommendations and, according to the Deputy Auditor General, Rhéal Chatelain, CIDA now has in place a "well-balanced plan" for tightening up its management.

Cart before the Horse. Underlying public skepticism about the management of our foreign-aid effort, however, is the largest question of all: Does Canadian aid, by and large, help the people it is intended for? Some projects have motivated people to take development into their own hands

and Canadian aid policies are moving, slowly, in this direction. But the decisions about big CIDA expenditures are still heavily influenced by the idea of benefits for Canada. Of the more than $963 million paid out in 1976, 49.59 per cent went into direct country-to-country aid, mostly capital equipment made in Canada; and two thirds of this bilateral aid *must* be spent in Canada. For the rest, 43.25 per cent is spent through United Nations agencies, leaving, after administration and research expenses, less than seven per cent for agencies such as CUSO, which specialize in foreign aid that gets right to the people.

Unfortunately, the priorities of government spending—of both the receivers and the donors of foreign aid—are still the big, glamorous capital projects, such as electronics equipment, generators, planes and trains. One of our major gifts to Bangladesh, for instance, has been an $8 million satellite station which plugs Bangladesh into international telecommunications. Yet there are only 90 000 telephones in that land of 80 million people, and only 38 000 TV sets. What's worse, 81 per cent of the population lives in villages that do not have adequate water supplies by Western standards. The cart has clearly been put before the horse.

Even food aid fails to be of real help. About three quarters of Canada's $47 million aid to Bangladesh is in the form of food. The food goes principally into the national food chain where it is sold, not given away, to ration-card holders. This system provides subsidized food on a priority basis to the military, police and civil servants first, then to the five major urban areas and finally to the rural areas. Sister Pauline, a Holy Cross missionary in a clinic near Chittagong, told me, "We often see malnourished mothers who have never heard of food aid."

Admittedly, this sale of donated food is

supposed to provide funds for development. But these funds are actually becoming absorbed in the Bangladesh government's struggle to pay the interest on its debts. Besides, food aid is proving to be counter-productive, since it weakens the incentive of the developing country to invest in its own agriculture. The current Bangladesh budget allocates only 19 per cent of government resources to agriculture; investment in industry is given a higher priority.

Disaffected Donors. Throughout the Third World, the fruits of development have gone to the minority in the upper economic levels, bypassing the vast number of villagers. The faster growth rate of the industrialized countries is resulting in a widening of the gap between rich and poor nations. The global statistics are startling:

- There are 460 million people who are malnourished, 200 million people unemployed, according to some estimates, and already dangerously overcrowded cities are growing twice as fast as the population as a whole.

- A large percentage of the people in the developing world do not have water within 100 yards [90 m] of their dwellings, and more than half have no electricity.

- Despite some progress with birth control, half the world's population today is under the age of 20; the additional people who will demand food, housing, jobs and services in the next two decades are already among us.

Too many people delude themselves that foreign aid can cure poverty. When it fails to do so, they question the validity of CIDA programs. But disaffection is no reason for us to turn our backs on these desperate problems. Nor are we excused by the fact that Canadian aid can only supply a fraction of the needs of the underdeveloped countries. We have a moral obligation to do what we can.

So what *can* we do? We can certainly insist that Canada follow policies genuinely designed to help close the gap between rich nations and poor. We must face the fact that aid by itself will *never* be an adequate response to the global poverty problem. There will have to be world trade and monetary reforms that enable developing nations to earn more from the export of their own commodities.

A serious effort to help Bangladesh, for example, would concentrate not on donating food but on improving the conditions for jute productivity, where the country's development future lies. I went to the largest jute mill in the world, employing 30 000 workers, and saw the overwhelming importance of jute to the Bangladesh economy: 85 per cent of foreign-exchange earnings are derived from jute, a fiber used for sacking, carpet-backing and a growing number of consumer products. But, unless Western nations reduce discriminatory quotas and tariffs that protect synthetic products, the prospects for jute are not good.

On a more human scale, we can help the people themselves by insisting that more of Canada's aid go to community development of the kind that I have seen in Bangladesh and Indonesia. We could even *reduce* our foreign-aid budget and spend it more effectively if a higher proportion went to train people to take their lives in their own hands.

Rahat took me to a second Proshika village where I met 15 young men who had started a co-operative with a total of $6. They bought fish to stock an unused ditch, and later sold the fish for a profit. Then they started a common vegetable garden and, with the profits, enlarged the garden and started a new fish pond. I asked one man what the co-op meant to him. "I know I am better off," he replied. "I do not deal with moneylenders any more. I feel more secure."

Small accomplishments, yes. But as I looked into his face and saw his pride and hope—which I had certainly not seen in the slums of Dacca—I felt exhilarated. I felt that I was looking at a liberated man, who would have a chance to realize his potential in life. Foreign aid doesn't need to be big. And it can be beautiful.

[Douglas Roche, "Foreign Aid That *Really Works*", *The Reader's Digest*, February 1978. © 1978 Reader's Digest Magazines Ltd. Reprinted by permission.]

Guidelines for Inquiry

1. What is your reaction to Edmonds' plea for an "international social conscience"? Explain why you feel the way you do.
2. In two separate columns, note the advantages and disadvantages in Canadian aid programs that Douglas Roche identifies in his article. What policy proposals does he suggest to improve this situation? What do you think of Roche's proposals?

Part Four: Canada and the United Nations

In the first years of its existence, the United Nations formed the cornerstone of Canadian policy. The international ideals of the UN were consistently put forward as worthwhile Canadian objectives. Immediately after the Second World War, Canada was one of the world's wealthier nations compared to the war-torn countries of Europe and Asia. This relative wealth gave us influence internationally and an ability to make sizeable contributions to the United Nations and its agencies in the forms of money and personnel. Dr. Brock Chisholm, for example, was the first Director of the World Health Organization, and Dr. Hugh Keenleyside was the first Director-General of the United Nations Technical Assistance Administration. One of the principal United Nations agencies, the Food and Agricultural Organization, was founded in Québec City, and the head-quarters of the International Civil Aviation Organization was established in Montreal.

One of Canada's main roles in the United Nations was to act as a mediator between Western Europe and the United States, and between the Western powers and the non-aligned nations. (The latter group tended to trust us because we had no history of imperialism.) However, our greatest international reputation was associated with United Nations peace-keeping operations. In fact, as Secretary of State for External Affairs, Lester Pearson was instrumental in establishing UN peacekeeping forces. Canadians generally looked to the United Nations as a promising instrument for seeking world peace and international co-operation.

Today, however, the United Nations no longer plays this key role in our foreign policy. European and Asian nations recovered from the war and re-established their powerful positions internationally, and so Canada lost some of its prestige. In the 1960s many new Third World countries joined the UN and began to dominate the General Assembly and the specialized agencies. As a rich, industrialized country, Canada's views did not always correspond to the views of these members. And by the mid-1960s it became evident that as a peacekeeping agency the United Nations was not as effective as it was once hoped it could be, and so again Canada's role was diminished.

What role does the United Nations currently play in our foreign policy? What role should it play? In this section, you will be asked to review our participation in this organization and to evaluate the extent to which we should make a commitment to it in the years ahead.

1. The UN Record in Perspective

The following two articles provide an overview of the record of the United Nations since its founding. The first article concentrates on the UN's political role in attempting to avert war; the second article reviews some of the economic and social programs which have been undertaken by the UN.

(a) The United Nations as a Political Instrument

The United Nations is not of central importance in its individual members' search for peace and security. The hope for world order and stability has, in fact, rested for years on the effectiveness of the "balance of power" theory.

What relevance, then, has the United Nations in today's international political scene? What were the original objectives of the nations which founded the United Nations Organization out of the ashes of World War II? Has the UN lived up to its expectations?

FOUNDING OF THE UN

As the last days of World War II were drawing to a close in 1945, the leaders of the victorious Allies became more and more determined that the destructiveness of that war should never be repeated again. They reasoned, much like the leaders of the Allied forces after World War I, that they had fought hard to win peace in the world, and they didn't want to see it disrupted again.

The actual United Nations organization began as a wartime coalition among the major political and military powers fighting against Germany and Japan. A conference, held in 1944, among these powers set out the main guidelines for a body which would be an international forum for the solution of any future conflicts between members of that body.

It was not until the following year, however, that representatives of the victorious powers met in San Francisco. They adopted a United Nations Charter (set of rules) to create a permanent UN organization.

THE CHARTER

The Charter relies heavily on American ideas and political experience. Basically democratic in nature, the Charter gives each nation in the General Assembly one vote, regardless of the size or power of that nation. It also gives veto power to the nations making up the permanent Security Council. This is the power of one nation to reject a decision made by all the others.

The Charter, in fact, closely follows certain aspects of the U.S. Constitution. It provides for a separation of powers between the executive (Security Council), the legislative (General Assembly), and the judiciary (International Court of Justice). It is also closely related to the Covenant of the old League of Nations which had been set up at the end of World War I, but with one major difference. The League was set up mainly as an agency to enforce the peace treaties that followed World War I. However, the UN was set up primarily as a forum where grievances could be expressed, disputes could be discussed peacefully, and, where necessary, action could be taken on behalf of the UN members, acting as one.

The principal UN organizations set up under the Charter were the General Assembly, the Security Council, the Economic and Social Council, the Trusteeship Council, and the Secretariat. Of these, the Assembly and the Security Council had the greatest authority.

The Assembly, the general legislative body, was empowered to discuss and make recommendations only. These recommendations would be passed to the Security Council. Over the years the United Nations has come in for a lot of criticism, most of it over inactivity. How often do we hear people say, "Why doesn't the UN do something about it"? The fact is the General Assembly is powerless to take any action. It is merely a forum for debate and the making of recommendations. It is *not* a parliament of nations with the power to make or pass laws.

The Security Council was, in the view of the founding nations, to be given the "primary responsibility for the maintenance of international peace and security". It was to be composed of 11 members, five of which (the U.S., U.S.S.R., Britain, France, and China*) were to be permanent members of the Council. The other six were to be elected each year by the General Assembly from within its own ranks. This year [1977] Canada becomes one of the elected nations in the Security Council.

In 1965 the Charter was amended to increase the size of the Security Council. Now, in addition to the five permanent members, 10 non-permanent members are elected to serve two-year terms.

The Charter gave the Council the authority to settle international disputes by peaceful means. If peaceful methods failed, and the peace of the world seemed to be in danger, the Council was given power to use any means, including the use of armed forces supplied by member nations, to stop any state from breaking the peace.

SECURITY COUNCIL PROBLEMS

A glance at the history of the world since 1945, however, will show just how effective this has been. There have been a series of wars in various parts of the world which the Security Council has seemed unable to prevent. Why?

The permanent members of the Security Council were given the right of the veto. This, in effect, made the Council powerless to deal with infractions of the Charter made by the great powers, or by nations who were under the protection of the great powers. If any of these powers felt their interests were threatened, the veto would simply be used, ending discussion of the matter in the Council.

Hence, although having far less power than the Council, the General Assembly came to exercise more and more influence, at least in public. In fact, the General Assembly is the one forum where the

*Until 1971, Nationalist China. After 1971, the People's Republic of China.

smaller powers can state their case and receive publicity for their cause. Indeed, some member states seem less concerned today about the cause of world peace than they do about the opportunity to make speeches promoting their own self-interests.

We mentioned at the beginning that the United Nations is not a major consideration for member states' search for peace and stability. Why is this? One reason has to be the inability of the great powers to trust the UN's ability to guarantee peace, or to protect the national interests of those same powers. The great powers have, in effect, hedged their bets by forming military alliances (NATO, ASEAN, the Warsaw Pact). These organizations provided the balance of power so necessary for world stability in earlier years. The Charter specifically forbids the involvement of member states in the affairs of other members. However, over the past few years we have seen Russian tanks in Hungary and Czechoslovakia, American troops in Lebanon and the Dominican Republic, and British and French armies in Egypt. We won't even mention the Vietnam episode.

After all this, it would seem that the UN is going the way of its predecessor, the League of Nations. However, there are many nations that feel that the UN, perhaps in a reformed state, is the answer to the problems of the world. Foremost among these is Canada.

CANADA'S CONTRIBUTION

Canadian diplomats at the UN have always been respected for their support of a strong body to promote world peace. Canada maintained a relatively independent position in balance of power politics in the years after 1945. As a result, we have been able to speak at the UN on a level that has been relatively free of national self-interest.

The best example of this is the Suez Canal crisis of 1956. Egypt was threatening to close this vital water highway over the question of ownership, and the whole problem of Arab-Israeli relations. As the Canal was owned by various governments, principally Britain and France, these nations did not want to see Egypt take over control. Britain and France, therefore, decided to send troops into Egypt to guarantee their interests. When Israel attacked at the same time, matters came to a head.

Lester B. Pearson, then Minister for External Affairs for Canada, proposed to the UN that an "Emergency Force" be established. This was to be made up of troops from member nations, which would move in and patrol the danger area, eliminating the threat of a major war. The Canadian idea was accepted, and the UN peace-keeping force, including a Canadian unit, was established in Egypt.

Canada's role at the UN has, in fact, been an extension of her normal diplomatic aims of international peace. The UN provides her with a forum in which she can preach the advantages of cooperation among the people of the world. . . .

The United Nations was never intended to become a "super-state" or federal government for the world's nations. It was established as a forum for discussion among the world community in order to prevent another major, world conflict. In this, it must be judged to have been successful.

Although "brush fires" occasionally break out, such as in the Congo and Middle East, no major fight involving the great powers has erupted. This may have been because of UN action. It may be that the balance of power among nations is such that another world war is unthinkable. However, if we did not have an international meeting place to blow off steam and seek answers to political problems, the world could have seen much more military activity than it has since 1945.

[Bryan Shaw Rogers, "Forum for Debate", *Canada & the World*, March 1977]

BUSY BASEMAN

Why is Canada portrayed as a "busy baseman"? To what extent has Canada continued this "busy" role?

(b) The United Nations as a Social and Economic Instrument

The UN is involved in a wide range of activities that affect the citizens of the world directly. But it is this aspect of the UN's work that is often overlooked.

WORLD HEALTH ORGANIZATION

The World Health Organization (WHO) is the UN agency concerned with health matters. This organization recently announced that, due to its world-wide campaign, smallpox has totally disappeared. For centuries this disease has been the cause of hundreds of millions of deaths. It was finally defeated by an international program of research, education and vaccination run by the WHO. It is worth noting that during the last seven years the WHO spent $83 million in its battle against smallpox. During the same seven-year period, $675 million was spent on developing the F-16 fighter plane.

The WHO operates a warning system to signal the onset of flu epidemics. It also conducts research into cancer, blindness and heart disease and runs specific health-related projects in many countries.

In addition, April 7 each year has been designated World Health Day. The theme this year [1977] is "Immunize and Protect Your Child". In his message, the Director General of WHO says that "vaccination has been outstandingly successful in many countries in controlling diptheria, whooping cough, infantile paralysis and measles, while tetanus and the childhood forms of tuberculosis are also becoming rare diseases—in part due to vaccination". . . .

COMMUNICATIONS AND THE UN

The list of UN agencies is almost endless, and space will not permit going into detail on them all. It is, however, worthwhile looking at a few of them more closely.

What about civil aviation? The International Civil Aviation Organization (ICAO) is headquartered in Montreal. Did you know that? If there were no standard rules covering the operation of aircraft that cross international boundaries, utter chaos could result. ICAO sets the rules and ensures that governments and airlines stick to them.

One of the major questions now facing ICAO is how to handle aircraft hijacking. No final solution has yet been found. However, ICAO recommendations to increase airport security have dramatically reduced the number of hijackings. There are many other aspects of international aviation with which ICAO is concerned. . . .

The Universal Postal Union (UPU) regulates the operations, at the international level, of post offices. Under agreements negotiated through the Union, a letter posted in one country, with a stamp of a certain value, will get to its destination in another country.

The International Telecommunications Union (ITU) sets the frequencies for all international telecommunications by radio, telephone, television or satellite. In some Canadian cities you can already dial direct to Paris, London, Rome, Geneva and other cities. The complications that are arising in more sophisticated fields of communication are in need of regulation and control.

WORLD CONFERENCES

In many fields where the UN works, cooperation is absolutely essential. The UN, however, felt that a number of wider questions, where international cooperation was not so obviously essential, needed close examination by member countries. These issues also needed to be brought to the attention of the ordinary citizens of the world. So, the UN organized a number of big, noisy, well-publicized world conferences on special themes. The first of these was in 1972, in Stockholm, when the United Nations Conference on the Environment was held.

Out of the conference grew the United Nations Environment Program (UNEP), with headquarters in Nairobi, Kenya. The first Executive Director of UNEP was a Canadian, Maurice Strong. UNEP was organized because it became apparent to the nations of the world that the protection of the environment required action beyond the power of any single country.

During 1974, the UN called two conferences—one on population, in Bucharest, Romania, and another on food, in Rome.

The Bucharest conference took some quite unusual positions on the so-called population explosion. The conference rejected the idea that the poor countries alone had to reduce their population growth, while the rich could go on as they were. The conference brought out the facts that: (a) as a country becomes more advanced its rate of population growth drops, and (b) a child born in a rich country consumes food and other resources at six times the rate of a child in a poor country.

The conference said that we ought to concentrate on two issues, both of which were fairly simple to state but, of course, quite complicated to apply. First, the world should concentrate on improving the lot of the citizens of poor countries. Second, rich countries should take steps to control the rate at which they consume food and other scarce resources. To be honest, the world is trying to achieve the first, but we in the rich countries are not doing too well in limiting our consumption.

The Rome Food conference picked up on this theme. In 1974, it was estimated that 480 million people were going to bed hungry each night. Despite the fact that the world produces enough food to feed all the people it has now, and perhaps many more, a large number are living at close to starvation levels. Even greater numbers are malnourished, and millions are actually starving to death each year.

Efforts were needed to bridge the distribution gap between the food produced and the people who needed to be fed. This conference came up with a relatively new approach. A $1 billion fund (The International Fund for Agricultural Development) was set up to help countries achieve self-sufficiency in food production.

The food conference also confirmed what the population people had found. The real job of the UN and its agencies was to undertake co-ordinated programs to reduce the chronic poverty under which so many of the world's people were forced to live.

NEW INTERNATIONAL ORDER

These three conferences reinforced what was becoming increasingly apparent. The world had become so closely interdependent that no one country, or group of countries, could live in isolation from the world's problems. Many of these problems were, in fact, beginning to affect the lives of the citizens of the richest countries.

The United Nations is now trying to achieve the new international ideas that these conferences have called for. The New International Economic Order is now the main, long-term, priority of the UN. In fact, the latest thinking calls it the New International Order, because the proposed reshaping of relationships between countries goes far beyond purely economic matters.

As we go further into the new era of international interdependence and cooperation, the UN will have an even more important role to play. This role could be made easier if more people understood more about the UN and if more countries tried to see the world in less nationalist and self-interested ways.

[Geoffrey Grenville-Wood, "The Other United Nations", *Canada & the World*, March 1977]

Guidelines for Inquiry

1. Why is the United Nations no longer "a major consideration for member states' search for peace and stability"?

2. Why was 1956 a high point in Canada's role in the United Nations?

3. To what extent is it reasonable to expect the UN to put a stop to all warfare in the world? Can you suggest any ways in which the UN's power could be strengthened?

4. What contributions has the UN made in battling disease and aiding international communications?

5. What are the implications of the New International Economic Order for you and your family's life style?

United Nations

The permanent site of the United Nations was established in New York City in 1952; the picture above shows the General Assembly. How has Canada's role in the UN changed since the 1950s? Why?

(c) Has Canada Failed the United Nations?

"When the Suez crisis blew up in 1956," said the ex-RCAF pilot, taking a thoughtful pull at his beer, "Lester Pearson had this brilliant idea of sending in a UN emergency force, so the word went out that Canadian troops were going to stand between the Israelis and the Egyptians. As far as the military were concerned, troops meant infantry, and they looked around for the outfit in the best state of readiness. That turned out to be the Queen's Own Rifles, stationed in Calgary. So we spent a week flying these guys from Calgary to Halifax, so they could get on a troopship and go to Egypt. Then Nasser heard that an outfit called the Queen's Own was coming to save him from the Israelis. Hell, for Nasser the British were worse than the Israelis; there was no way he was going to have the Queen's Own standing on guard for him, so we spent another week transporting the poor buggers back to Calgary. It turned out to be the best thing we could have done. The infantry would have gone wandering out into the desert, and God knows what would have happened. Instead, we sent technicians on the logistics side, transport people, communications people, and they did a hell of a fine job. It was the one function Canada could provide better than any other small UN nation, and that was the beginning of our reputation as peacekeepers. Every time I think about the UN, I think of that. Whenever anything works out, it's about one-third mistake and two-thirds dumb luck."

The pilot went to Egypt with the UN, ferrying troops, supplies and bureaucrats around the area. (He saw the Canadians get back at Nasser: the radio beacon at the airport on the Egyptian side of the Sinai was coded ER, for Elizabeth Rex. The Egyptians never tumbled.) He developed a healthy respect for the United Nations, but he also saw its major problem at first hand: every country supports the world body until its own interests are at stake: then it is outraged by "outside interference". The British were not happy with the UN role in Egypt. "When we went to the U.K., we nearly got into two fights just on the bus ride to our hotel. It was so bad we cut off our UN arm flashes, and left them off all the time we were in England."

I went to see the ex-pilot in Ottawa (he is now a federal civil servant) to find out how somebody who actually worked for the United Nations, risked his life for it, felt on the eve of its thirtieth anniversary. He was as puzzled, as hesitant, as on-the-one-hand-this-on-the-other-hand-that as the experts. And no wonder. The UN is under severe scrutiny. Even its best friends are beginning to voice doubts. Allan MacEachen, Secretary of State for External Affairs, says, "I ask myself, as you are obviously asking yourself, just what validity has the UN?" A senior UN official says: "There has been a growing sense of unease . . . we have been through some bad patches." Andrew Brewin, an NDP Member of Parliament and staunch internationalist, says: "As long as I do a good job on my constituency work, the voters will forgive me for being involved with the UN." Tory MP Doug Roche worries about "the poor people of the world being used as poker chips in the UN game," and his colleague David MacDonald worries that "nations are turning their backs on the UN, making their own rules." All these people are staunch UN supporters. Behind them, newspaper headlines thunder HYPOCRISY TEARS UN APART and CANADA MUST REEXAMINE ITS UN ROLE. . . .

If the United Nations has an obvious task, it is to prevent war, but since its founding in 1945, there have been more than 50 wars, ranging from comparative brush fires to major conflagrations—in Yemen, Korea, Vietnam—that rival World War II. If we have escaped World War III it is probably not because of the UN but because of the balance of terror between the superpowers. In fact, in some of doomsday's close calls, the Security Council has stood around as helplessly as the rest of us, waiting to see if there would be a tomorrow after all. The Cuban missile crisis in 1962 was strictly, in the phrase of the day, an "eyeball to eyeball" confrontation between the United States and Russia. Vietnam was kept off the General Assembly agenda for decades, and it is fair to ask: what is the use of a group pledged to keep peace on earth when it can't even find a war that has gone on for years?

People used to talk of the UN as the "world's policeman," a phrase as dated as the zoot-suits and jitterbugs of the era from which it sprang. The organization has tried to bridge the gap between its mandate and its record by denying its mandate. In a speech to correspondents on September 15, Secretary-General Kurt Waldheim noted, "There is a widespread expectation . . . that when hostilities break out in the world the United Nations should meet, order them to stop, and peace should thereby be restored. When this does not happen, there is a feeling that the United Nations isn't working." The UN charter begins with the words, "We the people of the United Nations, determined to save succeeding generations from the scourge of war . . ." Article One gives it the right and duty "to maintain international peace and security," and chapter seven spells out how the job is to be done. It is a measure of the UN's futility that its ranking officer assumes that these grand phrases are so much wasted paper.

In fact, only once has the UN assembled an army to enforce an order of the Security Council. That was in Korea, and it came about because the Russians, who would have vetoed the move, had pulled out in a huff. The more usual pattern is for two nations to hurl themselves at each other while the UN meets in emergency session and then, when their fury is spent or the issue has been decided, an international brigade is called in to help clean up the mess. The UN has not been able to stop the arms race, nor to prevent the proliferation of nuclear arms, and the nuclear safeguards of its International Atomic Energy Agency are a rich joke. . . .

Well, then, what does it do? It works on problems. It tries to control world population, to catch up with pollution, to succor the refugees of the wars it cannot halt, the famines it cannot prevent. It seeks to expand world food supplies, to divide the world's spoils more evenly between the rich and poor, to settle future development of resources now beyond human reach. But does anyone think the world's population problem has been licked, or that we are gaining on famine or pollution, or that the tremendous gap between the rich and the poor is getting any narrower?

The UN works splendidly in the abstract. It can agree that there should be no war, no starvation, no discrimination. It is less successful in coming to grips with reality. Stern resolutions denounce white racism in South Africa, but glide past black racism in Uganda. Colonialism is deplored in Angola, but not in Czechoslovakia. Terrorism is outlawed in theory, and the arch-terrorist Yasser Arafat, is invited to address the assembly, to show his guns and strut his stuff. China is at last admitted to the UN, on the theory that it is better to talk to regimes, even if their policies are repugnant, than to shut them out in the hostile cold; then South Africa is suspended and Israel is threatened with expulsion. We have an agreement on the peaceful uses of outer space, but none on who can fish off the coast of Newfoundland.

"The UN is not a world government," says external affairs minister Allan MacEachen, and Saul Rae, Canada's UN ambassador, adds: "If the major powers do not choose to use the UN, there is little it can do to interpose itself. . . . If country X decides it wants to do something on its own, this body may not be able to do much about it." Since 1945, we seemed to have developed a world full of country Xs.

When the charter was being planned, World War II was in its final throes, and the notion of an agency charged with keeping peace, and able to do so, sounded attractive. But soon the cold war had broken out, the veto power in Security Council votes was being used to stifle international action and power blocs were hardening at the edge. In 1948, Prime Minister Louis St. Laurent acknowledged: "We are fully aware . . . of the inadequacy of the United Nations at the present moment to provide the nations of the world with the security they require. . . . It is possible for the free nations of the world to form their own closer association for collective self-defense." That "closer association" turned out to be the North Atlantic Treaty Organization, which was balanced by the Warsaw Pact. Soon the world was dominated by blocs, pacts, alliances and economic communities, all lined up into opposing camps, all exercising independent options, all undercutting the failing functions of the UN. As power ebbed from the centre (if, indeed, there was ever any real power there), it became normal to bypass the UN on major issues, including the issues of peace and war. Tales of massacre, of starvation, of repression, were brought to New York and trotted out before the assembly, not in the belief that the injuries would be redressed—who

could believe, after Hungary and Biafra and Bangladesh and Vietnam?—but to register a complaint. If the UN could not be a policeman, it could be at least a tattletale.

In fact it became a bureaucratic convenience. "If there were no UN, "said a senior official of the Secretariat, "it would be necessary to invent one." The UN provides a debating forum (with certain subjects taboo), a meeting place, a convention bureau. Next year, there will be about 10 000 meetings held under UN auspices in New York, Geneva, Vienna and other regional centres around the world. That is a powerful amount of talking, but what will be the result? Probably, agreement to hold 11 000 meetings in 1977.

Never mind, say its supporters, the real hope for the UN lies in the emergence of the "new majority". With the decolonization of Africa—in which the UN played a strong supporting role—and the formation of the Arabian power bloc, control of the assembly (though not the Security Council) has passed to the Group of 77, a shifting alliance of developing countries that contains anywhere from 102 to 110 nations. (If the UN can't even count, how can it run the world?) Each country has an assembly vote, so that Qatar, population 115 000, and Red China, population 800 million, have an equal say in the parliament of the UN. One result is that the demands of the emerging peoples are given more prominence. Another is that it is harder and harder to take the assembly seriously. Does Idi Amin of Uganda really represent the last best hope of mankind? What are his credentials anyway? Do we really believe that the raucous, unstable coalition of new leaders—most of whom have told us how much they hate us and all we stand for— are worthy custodians of our future?

When I put this to a top UN official, he replied, "Ah, but was Canada ready to

Canada's Contribution to the UN, 1945 to end of 1974

Canada's total contributions to the UN from its founding represent less than one-half of 1 per cent of this year's Gross National Product, or about 22 per cent of this year's federal government estimates.

I Regular UN Budget		$ 76 163 000
II Peacekeeping		41 387 000
1. Mideast Border Patrol, 1956-67	$ 5 910 000	
2. Congo, 1960-64	9 187 000	
3. Cyprus, 1964-present	21 029 000	
4. UN Special Account, 1965-66	4 307 000	
5. Mideast Buffer Zone, 1973-present	954 000	
III Social and Economic Programs		416 145 000
1. UN Development Program	114 371 000	
2. Special Fund	21 378 000	
3. Technical Assistance	26 376 000	
4. Refugees	38 182 000	
5. UNICEF	27 875 000	
6. Relief and Works Agency	30 253 000	
7. Training and Research Institute	540 000	
8. Education, Training, South Africa	299 000	
9. World Food Program	127 513 000	
10. Family Planning Assistance	7 052 000	
11. Congo Fund	4 489 000	
12. Racial Discrimination Committee	8 000	
13. Trust Fund for South Africa	40 000	
14. Drug Abuse Control Fund	550 000	
15. Miscellaneous	16 215 000	
16. Environment	1 004 000	
IV UN Agencies, Organizations, and Unions		100 560 000
1. International Labour	15 309 000	
2. Food and Agriculture	20 216 000	
3. World Health	28 078 000	
4. UNESCO	17 673 000	
5. International Civil Aviation	5 732 000	
6. Intergovernmental Maritime	225 000	
7. International Telecommunications	3 598 000	
8. World Meteorological	969 000	
9. Universal Postal Union	744 000	
10. International Atomic Energy	5 234 000	
11. GATT	2 690 000	
12. Miscellaneous	92 000	
V UN Association in Canada		373 000
		634 628 000

assume a world role in 1867?" No, it was not. Nor was it allowed to. Our apprenticeship in foreign policy lasted decades. For the new nations, it lasts minutes. Perhaps that is both inevitable and just, but it makes the rich and established nations—including Canada—nervous, and reinforces the natural tendency to support the UN when we agree with it and to say to hell with it when we don't.

Last year, the new majority rammed through a belligerent resolution calling for a new economic order in the world. The debate was bitter, brutal and rude. This fall, the subject was raised again, in a more conciliatory mood, at the seventh special session, and at the end of 16 days of forceful but reasoned debate, a resolution was passed aimed at "redressing the economic imbalance" in the world. The passage of that resolution, and the contrast between last year's snapping and braying and this year's intelligent debate, produced a mood of euphoria at the Secretariat in New York. "At last," said a senior UN official, "we have had a breakthrough. We are committed. The UN is working."

Perhaps he is right, although it is hard to hear, in the windy phrases of that 16-page resolution, the heralds of a bright new dawn, or to accept, in the face of the futility of so many previous UN resolutions, that this one can be made to work. For, if the UN has been less than successful, the fault appears to lie not in its structure, charter or language, nor in the lack of talent—it has talent to spare—but in the fact that none of its members have put enough into it to make it work—in money, in men, in sovereignty, in commitment.

Canada is one of the foremost members of the UN. We provide 3.18 per cent of its general budget. We are eighth on the list of contributors, just behind Italy. We are also generous in our support of the special

agencies, social and economic programs, and peace-keeping. But our total contributions to the UN, from its founding, come to more than $630 million, less than one-half of 1 per cent of this year's [1975] gross national product. The general budget for the UN in 1974-75, $606 million, is about one-fifth of what the Ontario Ministry of Health spends annually. Our permanent mission to the UN in New York consists of 14 officers, and we have another 11 stationed in Geneva: you could run the whole thing with a LIP grant.

By contrast, Canada will be shoveling out $742 million this year alone in official development assistance, mainly through the Canadian International Development Agency. External Affairs Minister MacEachen's explanation is that "we still have national objectives and our foreign policy reflects these." Much of our bilateral aid is tied to trade agreements, much of our food aid is designed to help our own farmers as well as its starving recipients, much of our technical aid provides more jobs in Canada than overseas. (For example, our bilateral aid in 1974-75 comes to $339 million: we are exporting $1.5 billion worth of goods for sale to the main recipients.) We can get cash or credit or glory by making direct gifts with strings attached rather than turning the aid over to the UN, who might squander it on the undeserving and wreck our balance of trade.

Like any other nation, Canada is more interested in the profits of charity than its end results. In fact, at the Law of the Sea Conference where Canada has been holding out for control of an economic zone reaching out hundreds of miles into the Atlantic (and to hell with the poor nations who think benefits beyond a coastal zone should be shared), we argued that it was in the world's interest for us to grow even richer. Or, in the jargon of our experts, "self-interest requires the betterment of Canada and it implies a world order which is favorable to or compatible with such betterment. The promotion of national self-interest fuses the planes on which government objectives are pursued." The robber barons of an earlier age would have recognized the sentiment, although they weren't much for the fusing of planes. It is the old "trickle down" theory of Victorian economics: as the rich get richer the quality of crumbs dropping off the table to the bums beneath improves with each passing year. And Canada is, always has been, one of the good guys at the UN. . . .

Perhaps there are changes in store. Perhaps, as one Canadian who has worked with the UN off and on since the heady days of its first meeting in San Francisco says: "There is a lot of movement under the surface. More and more subjects are being brought here for discussion. Things that might have caused a war some time ago now cause a debate instead. Procedures are being installed, regulations are building up. We're not going to abolish war or poverty overnight, but maybe, over the years, we'll kind of nibble them to death."

Perhaps. It seems just as possible, however, that it is the UN that is being nibbled to death. After all, there doesn't appear to be much time: the world's problems—in resources, energy, development, pollution, population, poverty and war—seem to have and to meet them we have an organization none of us really believes in with little money and less clout. We want to rebuild the world with Plasticine and a tack hammer, and we are unhappy because the job is taking some time.

One alternative is to step up our commitment to the UN, to give it a chance to function. In theory, that is an attractive option, but it raises the vexing issue of whether we believe the new majority is any smarter or more trustworthy than the old one. In theory, we are all for more equal sharing of power and resources, but what will we do if the assembly throws Israel out, or demands more open immigration policies, or insists that we share the land we have with others who have none? Are we willing even to face these questions, much less to leave the answering to others?

The other alternative is to back off, not by quitting the UN, but by going our own way outside it. Give money, but not votes. File the resolutions, but go about our own business.

Our tendency is to talk in terms of the first alternative, and to act in terms of the second. Canada expressed grave reservations about the New International Economic Order when it was being discussed in 1974, then worked hard to make the special session work in 1975. We are, officially, pleased with the results and committed to more equal sharing. We are also standing firm on the law of the sea. We are, as always, all for the United Nations, but no closer than ever to trusting it with real power. And the hell of it is, who knows if that's a good thing or bad?

[Walter Stewart, "The Thirty-Year Flop", *Maclean's*, October 20, 1975. © 1979 by *Maclean's* Magazine. Reprinted by permission.]

Guidelines for Inquiry

1. With which of Walter Stewart's alternatives do you agree—to "step up" our commitment or to "back off"? Why?
2. (a) What should be the role of the United Nations in Canadian foreign policy?

(b) Explain your view of Canada's role in the United Nations in relation to the factors influencing our foreign policy outlined in Part One of this unit.

Part Five: Canada and China

After the victory in 1949 of the Communist forces in the Chinese Revolution, Canada continued to recognize the defeated Nationalist government, which had retreated to the island of Taiwan, as the rightful government of China. The Canadian government considered giving diplomatic recognition to the People's Republic of China at various times, but it did not actually do so until 1970. The Korean War in the 1950s and strong American pressure during the 1960s were two of the factors that delayed this step.

In the early 1960s Canada negotiated sizeable wheat sales to China. In addition, the Chinese were becoming more concerned with threats from the Soviet Union and the possibility of détente between that country and the leading Western nations. China feared isolation and knew that Canadian recognition might enhance its chance for membership in the United Nations and open up contacts with the United States through Ottawa.

After twenty months of negotiations the two countries exchanged diplomatic representatives. For Canadians, the exchange with China created the opportunity for trade and cultural relations with a fascinating country that houses 25 per cent of the world's population. The opening up of diplomatic relations also served to help Chinese-American relations. Gradually, more contact developed between the United States and China, and in 1979 these two countries established diplomatic relations with each other.

1. Canadian-Chinese Relations Since 1970

EARLY CONTACTS

Diplomatic recognition immediately produced benefits in the area of trade. Two weeks after it occurred, in fact, Canada negotiated a contract with China for what was at the time the largest wheat deal ever made. In the spring of 1971, barely two weeks after the first Canadian Ambassador to China, Ralph Collins, assumed his duties in Peking, the first Canadian Government trade mission arrived, headed by Jean-Luc Pépin, then Minister of Industry, Trade and Commerce.

According to Mr. Pépin himself, the purpose of the mission was essentially economic, and in September 1971 he submitted an extremely positive report to the Standing Senate Committee on Foreign Affairs. At the end of the trip, the Chinese leaders assured the Minister that they would continue to consider Canada as China's main supplier of wheat. This meant, above all, that China would call on Canada first as a favoured partner when it wanted to import wheat. This promise has never been broken. In 1973 the Peking Government concluded an agreement with Canada to buy 224 million bushels [6097 t] of wheat over the following three years.

The ministerial missions that followed the one headed by Mr. Pépin also gave cause for satisfaction. In August 1972, the Secretary of State for External Affairs, Mitchell Sharp, opened in Peking the largest trade fair that Canada had ever held abroad. However, Mr. Sharp's large delegation was clearly political and served to counterbalance the previous mission of the Minister of Industry, Trade and Commerce. These visits, as well as subsequent ones by Cabinet Ministers Donald Macdonald and Jeanne Sauvé, helped to weave a network of contacts, agreements and exchanges that enabled Canada to benefit from a full range of international relations with China.

Prime Minister Trudeau's visit in October 1973 put the finishing touches to these efforts. The warm relations established with China's leaders, and the results achieved, made this trip a great success, both for the Prime Minister's personal prestige and for Canadian diplomacy. A trade agreement was signed that included a most-favoured-nation clause, conveyed the intention of both sides to increase the number of their exchanges and established a joint trade committee that would meet annually. Another result of this trip was that the Canadian and Chinese Governments reached an immigration agreement allowing citizens of the People's Republic of China to come to Canada as part of a program of reuniting families. It is interesting to note that China has never made this kind of agreement with any other country. Since 1973, 2000 Chinese have taken advantage of this agreement.

Though it is obviously impossible to list all the achievements that might give Canada reason to rejoice, it may safely be said that, in general, diplomatic recognition of the Peking Government has benefited Canada. While it is difficult to evaluate actual political gains, one can see that there has been a steady increase in the volume of trade since 1970, except for the last two years. There has also been a very significant increase in scientific, technological, cultural and sports exchanges. The question now is whether it is possible to do more in the future. For almost two years relations between the two countries seem to have had difficulty in finding their "second wind". The factors that have led to this situation, on both the Canadian and Chinese sides, have to be examined.

The enthusiasm reflected in recent

Peter Bregg, Photographer, Canadian Press

Canada officially recognized the People's Republic of China in 1970. On a state visit to China in 1973 Prime Minister Pierre Trudeau and Premier Chou En-Lai toasted Canadian–Chinese relations. To what extent did Canada's new relationship appear to affect American foreign policy? How has this situation presented a difficult challenge for us?

reports of Canadian missions to China would seem to represent something of a change from the realism of the early Seventies. This seems to be especially true in the realm of trade. A simple perusal of the annual figures for trade with China since 1970 shows that there was a significant imbalance between exports and imports that was very much in Canada's favour. Even more interesting is the fact that, from 1961 to 1969, grain sales always represented more than 96 per cent of all

Canadian exports to China, and in some years the figure was as high as 99.9 per cent.

Since the time of Canada's diplomatic recognition of China, both parties have tried to correct these imbalances by considerably increasing Chinese imports to Canada. In spite of these efforts, officials of the Department of Industry, Trade and Commerce have estimated that it would still be possible to increase Canadian exports. In fact, when Jean-Luc Pépin returned from China, he stated that the

Chinese wished to export a wide variety of products but were not insisting on objectives such as the balancing of trade, equal increases in exports or anything of that kind. A working group was set up to coordinate action taken to tap the potential of the Chinese market. Its object was clear: to increase trade between the two countries, and Canadian exports to China, by selling a wider range of products. These efforts were not fruitless, since the proportion of grain exports has decreased progressively since 1971, with a cyclical exception in 1975, and Canada has sold more aluminum, timber products, potash and telecommunication and railway equipment.

However, despite the Chinese Government's assurances that it could easily buy from Canada manufactured products it now obtains elsewhere, orders have still been given to other countries. For example, though China presented the Canadian Government—and even Prime Minister Trudeau, during his visit in 1973—with the prospective purchase of "turn-key" factories, this kind of project does not yet seem to have materialized. In 1975 China imported 11 full units from Japan, West Germany, Britain, Italy and the United States.

TRADE DECLINING

Over the last two years for which figures are available (1975-1976), the volume of trade between Canada and China has decreased. Several factors may serve to explain this downward trend. The main ones seem to be the Chinese Government's need to reduce its trade deficit and, even more important, China's growing interest in its political and trade relations with Western Europe. China demonstrated this interest when it decided, in May 1975, to establish diplomatic relations with the Commission of the European Communities in Brussels. Canada and the United States

inevitably suffered because of this new direction in Chinese foreign policy.

There has also been a change in the kinds of product imported by China during this period; the proportion of agricultural products has decreased, while that of machinery and equipment has increased. These factors partly explain why the Peking Government has preferred an annual rather than a long-term renewal of the 1973 agreement on the purchase of Canadian wheat. Experts on China's economy estimate that sales of wheat should continue for several years, and Canada will undoubtedly remain a favoured partner. However, the sums involved in these sales and the obvious imbalance in trade between the two countries may prevent a further development of trade relations. It is, therefore, just as important for Canada to know what China does not want to buy as it is for China to know what it can sell.

CANADIAN INITIATIVES

Although Canada, a "second world" country in Chinese political terminology, seems to rank very high in the estimation of the Peking Government, it cannot expect to supersede countries the Chinese leaders feel are politically and economically more important. This may partly explain why the initiative has nearly always come from the Canadian side.

One of the characteristics of Chinese diplomacy is that it is not averse to being courted. To take a simple example of this well-known fact, since 1970 the Chinese have sent the Minister of Foreign Trade, in 1972, and a deputy minister, in 1976, to visit Canada—whereas no fewer than nine Canadian ministers and prominent Parliamentary figures—including, in 1973, the Prime Minister—have visited China during the same period. This fact may seem inconsequential but the constant necessity of rekindling friendship by means of the symbolic gestures that still greatly influence the Chinese must be appreciated. It is also interesting—almost amusing—to note that the federal government spent a quarter of a million dollars on restoring the home of Dr. Norman Bethune in Gravenhurst, Ontario. Although before that time probably at least 95 out of 100 Canadians had never heard of Dr. Bethune, who died for the revolution in China in 1939, he is a well-known figure to all Chinese citizens and since his death has become a symbolic bond between China and Canada.

It is somewhat unjust to reproach the government for too much initiative in its diplomatic policy in this area, since all the countries that have relations with China know that this is the price they have to pay in order to establish links with a socialist country in which traditional behaviour is still firmly anchored. The very obvious strengthening of cultural relations during the last two years seems to suggest that the time has arrived for individuals, groups and provinces to become more involved than the countries themselves. Perhaps the Canadian Government should allow others to take more responsibility for launching programs under the agreements it has concluded. The attempt to involve China in a network of transnational relations would be futile, but it is possible to make China more aware of the complex reality of Canada.

The efforts that have been made in the cultural and scientific fields seem to have produced very positive results, as is shown

"THERE'S SOMETHING I'VE BEEN MEANING TO ASK YOU"

M. R. Tingley *London Free Press*

What is this cartoon saying about Canada's relations with China in 1970?

by the success of the Shanghai Ballet's visit to Canada and the Canadian Brass's tour of China. Since China seems to be giving priority to modernization and scientific research, it would be advisable to encourage exchanges in these fields. . . .

[Gérard Hervouet, "Sino-Canadian Relations: Resignation and Optimism", *International Perspectives*, November/December 1977, Department of External Affairs]

Guidelines for Inquiry

1. (a) Describe the nature of Chinese-Canadian relations between 1970 and 1975.
   (b) How has the situation changed since 1975? Why?
2. What is the significance of Dr. Norman Bethune to Chinese perceptions of Canada?
3. What are the potential future directions for relations with China?

Part Six: Canada and Nuclear Disarmament

Canada participated in the original Manhattan Project, which was responsible for the technology of the first atomic bombs; these bombs were detonated in 1945. The effects of the A-bomb were devastating, however, and the Canadian government decided not to produce atomic or thermonuclear weapons. Instead, Canada has specialized in the development of nuclear power as a source of energy, using our own nuclear device, the CANDU reactor. In the meantime, however, those nations already possessing nuclear weapons have increased their arsenals. Today these countries possess the nuclear capabilities to destroy the world's population 100 times over. As the years pass, more and more nations are acquiring the necessary technology to produce nuclear weapons; and as the number of countries with nuclear weapons increases, so do the odds that some country will decide to use them.

As one of the leaders in nuclear technology, Canada is faced with a serious dilemma. Our CANDU reactor is a potentially significant source of export revenue for us as the world seeks to offset its dependence on oil and gas for energy through the use of nuclear power. However, instead of using the reactor for energy purposes, some countries may use it for nuclear weaponry. In 1974, for example, India exploded its first nuclear device, and there is little doubt that a CANDU reactor was used to develop the nuclear weapon. The Canadian government was extremely critical of India's actions, and embarrassed for having

The picture above shows the first atomic bomb. This was the type of bomb the United States dropped on Hiroshima during the Second World War. What role did Canada and Canadians play in the development of this bomb? Do you think it was right for us to become involved in this undertaking?

The picture above shows the total destruction of Hiroshima after the A-bomb; the destructive power of the present H-bomb is many times greater. What policy do you think the Canadian government should pursue to ensure that nuclear bombs are never used? What can we, as individuals, do to curb the threat of nuclear destruction?

supplied that country with the vital materials. What should our policy on these matters be? How can our government help curb the growth in the number of countries possessing nuclear technology? What can we do to reduce the existing stockpiles of nuclear weapons, stockpiles so large that they could put an end to human existence as we know it?

1. Canada and the Nuclear Nightmare

Mankind has been living with the Bomb for more than three decades now and, like the progress report offered by the apocryphal fellow in mid-plunge from a skyscraper, it's been a case of "so far, so good." Dire predictions to the contrary, no one yet has set off a nuclear spark and blown up the planet. But with almost every passing day new fears arise, as nuclear technology and weapon-making capability proliferate through an energy-short world. The nuclear club is no longer exclusively made up of superpowers: besides the United States and Soviet Union, Britain, France, China and India are stockpiling weapons. Moreover, several smaller, less stable nations appear to have reached the club's threshold, if not its checkroom. The fact that several of these prospective members—Israel, Egypt, Taiwan, South Korea, South Africa, Argentina and Brazil—feel menaced by their neighbors has led some scientists and diplomats to worry aloud that they might be driven to use the Bomb in a local crisis. All, naturally, deny any intention to bring an Armageddon prematurely, but skepticism persists.

The high-technology nations are in a quandary, at least partly because the mushroom-shaped cloud has a golden lining. The selling of nuclear technology is a competitive business—Canada, with its CANDU reactor, is a leading exporter—that seems likely to go on growing as the world turns increasingly away from fossil fuels for energy. (Canada expects to have no fewer than 115 nuclear power stations in operation by the year 2000; the U.S. Atomic Energy Commission forecasts that nuclear plants will generate 33 per cent of U.S. electric power by 1980, whereas they contributed only 2 per cent in 1973). But with every sale the problem of safeguards grows more complicated. The International Peace Research Institute in Stockholm recently reported that 19 nations now have the scientists to produce nuclear weapons, and it predicted this number would grow to at least 30 by 1980: "Mankind may be slowly drifting toward World War III."

The moral dilemma confronting exporters arises from the potential benefits of nuclear energy for peaceful purposes and whether or not these benefits can be safely shared by less developed nations. As Prime Minister Pierre Trudeau once put it: "They [the developing nations] should not be required to re-invent the wheel." However, the problems posed by nuclear power plants are dishearteningly enormous. The radioactive life of plutonium, a nuclear by-product, has been estimated at a minimum 200 000 years—which obviously poses a disposal-and-storage nightmare. One U.S. scientist, Alvin M. Weinberg, has suggested that mankind will have to develop a nuclear priesthood to stand guard over man's radioactive legacy. "The price we demand of society for this magical energy source is both a vigilance and a longevity of our social institutions that we are quite unaccustomed to," he observes.

In recent weeks, the debate over proliferation of technology and, inevitably, weapon potential has intensified as France sold a reactor to South Africa, as U.S. intelligence reports (since strenuously denied) suggested

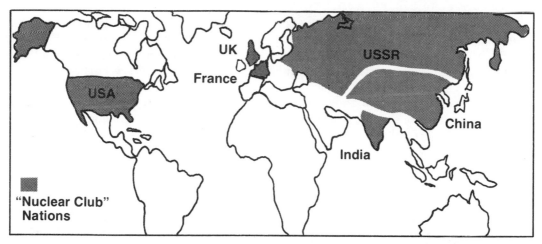

"Nuclear Club" Nations

Potential New Members

Argentina	Israel	Pakistan
Egypt	S. Korea	Iran
Taiwan	S. Africa	Brazil

that Taiwan had secretly built a facility to re-process uranium for use in bombs, as West Germany pressed ahead with plans to sell technology to Brazil and as an alarmed United States sought to put the brakes on further expansion of the club's membership. All exporting countries, including Canada, promised under a 1968 treaty not to help other nations acquire nuclear weapons. But, as University of Chicago professor Albert Wohlstetter notes: "They are not precisely and explicitly prohibited from exporting facilities and materials that might bring an importing country to within a few hours of a capability to explode a bomb."

Embarrassed two years ago when India surprised the world by detonating a nuclear device (after having bought a Canadian reactor), Canada has been insisting on enhanced safeguards from its customers. Proposed sales to South Korea and Argentina, for example, were held up while Ottawa officials negotiated guarantees. Earlier this year, External Affairs Minister Allan MacEachen told the Commons he was satisfied that both Seoul and Buenos Aires had made commitments "which fully meet international standards and Canadian safeguards policy." Canada and Pakistan, which is forever looking nervously toward India, have been engaged in protracted discussions over safeguards. The Pakistanis, meantime, have been negotiating with the French government to purchase facilities.

Even as they continue to market their wares, the leading nuclear nations fret about the consequences of proliferation. They have banded together in a so-called Nuclear Suppliers Conference—the original members were the United States, Soviet Union, Britain, Canada, France, West Germany and Japan—and have been holding closely guarded discussions in London.

The United States has been leading the campaign for tighter restrictions. According to the Americans, selling re-processing equipment is tantamount to selling bomb capability.

Concern is not limited to governments. Literally hundreds of scientists around the world have deplored the expansion of the nuclear club. Protest groups, such as Canada's Coalition for Nuclear Responsibility, seek to stimulate the debate. Consumer crusader Ralph Nader has increasingly turned his attention to the perils of the nuclear age. And such prominent intellectuals as British economist Barbara Ward and Lord Calder have sketched doomsday scenarios if the slide toward global nuclearization continues. Uniting the worriers, who, having failed in the 1950s to ban the bomb, would now at least like to curb it, is their unspoken belief in Murphy's Law: "If something can go wrong, it will." It is a chilling prospect to consider.

[William Lowther, "The Bomb and How to Get It, the Threat and How to Curb It", *Maclean's*, September 20, 1976. © 1979 by *Maclean's* Magazine. Reprinted by permission.]

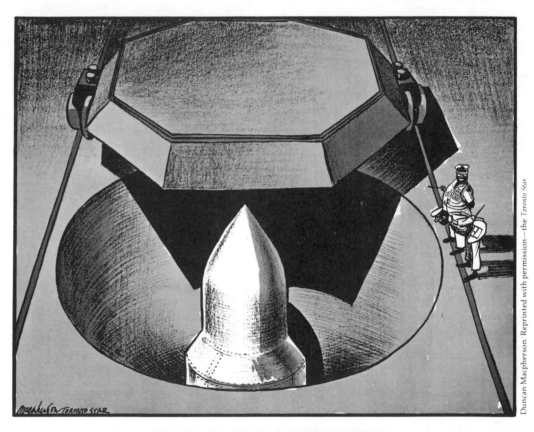

Duncan Macpherson. Reprinted with permission—the *Toronto Star*

"OFFICIALLY, IT'S A NUCLEAR REACTOR FROM CANADA"

How does this cartoon point out the dilemma we face in exporting nuclear reactors?

2. Trudeau Speaks Out, But Who Is Listening?

The following article outlines an address by former Prime Minister Trudeau to a special United Nations session on disarmament in 1978.

Prime Minister Pierre Trudeau advocated a gradual process of suffocation as the best way to take the life out of the international arms race when he addressed the special United Nations session on disarmament yesterday.

Although the speech contained no radically new theories, it did place Canada strongly in favor of comprehensive bans on the testing of new nuclear weapons and the vehicles to deliver them. . . .

Mr. Trudeau also suggested that no more fissionable material be produced for use in weapons systems. (There are already at least 14 000 nuclear warheads in the arsenals of the United States and Russia, with 500 more controlled by Britain, France and China—more than enough to wipe out the existing world population 100 times over.)

Mr. Trudeau's suffocation proposal includes an agreement by the nuclear powers to limit and then progressively reduce military spending on new strategic nuclear weapons systems. . . .

[He] recounted how Canada had become the first country possessing nuclear weapons that had subsequently removed them.

Canada was also the first country with the capacity to produce thermonuclear weapons that chose not to do so, he told the first major UN meeting on disarmament since the Second World War. . . .

Mr. Trudeau spoke with some feeling about the arms race which "defies the logic of an interdependent world" and warned that "beggaring our neighbors is the surest way of beggaring ourselves.

"It is hardly credible that nations which have learned that their destinies are linked, that national aims can no longer be wholly realized within national boundaries . . . should have discovered no better alternative to assuring their security than an escalating balance of terror.

"And it is even less credible that, in a world of finite resources, and in so many parts of which basic human needs remain unsatisfied, nearly $400 billion in resources should have to be spent year by year for security," [he said in] reference to one estimate of the world's total annual defence budgets.

Mr. Trudeau set his sights on "a reasonable consensus on broad objectives and on a plan of action for the next few years," rather than on more dramatic proposals that might have less chance of success.

"A strategy of suffocation seems to me to have a number of advantages. It is not merely declaratory, because it will have a real and progressive impact on the development of new strategic weapons systems. . . . It is also a realistic strategy because it assumes that, for some time to come, at least, total nuclear disarmament is probably unattainable in practice."

Mr. Trudeau also spoke extensively about the need to develop nuclear energy because the world is "hovering on the threshold of a plutonium economy," but he reiterated the need for tough controls to ensure that plutonium is not diverted into weapons. . . .

[Hugh Winsor, "PM Urges Nuclear Bans in UN Speech", *Globe and Mail*, Toronto, May 27, 1978]

Guidelines for Inquiry

1. (a) What difficult moral dilemma do the exporters of nuclear technology face?
   (b) How are these countries trying to avoid the perils of an expanded "nuclear weapons club"?
2. (a) What did Trudeau mean when he advocated "a gradual process of suffocation" in order to curb the nuclear arms race?
   (b) What do you think Canada should do to help reduce the possibility of nuclear warfare?

Part Seven: Canadian Foreign Policy—What Should It Be?

You have now had an opportunity to examine some specific foreign policy issues, and so you should be aware that there are many different viewpoints. You also should have some idea of the wide range of Canadian foreign policy interests. As you read this last section, think about the many aspects of Canada's foreign policy and decide what you would do if you had the opportunity to direct the course of Canada's foreign relations.

1. Lester Pearson Speaks Out as Minister of External Affairs, 1949

IRWIN: May we ask, Mr. Minister, what is our foreign policy, where is it going and what are its objectives?

THE MINISTER: That's a good question, but it's not an easy one to answer for a country like Canada. Let me try it this way. In economic policy the objective of our foreign policy is simple. It is to bring about the widest possible area and volume of trade on a multilateral basis. It always has been. So far as other aspects of foreign policy are concerned our basic objective is peace and the avoidance of conflict. You may say that peace isn't a policy, it's a prayer. Maybe. But that prayer should be the ultimate objective of everything we do in our relations with other countries—to avoid conflict and maintain peace.

FRASER: Not at any price, though?

THE MINISTER: No, not at any price. Peace with liberty, and, if you like, with justice. If our freedom were in danger we would protect it. If we were attacked, of course, we would defend ourselves. But we haven't many concrete objectives in our foreign policy in the sense that some countries have.

We have no territorial ambitions; we have no old grudges that shape our foreign policy. We have certainly no expansionist ideas. We have all the geography that we can handle, and we're not interested in ideological crusades.

IRWIN: Is it possible for a country like Canada to have a really independent foreign policy or are we just a tail to the American State Department or, say, the British Foreign Office?

THE MINISTER: I don't think we're the tail to any foreign office, the U.S. State Department or any other. There is some truth, of course, in your suggestion that we are influenced by the views of other countries. But no country can have complete independence today in its foreign policy, because no country can now guarantee its own security by its own actions. Not even the United States—

FRASER: Not even the biggest—?

THE MINISTER: Not even the United States. And if that is true, then *no* country, certainly no middle or small power, can follow a *completely* independent foreign policy. But that doesn't mean we are necessarily a satellite revolving in a fixed course around some larger planet.

["Straight Talk from Mike Pearson"— Interview between Lester Pearson and Arthur Irwin and Blair Fraser, *Maclean's*, October 15, 1949. © 1979 *Maclean's* Magazine. Reprinted by permission.]

2. Canadian-American Relations: President Kennedy's Viewpoint, 1961

Geography has made us neighbours. History has made us friends. Economics has made us partners. And necessity has made us allies. Those whom nature hath so joined together, let no man put asunder.

[John F. Kennedy, Address to Canadian Parliament, May 17, 1961, *House of Commons Debates*, Vol. v, 1960-61, p. 4963]

3. Prime Minister Pearson Comments, 1966

Our diplomacy—I keep using the word "powerful" because that is the word which has been running through your discussions—if not powerful, has at times been influential, partly because it has been the product of special circumstances of our origin and of our history and our associations.

We have acquired a special diplomatic reputation through the influence which we have been able at times to exert on the greatest centre of free-world power, the United States. We have acquired that kind of power because we do have an influence on the United States at times out of proportion to our size and our material strength. We have been able to use that influence constructively, and I hope we will continue to do so. But I am not going to get into any controversy, at this moment at least, whether we should use it quietly, or whether we should use it publicly. I think we should do both. I will say no more about that.

We have also acquired diplomatic power from a demonstrated desire and willingness to discharge our responsibilities as a member of the United Nations; and even more, I believe, from a desire to broaden and deepen that responsibility of the United

Nations. I think of our efforts, for instance, to build up peace-keeping machinery in the United Nations.

We also have a kind of diplomatic power and influence derived from our association with an imperial past, from the Empire and the Commonwealth. We are, in this sense, something unique in the world today. We combine a North American present with a British and a French past. One might even say that one reason why Canada is a strong middle power now is that its people have maintained from the past almost a "great power" psychology. This formulation could easily be misunderstood if it suggested some kind of arrogance or pride out of keeping with our real status. I don't think we suffer from that. If, however, it is understood in the more generous sense of accepting responsibility, and of confidence in being able to do something to discharge that responsibility because of our past history, as well as our present status, then I think this is relevant to the Canadian role.

[Lester B. Pearson, "Canada's Role As a Middle Power", from *Contemporary Affairs*, No. 35, 1966, J. King Gordon, editor. (Papers given at the Third Annual Banff Conference on World Development, August 1965.) Canadian Institute of International Affairs]

4. Prime Minister Trudeau and New Directions, 1968

We Canadians found a lot to be proud of in 1967, and also some things to question.

Above all, we became keenly aware in our centennial year that significant changes—political, economic, technological—have taken place in the world around us and within the body politic of our own nation. We found ourselves questioning long-standing institutions and values, attitudes and activities, methods and precedents which have shaped our international outlook for many years. We found ourselves wondering whether, in the world of tomorrow, Canada can afford to cling to the concepts and role-casting which served us in our international endeavours of three decades or more.

Those fundamentals of foreign policy did serve Canada well in circumstances of severe testing for us and for the world generally. This country played a leading part in shaping the multi-racial Commonwealth, in promoting and supporting a universal United Nations, and in trying to keep NATO attuned to changing strategic and political requirements. We made a significant contribution to international aid. . . . Reassessment has become necessary not because of the inadequacies of the past but because of the changing nature of Canada and of the world around us.

All of us need to ponder well what our national capacity is—what our potential may be—for participating effectively in international affairs. We shall do more good by doing well what we *know* to be within our resources to do than to pretend either to ourselves or to others that we can do things clearly beyond our national capability.

Canada's position in the world is now very different from that of the postwar years. Then we were probably the largest of the small powers. Our currency was one of the strongest. We were the fourth or fifth trading nation and our economy was much stronger than the European economies. We had one of the very strongest navy and air forces. But now Europe has regained its strength. The third world has emerged.

It is for us to decide whether and how we can make the best use abroad of the special skills, experience and opportunities which our political, economic and cultural evolution have produced in this rich and varied country.

Realism—that should be the operative word in our definition of international aim. Realism in how we read the world barometer. Realism in how we see ourselves thriving in the climate it forecasts. For we must begin with a concrete appraisal of the prevailing atmosphere—conscious always that rapid change is likely to be its chief characteristic.

[Pierre Elliot Trudeau, Policy statement issued May 29, 1968]

5. Views of Mitchell Sharp, Minister of External Affairs, 1972

The nations of the Third World, the world of the former colonies and the developing countries, no longer feel excluded by the fixations of the power blocs, and are playing a larger part in world affairs. China, though publicly rejecting the super-power role, seems to be assuming a position of leadership of the Third World. The new Europe is destined to be an economic power comparable in strength to the United States or the U.S.S.R.

It is in this world of changing political, economic and military relationships that Canada must find its place and hold it. It is in this world of change that one must attempt to answer the questions: How much independence can we have? How much should we have? How do we keep it? How do we use it? Why is it important to us?

. . . When this government came to power in 1968 one of its early decisions was to undertake a fundamental review of Canada's foreign policy. What came out of it was not so much a fundamental change in our policy as a reorientation of our thinking about Canada's place in the world and

an enlargement of our world view. Canada's angle of vision for historical reasons has been across the Atlantic to Western Europe, and southward to the United States. We decided that in these two directions we must extend our line of sight, eastward to the nations of Eastern Europe, southward to the countries of Latin America. We decided that we must look northward to our own Arctic and across the pole to our northern neighbor the U.S.S.R., westward across the Pacific to Australasia, Japan, China and the countries of Asia.

This may all sound somewhat grandiose, but it has very real meaning. Canada no longer sees itself primarily at the apex of the North Atlantic Triangle, but as an Atlantic, a Pacific, an Arctic and, above all, an American nation. This is bringing about changes of emphasis in our foreign policy. It is not a retreat into isolationism as some observers have suggested, rather it is a broadening of horizons. It is also a considered move toward a more independent position in terms of foreign policy.

[Mitchell Sharp, Address to the Women's Canadian Club, Toronto, January 14, 1972]

6. Is Nationalism Blunting Our Internationalism?

. . . Once Europe had fully recovered from the war, and West Germany was no longer an international pariah, Canada had to revert to being, as Ramsay Cook once put it, "a befuddled minor power yearning for past glories."

Still others, Hugh Winsor of the Toronto *Globe and Mail*'s Ottawa bureau for one, point to the October Crisis of 1970 as the *real* watershed. "I'd come back from Tanzania, from three years teaching journalism, fully expecting to specialize in

*"Gentlemen, it's just come to my attention that
Canada is not the only country in the world."*

foreign affairs," says Winsor. "But after the crisis, the writing was on the wall for internationalists like me. There just wasn't going to be that much space available any more, for any problems except our own."

Call it the New Isolationism, or the New Insularity, or the New Chauvinism. Whichever label you put on the phenomenon, Canadians have never before been so fascinated by themselves and, as a consequence, so switched off on everyone else. "Dangerous and disquieting," is the way External Affairs Minister Don Jamieson

describes the mood, "particularly at a time when the need for interdependence among nations never was more pronounced." Ivan Head, who, until he was named president of Ottawa's International Development Research Centre in March, had been Trudeau's personal advisor on international affairs, says "Canadians don't seem to realize that the fate of this country may be determined as much by foreign policy as by domestic. We are very, very vulnerable. Vulnerable to being overlooked and forgotten in the world, to being the silent victim of decisions taken elsewhere." . . .

Where did it all go? Pearson with his Nobel Prize? John Kennedy praising our foreign service as "the best in the world"? What happened to the creative imagination that was the mainspring behind NATO, behind the UN Peacekeeping Force, behind the kind of Commonwealth that could be redesigned to live on beyond imperial glories as a club in which white, black, brown, and yellow could get together and talk candidly in a way that's possible in no other forum? And what happens to us now? Can we amount to anything more than a junior North American partner allowed a flash of impertinence now and then—as in "Viva Castro"—because no one takes a junior partner seriously, least of all ourselves? Can we, even if a more independent role is possible, summon up the will to take it on, when the intellectual and emotional horizons of most Canadians are within Canada? . . .

[Sandra Gwyn, "Where Are You, Mike Pearson, Now That We Need You?" *Saturday Night*, April 1978]

Guidelines for Inquiry

1. Now that you have completed this unit on Canada in the world, we would like you to formulate your own foreign policy statement based on what you think is best for Canada now and in the immediate future. The information in the text combined with your own knowledge of current issues should help you to create your policy statement.

Acknowledgments

J. M. Beck, *Pendulum of Power*, Prentice-Hall of Canada Limited, Scarborough, 1968.

Léandre Bergeron, *History of Québec: A Patriot's Handbook*, trans. Baila Markus, New Canada Publications, 1971. A division of NC Press Ltd., Box 6106, Station A, Toronto.

Solange Chaput Rolland and Gertrude Laing, *Face to Face*, New Press, © 1972.

Jean-Paul Desbiens (Frère Untel), *The Impertinences of Brother Anonymous*, Harvest House, Montreal, 1962.

John R. English, "Charles de Gaulle in Canada", originally published in *Past and Present*, University of Waterloo. Reprinted by permission of the author.

Thomas A. Hockin, *Apex of Power*, Prentice-Hall of Canada Limited, Scarborough, 1971.

Bruce Kidd, "Canada's 'National' Sport", in *Close the 49th Parallel*, ed. Ian Lumsden, © University of Toronto Press, 1970.

"French Canadians and the West", trans. Philip Stratford, in André Laurendeau, *Witness for Quebec*, Macmillan of Canada, 1973.

René Lévesque, *Option for Québec*, McClelland and Stewart Limited, Toronto, 1968.

R. MacGregor Dawson, *William Lyon Mackenzie King: A Political Biography*, Vol. 1, 1874-1923, © University of Toronto Press, 1958.

Kenneth McNaught, "The National Outlook of English-speaking Canadians", in *Nationalism in Canada*, ed. Peter Russell, McGraw-Hill Ryerson Limited, © 1966. Reprinted by permission.

James M. Minifie, *Open at the Top: Reflections on U.S.-Canada Relations*, McClelland and Stewart Limited, Toronto, 1964.

Peter Newman, *The Distemper of Our Times*, McClelland and Stewart Limited, Toronto, 1968.

George Radwanski, *Trudeau.* © 1978. Reprinted by permission of the Macmillan Company of Canada Limited.

Richard Simeon, "Postscript", in *One Country or Two?* ed. R. M. Burns, © McGill-Queen's University Press, 1971.

Dale C. Thomson and R. Swanson, *Canadian Foreign Policy: Options and Perspectives*, McGraw-Hill Ryerson Limited, © 1971. Reprinted by permission.

"New Treason of the Intellectuals", trans. Patricia Claxton, in P. E. Trudeau, *Federalism and the French Canadians*, Macmillan of Canada, 1968.

Stanley R. Tupper and Douglas L. Bailey, *One Continent — Two Voices: The Future of Canada-U.S. Relations*, Clarke Irwin and Company Limited, 1967. Copyright held by Hawthorn Books, Inc., New York.

97 08 18 28 38 48 58 68 78 88 89 HR 10 9 8 7 6 5 4 3 2 1